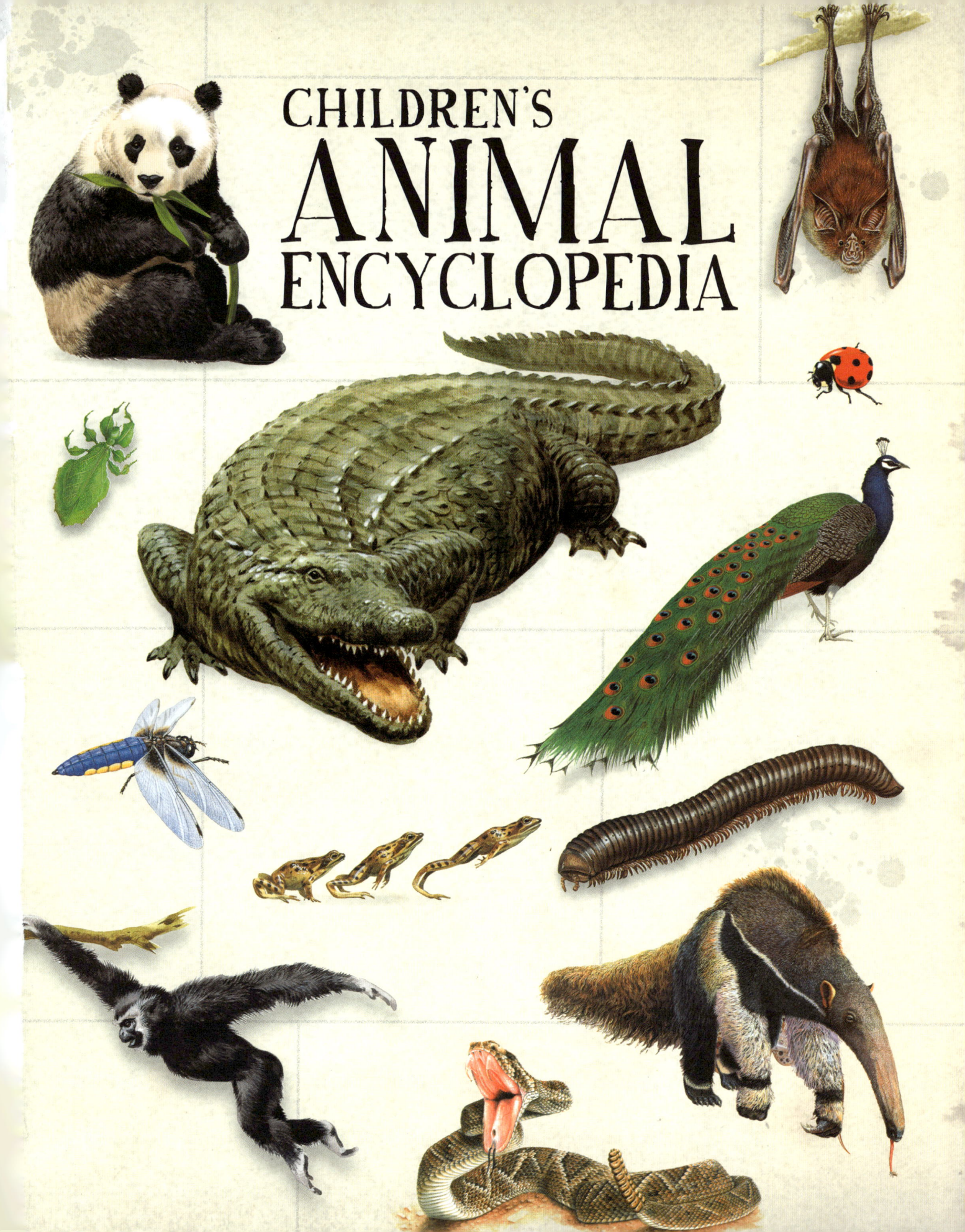

Created by Tall Tree Ltd.
Editors: Camilla Hallinan, Jon Richards
Designers: Marisa Renzullo, Malcolm Parchment

Art Director: Susi Martin
Publisher: Zeta Jones

Copyright © 2014 Marshall Editions

Copyright © Marshall Editions 2014
A Quarto Group company
The Old Brewery,
6 Blundell Street,
London, N7 9BH

Published in the UK by Marshall Editions

All rights reserved. No part of this publication may be reproduced, stored in a retrieval system, or transmitted in any form or by any means, electronic, mechanical, photocopying, recording or otherwise, without the prior written permission of the Publisher, nor be otherwise circulated in any form of binding or cover other than that in which it is published and wihout a similar condition being imposed on the subsequent purchaser.

A catalogue record for this book
is available from the British Library

ISBN 978 1 78171 737 0

Printed in China
by Toppan Leefung Printing Ltd

10 9 8 7 6 5 4 3 2 1

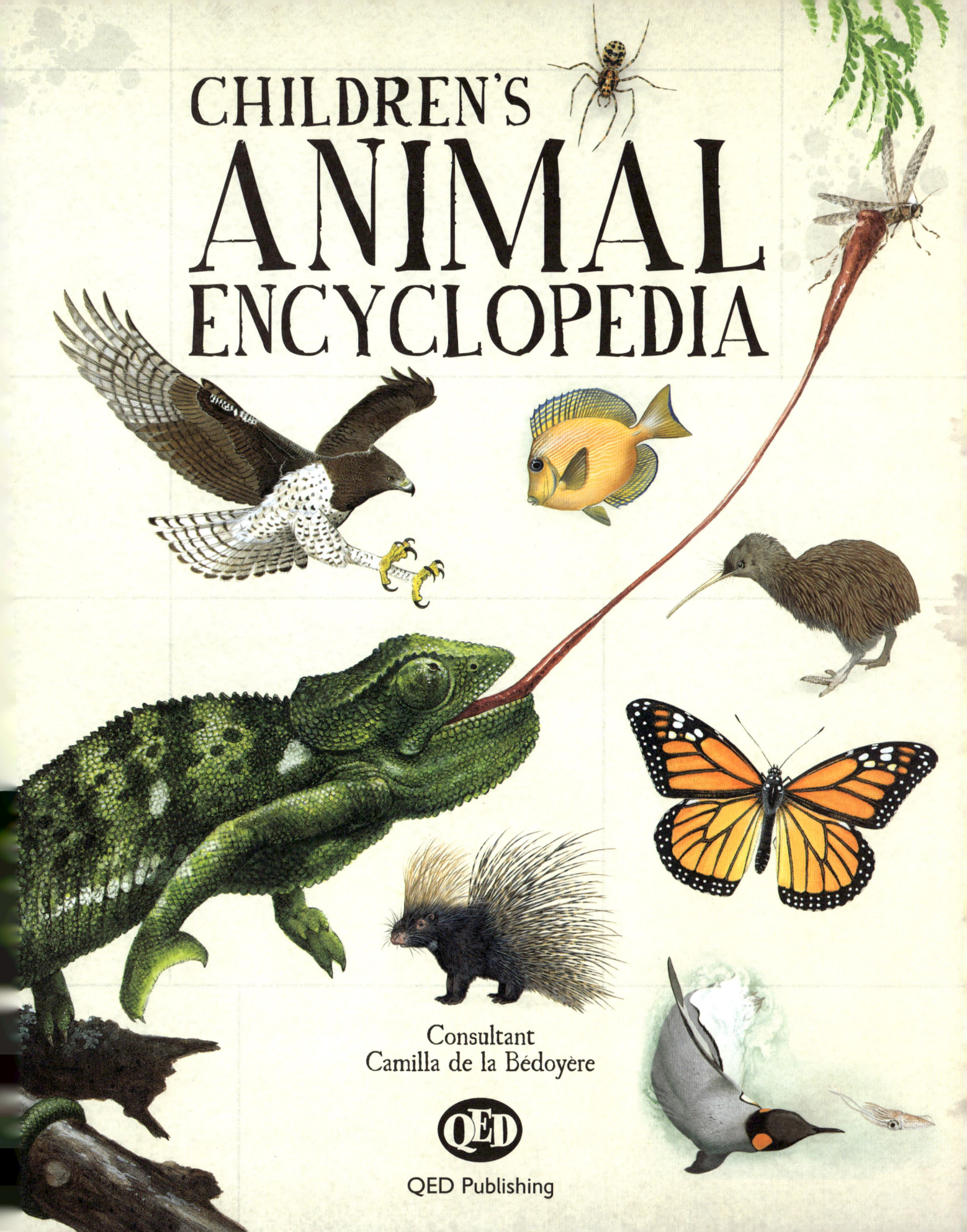

CONTENTS

MAMMALS

Mammals 6
What is a mammal? 8
Monotremes and marsupials 10
Anteaters and other insect eaters 14
Bats 16
Vampire bats 18
Primates 20
Carnivores 26
Tigers 34
Seals, whales and dolphins 36
Antarctic seals 38
Elephants 44
Hoofed mammals 46
Rodents and rabbits 54
Why do zebras have stripes? 62

BIRDS

Birds 64
What is a bird? 66
Game birds and ground birds 68
Waders, waterbirds, cranes
and seabirds 74
Penguins 84
Owls and birds of prey 86
Eagles 90
Birds of the trees and masters
of the air 92
Hummingbirds 98
Songbirds 100
Birds of paradise 106
How do animals communicate? 110

REPTILES

Reptiles 112
What is a reptile? 114
Crocodiles, alligators, turtles
and tortoises 116
Nile crocodiles 118
Lizards and snakes 124
Chameleons 128

AMPHIBIANS

Amphibians	134
What is an amphibian?	136
Newts and salamanders	138
Frogs and toads	142
Arrow-poison frogs	148
Poisons and venoms	150

FISH

Fish	152
What is a fish?	154
Lampreys, sharks and rays	156
Skates, rays and seabed sharks	158
Sturgeons, gars and relatives	160
Eels, tarpons and herring	162
Carp, bream and piranhas	164
Catfish and relatives	166
Electric eel, salmon, hatchetfish and pike	168
Cod, anglers and cusk-eels	170
Perch-like fish	172
Tuna	178
Flyingfish, lanternfish and lizardfish	180
Guppies, grunions and relatives	182
Oarfish, squirrelfish and relatives	184
Seahorses, stonefish and relatives	186
Flatfish	188
Coelacanth, lungfish, triggerfish and relatives	190
Why do some animals work together?	192

Children's Animal Encyclopedia

INSECTS, SPIDERS AND OTHER INVERTEBRATES

Insects, spiders and other invertebrates	194
What is an invertebrate?	196
Cockroaches, earwigs, crickets, grasshoppers and relatives	198
Mantids, dragonflies and relatives	202
Bugs, lice, fleas and beetles	206
Stag beetles	212
Flies, moths and butterflies	214
Hawk moths	220
Bees, wasps, ants and termites	222
Honeybees	226
Spiders and scorpions	230
Orb weavers	234
Snails, slugs and other land invertebrates	238
Sea creatures	240
Rock clingers	246
Why do animals build nests?	250
Index	252
Acknowledgements	256

Mammals

Children's Animal Encyclopedia

MAMMALS

Human beings are just one of about 5,500 mammal species. Mammals come in all shapes and sizes and are found in almost every part of the world, from the frozen Arctic to the hottest deserts, densest forests and biggest oceans. There are many different kinds of mammal, each with its own way of life. The tiger, for example, hunts prey in the depths of the forest, while dolphins swim through the sea, moles burrow underground, bats fly through the air, horses gallop across the ground and monkeys swing through the trees.

WHAT IS A MAMMAL?

Mammals are a diverse group of animals, but they all have certain things in common. They are warm-blooded, have lungs to breathe in air and a bony frame called a skeleton to support their bodies and protect their internal organs. Most also have relatively large brains, good senses and hair or fur.

TYPES OF MAMMAL

Most mammals give birth to live young. In most mammals, known as eutherians, the babies grow inside the mother's womb. They are supplied with food and oxygen by a special organ called the placenta, and are well-developed when they are born. Marsupials are very undeveloped at birth and crawl into a special pouch where they can grow stronger in safety. Monotremes are unusual – they lay eggs instead of producing babies.

Indian elephant

Mammals are warm-blooded animals – they can keep their body temperature constant, whatever the temperature of their surroundings. When they are too hot, many mammals sweat to cool down. Elephants cannot sweat, so they keep cool by staying in the shade, bathing in water and letting heat evaporate from their huge ears.

MARSUPIAL

Baby wallaby feeding in pouch
- Large head
- Young wallaby clings to teat
- Poorly developed legs
- Long, thick tail for balance
- Long face to make room for large, flat teeth used for chewing plants
- Young wallaby
- Powerful legs for bounding along fast
- Furry pouch

Ring-tailed wallaby

SENSES

Mammals generally have well-developed senses of sight, hearing, smell, taste and touch. These senses help them to locate food, avoid predators, find a mate and much more. The sense organs are often found in the head, near the brain.

- Acute hearing
- Sharp eyes
- Sensitive whiskers
- Keen sense of smell

Female wild boar with young

SUCKLING

A female mammal has mammary glands (also called breasts or udders) that produce milk, which the babies suck from teats. This is called suckling. The milk contains sugar, fat, proteins and vitamins, which the babies need to grow and stay healthy.

MONOTREME

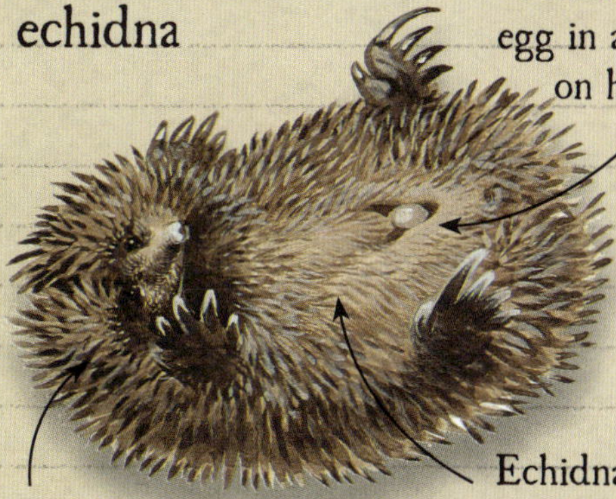

Short-beaked echidna
- Female carries egg in a groove on her belly
- Coat of protective spines
- Echidna has no teats – milk oozes from pores in skin

EUTHERIAN MAMMAL

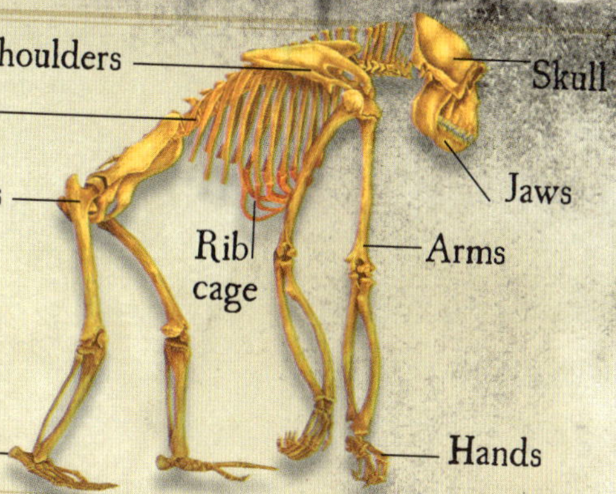

Pileated gibbon
- Long arms for swinging from tree to tree
- Forward-pointing eyes to judge distances accurately
- Fur covers skin
- Five-toed feet
- Short, strong legs

Gorilla skeleton
- Shoulders
- Vertebrae
- Hips
- Rib cage
- Skull
- Jaws
- Arms
- Feet
- Hands

Blue whale skeleton
- Jaws
- Shoulders
- Vertebrae
- Tail
- Rib cage
- Skull
- Flippers
- Hips, but no hind limbs

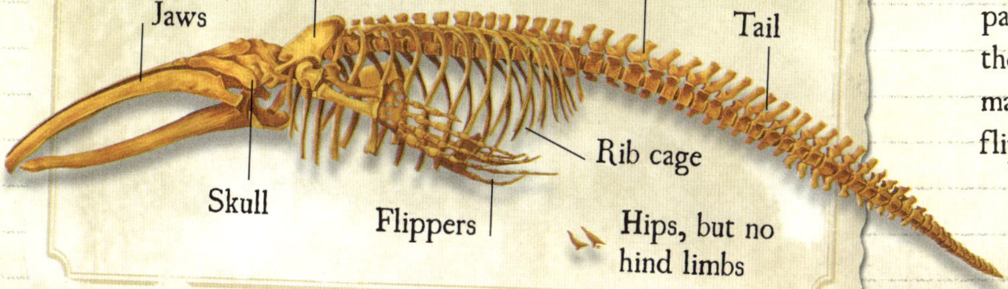

MAMMAL SKELETONS

Mammals are vertebrates, which means that their skeleton has a backbone made up of individual bones called vertebrae. A rib cage surrounds the heart and lungs, and a skull protects the brain. Some mammals have adapted parts of their skeletons to suit their particular lifestyle. Sea mammals, for example, have flippers instead of arms and legs.

MONOTREMES AND MARSUPIALS

In most mammal species, the young develop inside their mother's body for a long time before they are born. But monotremes and marsupials are different. Like their reptile ancestors, monotremes lay eggs, but when they hatch, the young feed on their mother's milk. Marsupials give birth to very undeveloped babies: some are no bigger than a grain of rice, and all are hairless and blind. Once it is born, a young marsupial develops in a furry pouch on the underside of its mother's body.

MONOTREMES

Monotremes consist of echidnas (or spiny anteaters) and platypuses. A female echidna lays a single, soft-shelled egg and puts it in a groove on her belly, where it is protected for seven to 10 days until it hatches. The platypus is one of the few venomous mammals: the male has a spur on each hind foot, for injecting venom into an enemy. A female platypus lays two or three eggs in a long tunnel; they take up to two weeks to hatch.

Size: body 45–77 cm (17¾–30¼ in); virtually no tail
Range: New Guinea
Habitat: tropical evergreen forest

Long-nosed echidna
Zaglossus bruijni

Echidnas have long, slender snouts. They have no teeth and weak jaws, so they lap up ants, termites and other small creatures with their sticky tongues and crush them against the roof of their mouths.

Platypus
Ornithorhynchus anatinus

The platypus spends most of the day in a riverside burrow. At dawn and dusk it comes out to feed on the riverbed, using its sensitive bill to probe the mud for insects, worms, grubs, crayfish and frogs. Its bill is a skin-covered framework of bone.

Size: body 46 cm (18 in); tail 18 cm (7 in)
Range: Australia, Tasmania
Habitat: fresh water

Size: body 35–50 cm (13¾–19¾ in); tail 9 cm (3½ in)
Range: Australia, Tasmania, southeastern New Guinea
Habitat: deciduous and tropical evergreen forest, temperate grassland, desert

Short-nosed echidna
Tachyglossus aculeatus

The echidna's spiny coat protects it from attackers. When threatened, it either curls itself up into a ball or, if it is on soft soil, digs straight downwards so that only its spines are visible.

MARSUPIALS

The word marsupial means "pouched mammal". A tiny marsupial baby has to wriggle its way through its mother's fur to reach her pouch. Once inside, it latches on to a teat and drinks her milk. The pouch gives the baby a safe place in which it can grow and develop until it is ready to face the outside world. There are more than 335 marsupial species.

Kowari
Dasyuroides byrnei

Size: body 16.5–18 cm (6½–7 in); tail 13–14 cm (5–5½ in)
Range: central Australia
Habitat: tropical grassland, desert

At home in grasslands and deserts, this small marsupial lives alone or in small groups in an underground burrow. At night, it hunts among the tussock grass for insects, lizards and small birds. Kowaris breed in winter and produce litters of five or six young. Due to overgrazing and loss of habitat, the kowari is now listed as vulnerable.

Water opossum
Chironectes minimus

Size: body 27–33 cm (10½–13 in); tail 36–40 cm (14¼–15¾ in)
Range: Mexico, Central and South America
Habitat: fresh water

The water opossum is the only marsupial that lives in water. It emerges from its riverbank burrow to swim and search for fish, shellfish and other small water creatures, which it carries back to the bank to eat. It swims with its webbed hind feet, and steers with its long tail. Its oily fur repels water, keeping it dry.

Brown bandicoot
Isoodon obesulus

Size: body 30–33 cm (11¾–13 in); tail 7.5–18 cm (3–7 in)
Range: southern and eastern Australia, Tasmania
Habitat: deciduous forest, desert

The brown bandicoot hunts by following the scent of its prey. It feeds on worms, insect larvae and underground fungi. It will even eat scorpions, biting off their poisonous tails before consuming them. In areas of dense vegetation, it hides from predators such as eagles and foxes.

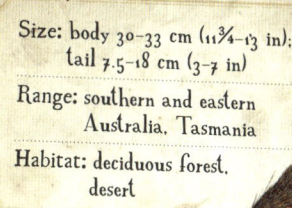

Virginia opossum
Didelphis virginiana

Size: body 32.5–50 cm (12¾–19¾ in); tail 25.5–53.5 cm (10–21 in)
Range: southeastern Canada, through USA to Central America
Habitat: deciduous and tropical evergreen forest, desert, inhabited areas and farmland

This is the sole North American marsupial. It often scavenges for food in refuse tips and rubbish bins. To escape a predator, such as a dog, eagle or bobcat, the opossum may "play dead", lying on its side with its tongue hanging out and its eyes shut or staring into space. Thinking it is already dead, the predator may lose interest, giving the opossum vital seconds to make its escape.

Marsupials

Koala
Phascolarctos cinereus

The koala spends up to 18 hours each day asleep. The rest of the time it feeds on the leaves of eucalyptus trees. It has a long gut, which enables it to digest the tough leaves and deal with the leaves' poisonous chemicals. Special pouches in its cheeks store the leaves until it needs to eat them.

Size: body 60–85 cm (23½–33½ in); virtually no tail
Range: eastern Australia
Habitat: deciduous forest, tropical forest

Tasmanian devil
Sarcophilus harrisii

About the size of a small dog, the Tasmanian devil moves slowly, but with cunning. Its keen sense of smell enables it to locate prey in the dark and take it by surprise. It feeds on reptiles, birds, fish and small mammals, and crushes the bones of its prey in its powerful jaws. Badly affected by disease, the species is now listed as endangered.

Size: body 52–80 cm (20½–31½ in); tail 23–30 cm (9–11¾ in)
Range: Tasmania
Habitat: deciduous forest, inhabited areas and farmland, coast

Size: body 32–58 cm (12½–22¾ in); tail 24–35 cm (9½–13¾ in)
Range: Australia, Tasmania; introduced into New Zealand
Habitat: deciduous forest, tropical evergreen forest

Common brush-tailed possum
Trichosurus vulpecula

Like most possums, this one is nocturnal. In its natural woodland habitat, it feeds on flowers, leaves, fruit, insects and young birds. In populated areas, it makes its home on buildings and feeds on rubbish. It breeds one young once or twice a year.

Size: body 70–120 cm (27½–47 in); virtually no tail
Range: eastern Australia, Tasmania
Habitat: deciduous forest, desert

Coarse-haired wombat
Vombatus ursinus

The wombat feeds on grass in forests and scrubland and can go without water for months. In summer, it shelters from the heat in a long, deep burrow. The female gives birth to a single young, which stays in her pouch for three months. Then it forages with her for several months before leaving to live independently.

Children's Animal Encyclopedia

Size: body 23–34 cm (9–13½ in);
tail 13–17 cm (5–6¾ in)
Range: northeastern Australia
Habitat: tropical evergreen forest

Size: body 1–1.6 m (3¼–5¼ ft); tail 90–110 cm (35½–43½ in)
Range: central Australia
Habitat: tropical grassland, scrub, desert

Musky rat-kangaroo
Hypsiprymnodon moschatus

This tiny kangaroo is unusual because it regularly gives birth to twins. Unlike other kangaroos, it prefers to move around on all fours like a rabbit. Both males and females produce a strong, musky smell, but no one knows why they do this.

Red kangaroo
Macropus rufus

The red kangaroo is the largest marsupial. It bounds along with huge leaps, on its back legs only, reaching speeds of up to 56 km/h (35 mph). It lives in Australia's hot, dry deserts and grassland. The female gives birth to a single baby called a joey, which emerges from her pouch after two months. If danger threatens, the joey dives back into her pouch.

Bridled nail-tail wallaby
Onychogalea fraenata

The nail-tail gets its name because it has a small, finger-like nail hidden in thick hair at the tip of its tail. It has a strange way of hopping, moving its arms in circles as it bounces along. Heavy grazing by sheep and cattle has destroyed much of the scrubland where it used to live and feed, and so this wallaby is now an endangered species.

Size: body 52–80 cm (20½–31½ in); tail 42–93 cm (16½–36½ in)
Range: northeastern Australia
Habitat: tropical evergreen forest

Lumholtz's tree kangaroo
Dendrolagus lumholtzi

The tree kangaroo spends most of its time high up in the forest trees, where it eats leaves and fruit. It can even sleep up there, crouched on a thick branch. This species is rarely seen because it is nocturnal and well-camouflaged in trees.

Size: body 45–67 cm (17¾–26¼ in); tail 33–66 cm (13–26 in)
Range: parts of eastern Australia
Habitat: scrub and grassland

ANTEATERS AND OTHER INSECT EATERS

Although these insect eaters are not all related to each other, they are perhaps the oddest-looking and most fascinating mammals of all. They include the armoured armadillos, the aardvark with its pig-like body, rabbit-like ears and kangaroo-like tail, the anteaters with their incredibly long snouts, and the small, furry moles, shrews and spiny tenrecs and hedgehogs.

AARDVARKS, ARMADILLOS AND ANTEATERS

Anteaters and armadillos belong to a group of animals called xenarthrans – a group that also contains sloths. Anteaters lack teeth, but some armadillos have up to 100 small, peg-like teeth. They do not need big biting teeth, because they feed on ants and termites, which they lick up with their tongues. Aardvarks have similar lifestyles to armadillos and anteaters, even though they are not closely related.

Size: body 1–1.6 m (3¼–5¼ ft); tail 44.5–60 cm (17½–23½ in)
Range: Africa, south of the Sahara
Habitat: tropical grassland

Aardvark
Orycteropus afer

The aardvark feeds on termites at night, finding them with its long snout and long, sticky tongue. During the day, it sleeps in its burrow, which it digs with its strong feet. The burrow may be long and complex, with many openings.

Giant anteater
Myrmecophaga tridactyla

This anteater sniffs out ants' nests and termite mounds, breaks them open with its claws and thrusts its long, sticky tongue inside. It is careful never to destroy a nest or eat all the ants, so it can return there to feed in the future.

Size: body 45–50 cm (17¾–19¾ in); tail 25–40 cm (9¾–15¾ in)
Range: southern USA, Central and South America
Habitat: grassland, forest, scrub

Nine-banded armadillo
Dasypus novemcinctus

When threatened, this armadillo rolls up into a ball so that its soft belly is protected and only its armour-plated back is exposed. It spends most of the day asleep in the safety of its burrow.

Size: body 1–1.2 m (3¼–4 ft); tail 65–90 cm (25½–35½ in)
Range: Central and South America, down to northern Argentina
Habitat: tropical evergreen forest, tropical grassland, fresh water

MOLES, TENRECS, SHREWS AND HEDGEHOGS

A number of smaller mammals, including moles, shrews, tenrecs and hedgehogs, feed almost exclusively on insects and other small invertebrates such as worms, centipedes, snails and spiders. Many of these mammals have long, narrow snouts in order to reach into the small spaces where insects hide. They also have sharp teeth and claws. They have poor eyesight, but an excellent sense of smell.

Short-eared elephant shrew
Macroscelides proboscideus

Elephant shrews get their name because of their extraordinary trunk-like noses. They walk on all fours, but when they need to move fast, they hop along on their back legs like miniature kangaroos. They feed on termites, seeds, fruit and berries in the daytime, but shelter from the midday sun in burrows.

Size: body 9.5–12.5 cm (3¾–5 in); tail 9.5–14 cm (3¾–5½ in)
Range: southern Africa
Habitat: temperate grassland, desert

Western European hedgehog
Erinaceus europaeus

The hedgehog roots around in hedgerows and undergrowth for small creatures to eat, making pig-like grunts as it goes. If it is attacked, it curls itself up into a ball, so that its prickly coat deters predators. In cold climates, it hibernates through the winter.

Size: body 13.5–27 cm (5¼–10½ in); tail 1–5 cm (½–2 in)
Range: western Europe; introduced into New Zealand
Habitat: inhabited areas and farmland, deciduous forest, desert

European mole
Talpa europaea

This small mammal spends almost its entire life underground, digging tunnels with its broad, spade-like front legs. It has poor eyesight, but good hearing. It feels its way around and finds worms and insects to eat by detecting the vibrations in the ground caused by their movements.

Streaked tenrec
Hemicentetes semispinosus

The streaked tenrec is covered in protective spines. The female produces a litter of seven to 11 babies. If she feels threatened, she raises a small patch of spines on her back and vibrates them rapidly. This makes a clicking noise to warn her young of approaching danger.

Size: body 16–19 cm (6¼–7½ in); virtually no tail
Range: Madagascar
Habitat: tropical forest

Size: body 9–16.5 cm (3½–6½ in); tail 3–4 cm (1¼–1½ in)
Range: Europe to Central Asia
Habitat: inhabited areas and farmland, deciduous forest, grassland

BATS

Bats are the only flying mammals. They power themselves through the air on smooth wings of skin, making sudden mid-air turns and twists. Most bats spend the day asleep, hanging upside down, out of reach of predators. At night, they launch themselves into the air to hunt for food. Some bats make high-pitched sounds that bounce, or echo, off nearby objects and are picked up by the bats' large ears. The bats use this echolocation to detect prey and avoid obstacles. Others, such as fruit bats, rely more on their sense of smell.

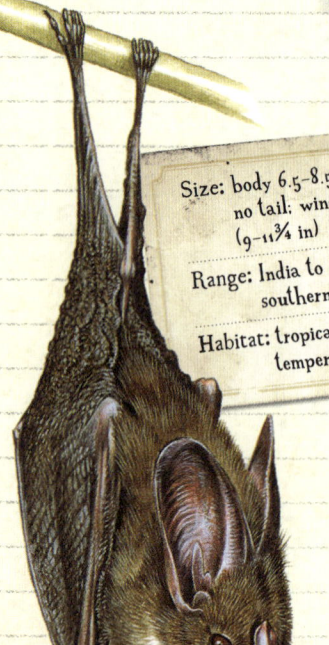

Size: body 6.5–8.5 cm (2½–3¼ in); no tail; wingspan 23–30 cm (9–11¾ in)
Range: India to Burma (Myanmar), southern China, Malaysia
Habitat: tropical evergreen forest, temperate grassland

Spear-nosed bat
Phyllostomus hastatus

The spear-nosed bat will eat insects and fruit, but prefers the flesh of mice, birds and small bats. The spear-nosed bat, in turn, is preyed upon by false vampire bats. It has a broad, spear-shaped flap of skin sticking up from its nose. Huge flocks of this heavy-bodied bat like to shelter in buildings and caves. Flocks emerge at dusk to fly to their feeding grounds. The female gives birth to a single baby, once or twice a year.

Size: body 10–13 cm (4–5¼ in); tail 2.5 cm (1 in); wingspan 44–47 cm (17¼–18½ in)
Range: Central and northern South America
Habitat: tropical evergreen forest

Greater false vampire bat
Megaderma lyra

The greater false vampire is one of the largest of all bats. It feeds largely on insects and spiders, but also on rodents, frogs, fish and even other bats. It roosts in caves in groups of three to 50 bats. Unlike true vampire bats, false vampire bats do not drink blood.

Size: body 4–5 cm (1½–2 in); tail 3–4.5 cm (1¼–1¾ in); wingspan 23–28 cm (9–11 in)
Range: northern Europe eastwards to China and Japan
Habitat: deciduous forest

Common long-eared bat
Plecotus auritus

This bat's ears are nearly as long as its head and body combined. The bat uses its sensitive ears to detect the calls and movements of insect prey, and to find its way by echolocation. The long-eared bat hibernates in caves during winter. In summer, it roosts in colonies of 50–100 bats in buildings and trees, feeding at night mainly on moths.

Children's Animal Encyclopedia

Size: body 20–25 cm (8–10 in); no tail; wingspan 1.5 m (5 ft)
Range: southern and Southeast Asia
Habitat: tropical forest, swamp

Indian flying fox
Pteropus giganteus

The largest wings of any bat belong to the greater fruit bat. By day, it roosts in trees in flocks of several thousand bats, taking flight at dusk to find juicy fruit to eat or sweet flower nectar to sip. Fruit trees are able to reproduce as their pollen, sticking onto the bat's fur, is moved from flower to flower. Fruit seeds it spits out or passes in its droppings take root and grow into new fruit trees.

Ghost bat
Macroderma gigas

The ghost bat, a type of false vampire bat, gets its name from the eery colour of its pale fur at night. It feeds on mice, birds, geckos and other bats. By day, it roosts in caves, rocky clefts and old mine shafts. It is rare because quarrying (removing stone) has destroyed some of its major roosts.

Size: body 11.5–14 cm (4½–5½ in); no tail; wingspan 40–60 cm (15¾–23½ in)
Range: northern and western tropical Australia
Habitat: tropical evergreen forest, desert

Size: body 7–12 cm (3–4¾ in); tail 1.5–2.5 cm (½–1 in); wingspan 20–28 cm (8–11 in)
Range: Papua New Guinea and Solomon Islands
Habitat: tropical evergreen forest, inhabited areas, farmland

Size: body 11–13 cm (4½–5 in); tail 2.5–4 cm (1–1½ in); wingspan 33–35 cm (13–13½ in)
Range: Europe, Asia, northern Africa
Habitat: inhabited areas, farmland, deciduous forest, temperate grassland

Dobson's tube-nose bat
Nyctimene major

The scroll-shaped nostrils of this bat stick out on each side of its head. They probably help the bat to find ripe fruit, such as guavas, figs and even young coconuts. Using its sharp teeth, the bat chews the fruit to extract the juice.

Greater horseshoe bat
Rhinolophus ferrumequinum

This bat feeds on beetles, swooping down to snatch them off the ground with pin-point accuracy. It roosts in caves, trees and the roofs of old buildings. But as caves are explored, trees felled and buildings pulled down, the bat finds it harder to find suitable homes. It is now rare or extinct in some parts of northwestern Europe.

17

VAMPIRE BATS

The only mammals to feed entirely on blood are vampire bats, which live in the tropical countries of Central and South America. The common vampire bat (*Desmodus rotundus*) preys on sleeping animals – usually cattle and horses – and sometimes even people. The two other vampire species, *Diaemus youngi* and *Diphylla ecaudata*, prey on large birds such as chickens. The common vampire feeds on its victim for about 30 minutes. The victim does not lose a dangerous amount of blood, but the bat's bite can spread disease and infection. Over the course of a year, a colony of 100 bats drinks a volume equal to the blood of 25 cows or 14,000 chickens.

The body of the common vampire bat is 9 cm (3½ in) long, and its wingspan is 18 cm (7 in). It has no tail, a snub-nose, and short, pointed ears. It has fewer teeth than most bats, since it has no need to chew or grind up food.

YOUNG BATS

At birth, a baby vampire bat is helpless, but its strong claws and hooked milk teeth allow it to cling tightly to its mother, even when she flies. At first, the young bat feeds entirely on her milk. Then she gradually introduces blood into its diet, feeding it a few drops at a time.

FEEDING

A vampire bat lands on the ground close to its victim and then creeps towards it on all fours. A heat sensor on the end of its nose helps it to locate an area of skin where warm blood flows close to the surface. The bat bites into its victim with its razor-sharp teeth and laps up the blood that flows from the wound. The bat's saliva stops the blood from clotting.

Hoof

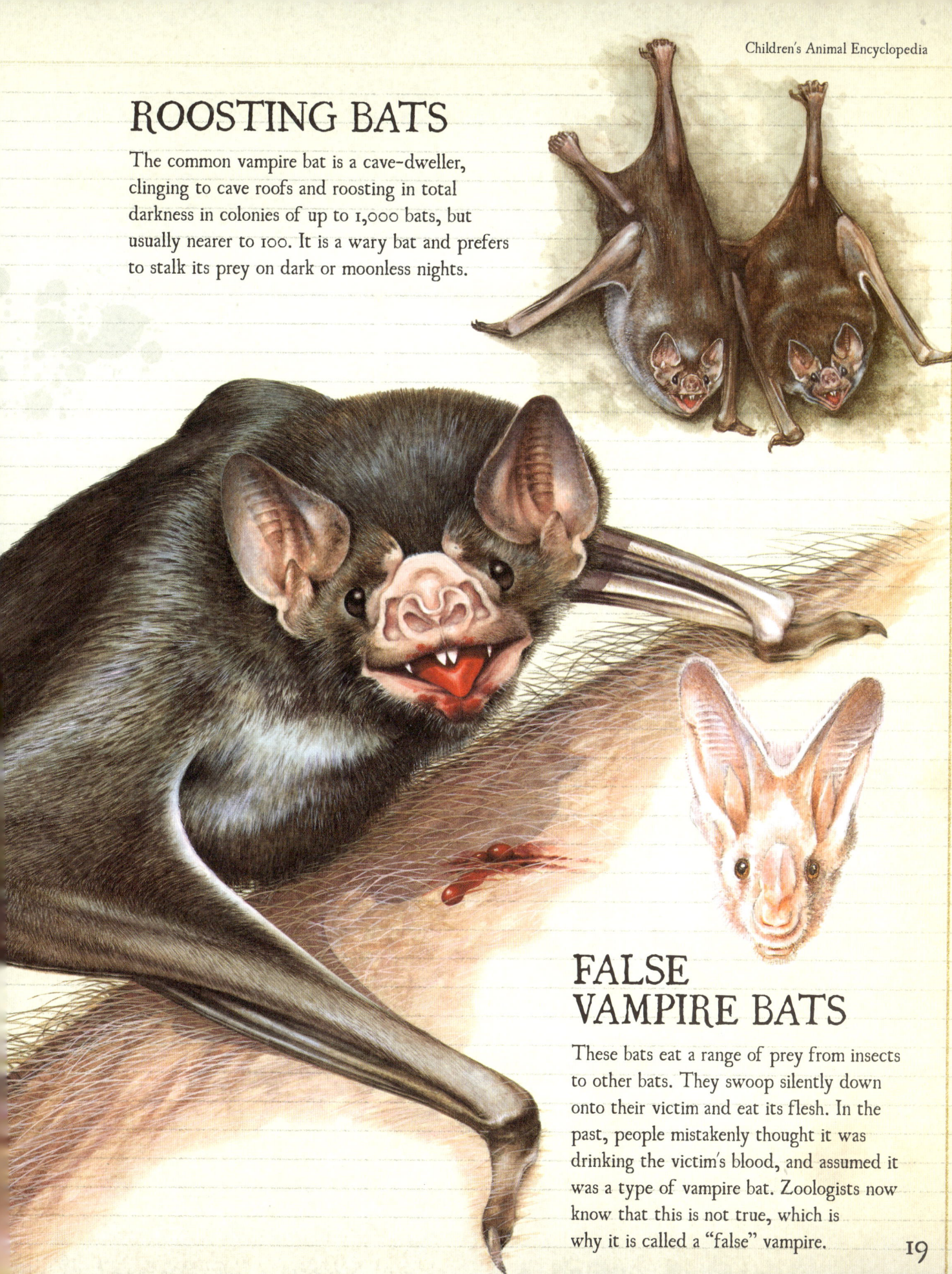

ROOSTING BATS

The common vampire bat is a cave-dweller, clinging to cave roofs and roosting in total darkness in colonies of up to 1,000 bats, but usually nearer to 100. It is a wary bat and prefers to stalk its prey on dark or moonless nights.

FALSE VAMPIRE BATS

These bats eat a range of prey from insects to other bats. They swoop silently down onto their victim and eat its flesh. In the past, people mistakenly thought it was drinking the victim's blood, and assumed it was a type of vampire bat. Zoologists now know that this is not true, which is why it is called a "false" vampire.

PRIMATES

Humans, monkeys, apes, lorises, tarsiers and lemurs all belong to a group of about 233 species called primates. With relatively large brains, these mammals are intelligent and quick to learn new skills. Many have opposable thumbs, which means that their thumbs can move across their palms to press against their fingers, allowing them to grasp objects firmly. Some also have opposable big toes. Most primates live in trees, and they have forward-pointing eyes to help them judge the distances between branches.

Size: body 14–16 cm (5½–6¼ in); tail 15–20 cm (6–7¾ in)
Range: South America: upper reaches of Amazon River area
Habitat: tropical evergreen forest

Pygmy marmoset
Cebuella pygmaea

One of the smallest of all the primates, the pygmy marmoset is often attacked by large birds, so it tries to keep out of sight. It moves either in short dashes or by creeping along very slowly, sometimes staying very still to avoid being spotted.

LEMURS, AYE-AYES, LORISES, BUSHBABIES, TARSIERS, MARMOSETS AND TAMARINS

Lemurs, aye-ayes, bushbabies, lorises and tarsiers are found in parts of Africa and southern Asia. They have smaller brains than monkeys and apes, and their skeletons resemble those of small, tree-dwelling, shrew-like animals, which were probably the first primates to evolve. The fast-moving marmosets and tamarins of the South American rainforests often have colourful fur and unusual "hairstyles".

Ring-tailed lemur
Lemur catta

The ring-tailed lemur climbs up to the tops of trees to bask in the early morning sunshine after a cold night. It marks out its territory with smelly secretions from scent glands.

Size: body 45 cm (17¾ in); tail 55 cm (21½ in)
Range: Madagascar
Habitat: deciduous forest, tropical evergreen forest

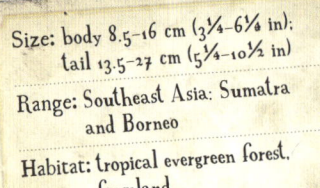

Size: body 8.5–16 cm (3¼–6⅜ in); tail 13.5–27 cm (5¼–10½ in)
Range: Southeast Asia: Sumatra and Borneo
Habitat: tropical evergreen forest, farmland

Western tarsier
Tarsius bancanus

The tarsier's large, bat-like ears and huge eyes make it a ruthless night-time hunter, but the eyeballs are too big to move in their sockets. To make up for this, the tarsier can turn its head right around.

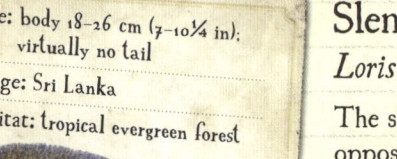

Size: body 18–26 cm (7–10¼ in); virtually no tail
Range: Sri Lanka
Habitat: tropical evergreen forest

Slender loris
Loris tardigradus

The slender loris's opposable thumbs and big toes enable it to grip tightly onto branches as it creeps through the trees, grabbing insects, lizards, birds and eggs with both hands.

Children's Animal Encyclopedia

Golden lion tamarin
Leontopithecus rosalia

This beautiful primate gets its name from the silky, lion-like mane that covers its head and shoulders. It lives in family groups and at night shelters in hollows in old trees. It is a nimble creature and leaps from branch to branch searching for insects, lizards and birds to eat.

Size: body 18–21 cm (7–8¼ in); tail 25–32 cm (9¾–12½ in)
Range: western Brazil, Peru, Bolivia
Habitat: tropical evergreen forest

Emperor tamarin
Saguinus imperator

The emperor tamarin is easily recognized by its long, drooping "moustache". Small troops of these tamarins dart through the trees looking for insects, fruit, tender leaves and flowers to eat. They also lap up tree sap and steal birds' eggs.

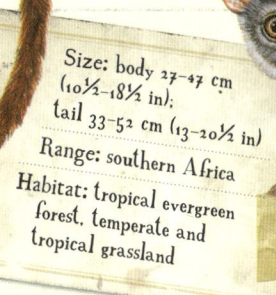

Size: body 27–47 cm (10½–18½ in); tail 33–52 cm (13–20½ in)
Range: southern Africa
Habitat: tropical evergreen forest, temperate and tropical grassland

Greater bushbaby
Otolemur crassicaudatus

The bushbaby gets its name because its call sounds like a child crying. It eats plants but also preys on reptiles and birds, pouncing and killing its victims with one bite. A night hunter, the bushbaby's keen eyes can focus on prey in moonlight or starlight.

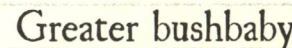
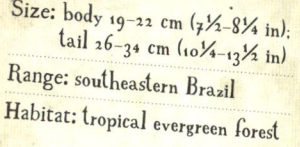

Size: body 19–22 cm (7½–8¼ in); tail 26–34 cm (10¼–13½ in)
Range: southeastern Brazil
Habitat: tropical evergreen forest

Size: body 36–44 cm (14½–17½ in); tail 50–60 cm (19¾–23½ in)
Range: Madagascar
Habitat: tropical evergreen forest, deciduous forest

Aye-aye
Daubentonia madagascariensis

The aye-aye is a nocturnal insect-eater. It taps on trees with its long middle finger, listens for the sound of insects moving under the bark, gnaws a hole and then uses the same finger to hook the insects out. Local tradition says that if you see this strange-looking animal you will have bad luck. Sadly it is often killed.

OLD WORLD MONKEYS

The monkeys in Asia and Africa are known as Old World monkeys. They have close-set downward-pointing nostrils. On their buttocks are pads of hard skin that allow them to rest their weight on the bottoms comfortably while they sleep sitting upright. They tend to be larger than the New World monkeys of the Americas. Unlike the New World monkeys, they do not have prehensile (gripping) tails. Most Old World monkeys are active in the daytime and sleep at night. They have excellent eyesight, hearing and sense of smell.

Diana monkey
Cercopithecus diana

This elegant colourful monkey is an excellent climber and spends almost all its time high up in the trees of the rainforest. Troops of up to 30 monkeys live together, led by an old male. They feed mainly on plants, but also eat insects and the eggs and young of birds.

Size: body 40–57 cm (15¾–22½ in); tail 50–75 cm (19¾–29½ in)
Range: western Africa
Habitat: tropical evergreen rainforest

Size: body 55–95 cm (21¾–37½ in); tail 7–10 cm (2¾–4 in)
Range: western central Africa
Habitat: tropical evergreen rainforest

Japanese macaque
Macaca fuscata

Japan's mountain forests are home to macaque monkeys, which are also known as snow monkeys. In cold winters, these monkeys warm themselves in volcanic springs, where water heated deep below ground bubbles up to the surface to form steaming pools. Macaques eat fruit, leaves, insects and small animals.

Mandrill
Mandrillus sphinx

The forest-dwelling mandrill is unmistakable, with its flaming red nose and blue cheeks. The male mandrill is the largest of all monkeys. A female mandrill gives birth to a single baby, which she carries around with her, either on her back or clinging to her belly. Adults are bad tempered and aggressive and have even been known to attack humans.

Size: body 50–75 cm (19¾–29½ in); tail 7–12 cm (2¾–4¾ in)
Range: Japan
Habitat: tropical forest, marsh, high ground

Children's Animal Encyclopedia

Size: body 53–76 cm (20¾–30 in);
tail 55–76 cm (21¾–30 in)
Range: Southeast Asia: Borneo
Habitat: tropical evergreen rainforest, fresh water

Proboscis monkey
Nasalis larvatus

The male proboscis monkey has a long fleshy nose, which straightens out when he makes his loud honking call. The nose probably acts like a loudspeaker, to warn other monkeys of danger. It also goes red or swells when he is angry or excited. The proboscis monkey lives in mangrove swamp jungle, where it climbs nimbly through the trees.

Olive baboon
Papio anubis

Orderly troops of up to 150 olive baboons move around Africa's savanna, eating leaves, shoots, seeds, roots, bark, fruit, insects, eggs and lizards. These large, heavily built baboons also hunt small mammals such as young antelopes. They spend much of their time grooming each other's fur to keep it clean. They mainly live on the ground, but sleep at night in trees or on rocks.

Size: body up to 1 m (3¼ ft); tail 45–75 cm (17¾–29½ in)
Range: western, central and eastern Africa
Habitat: tropical grassland, tropical evergreen forest

Size: body 46–70 cm (18–27½ in); tail 42–80 cm (16½–31½ in);
Range: western, central and eastern Africa
Habitat: tropical evergreen forest

Red colobus
Procolobus badius

This monkey lives in troops of 50 to 100 animals. The troop contains many small family groups, each consisting of a male and several females with their young. The red colobus makes spectacular leaps between the branches of trees as it searches for fruit, leaves and flowers to eat. Chimpanzees sometimes band together in hunting parties to prey on the red colobus.

Size: body 40–50 cm (15¾–19¾ in); tail 45–55 cm (17¾–21¾ in)
Range: western Africa
Habitat: tropical evergreen rainforest, fresh water

Allen's swamp monkey
Allenpithecus nigroviridis

This little-known monkey lives near rivers and in swamps. Though it eats mainly leaves and fruit, it also goes into the water to snatch crabs and even fish. It, in turn, is hunted by local people for meat and because it sometimes raids farmers' crops. It is now an endangered species.

23

NEW WORLD MONKEYS

The monkeys that live in the lush rainforests of Central and South America are known as New World monkeys. Their long tails help them to balance when they are high off the ground. Many – such as the capuchin, howler and spider monkeys – have prehensile (gripping) tails, which they can wrap around branches and use like an extra limb. They have long fingers and strong feet that grip well, and are excellent runners and leapers. Unlike their Old World relatives, they have broad nostrils that open to the sides and no sitting pads on their buttocks.

Size: body 61 cm (24 in); tail about 67 cm (26¼ in)
Range: southeastern Brazil
Habitat: tropical evergreen forest

Red howler
Alouatta seniculus

Red howler monkeys live in the rainforest in troops of up to 30. Sometimes, all the males in a troop join together in a dawn chorus of howling that can be heard 3 km (1¾ miles) away, telling other monkeys to stay away from their territory. The male's large throat has a special chamber that amplifies its call.

Size: body 80-90 cm (31½-35½ in); tail 80-90 cm (31½-35½ in)
Range: South America
Habitat: tropical evergreen forest

Woolly spider monkey
Brachyteles arachnoides

This monkey moves around the rainforest by using its long arms and prehensile tail to swing from branch to branch. Its numbers are falling because its rainforest home is being destroyed, giving them little refuge from hunters who kill it for meat.

Monk saki
Pithecia monachus

The monk saki has long shaggy hair around its face and on its neck, and a thick bushy tail. This shy wary monkey lives high in the trees and never ventures down to the ground. It usually moves on all fours, but may sometimes walk upright on a large branch. It can make large leaps between branches. These monkeys spend their time in pairs or small family groups.

Size: body 30-38 cm (11¾-15 in); tail 38-50 cm (15-19¾ in)
Range: South America: upper reaches of Amazon River area
Habitat: tropical evergreen forest

White-fronted capuchin
Cebus albifrons

This intelligent monkey is always picking up things, hoping they may be edible. It feeds on shoots, fruit, insects, young birds and birds' eggs. It soaks its hands and feet in urine and uses the scent to mark its territory as it moves through the trees.

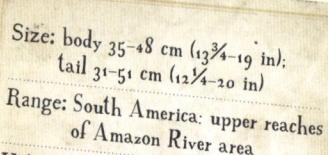

Size: body 35-48 cm (13¾-19 in); tail 31-51 cm (12¼-20 in)
Range: South America: upper reaches of Amazon River area
Habitat: tropical evergreen forest

GIBBONS AND GREAT APES

Gorillas, chimpanzees and orang-utans are called great apes. They are our closest living relatives. After humans, they are the most intelligent primates, but they are endangered, because of hunting and habitat loss. Gibbons are smaller, and are known as lesser apes. Apes live in family-based groups. They walk on all fours, using the knuckles of their hands rather than flat palms, but they can also walk upright, on their hind legs.

Size: height 1.2–1.5 m (4–5 ft); no tail
Range: Borneo
Habitat: tropical forest, swamp

Bornean orang-utan
Pongo pygmaeus

After the gorilla, the orang-utan is the second largest primate. It builds a platform of sticks to form a tree nest in which it sleeps, which may be a different one each night. A female orang-utan gives birth to a single baby, which clings to her fur as she moves around in the treetops.

Size: body 42–58 cm (16½–22¾ in); no tail
Range: Southeast Asia
Habitat: tropical evergreen forest

Size: body 64–94 cm (25¼–37 in); height 1.2–1.7 m (4–5½ ft); no tail
Range: western and central Africa
Habitat: tropical forest, scrub, grassland

Lar Gibbon
Hylobates lar

The lar gibbon lives in trees and rarely descends to the ground. As it swings through the trees and runs upright along branches, it has to look out for weak or dead branches, because a fall from this height could be fatal. Lar gibbons live in small family groups, and are now an endangered species.

Chimpanzee
Pan troglodytes

The chimpanzee mainly eats plants, but occasionally insects and meat. It makes many noises, gestures and facial expressions. It has learned to use everyday objects as simple tools: stones, for example, are used to smash open nuts, wads of leaves to mop up drinking water and sticks to prise grubs out of rotten wood and extract ants and termites from their nests.

Size: height 1.4–1.8 m (4½–6 ft); no tail
Range: western central Africa
Habitat: tropical evergreen forest

Western gorilla
Gorilla gorilla

Gorillas spend most of their time on the ground. They feed on leaves, buds, stalks, berries, bark and fern. They live in troops of up to 30 animals, made up of a leading adult male, a few young males and several females and their young. Young gorillas travel on their mother's back until they are two or three years old.

Carnivores

CARNIVORES

This group of flesh-eating mammals includes dogs, bears, raccoons, mustelids, mongooses, civets, hyenas and cats. Most carnivores have agile bodies and finely tuned senses of sight, hearing and smell, so they can find their prey before it detects them. The main difference, however, between carnivores and other mammals is that they have special teeth that can shear flesh from bone, the way scissors cut paper.

Size: body 1.2 m (4 ft); tail about 30 cm (11¾ in)
Range: South America
Habitat: temperate grassland, fresh water

DOGS

All domestic dogs are descended from wolves. Wolves and other wild dogs have long legs for chasing prey and sharp teeth for killing it. A dog's most developed sensory organ is its nose, which it uses to detect the scent of prey, find a mate, identify other animals and even tell whether they are afraid or relaxed.

Maned wolf
Chrysocyon brachyurus

The maned wolf is similar to the red fox in appearance, but with longer legs and a longer muzzle. A wary creature, the maned wolf lives in remote areas and hunts mainly at night. It preys on large rodents, birds, reptiles and frogs.

Bush dog
Speothos venaticus

With its stocky legs, short tail, squat body and broad face, the bush dog looks more like a small bear than a dog. It inhabits grasslands and open forests, hunting in packs (family groups) during the day for rodents. It spends most of the night underground in a den.

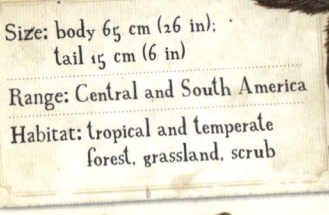

Size: body 65 cm (26 in); tail 15 cm (6 in)
Range: Central and South America
Habitat: tropical and temperate forest, grassland, scrub

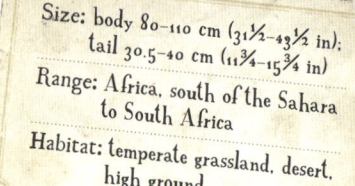

Size: body 80–110 cm (31½–43½ in); tail 30.5–40 cm (11¾–15¾ in)
Range: Africa, south of the Sahara to South Africa
Habitat: temperate grassland, desert, high ground

Hunting dog
Lycaon pictus

These dogs hunt together as a pack. They chase a group of animals, such as wildebeest, split one from the fleeing herd and then move in for the kill. Once found across the African savanna, hunting dogs were shot by farmers protecting their cattle and now live in only a few scattered places.

Children's Animal Encyclopedia

Size: body 37–41 cm (14½–16¼ in);
tail 19–21 cm (7½–8¼ in)
Range: northern Africa,
Middle East
Habitat: desert

Fennec fox
Vulpes zerda

The fennec is the smallest fox. Its large ears, up to 15 cm (6 in) long, allow heat to escape from its body, keeping the fox cool in the hot deserts where it lives. It hunts at night for small rodents, birds, insects and lizards. During the day it shelters in burrows in the sand.

Size: body 1–1.4 m (3¼–4½ ft);
tail 30–48 cm (11¾–19 in)
Range: Canada, northern USA,
Europe, Asia
Habitat: northern forest, temperate
grassland, tundra

Grey wolf
Canis lupus

The largest of all the wild dogs, the grey wolf preys on hoofed mammals, such as bison, moose and musk oxen. Packs vary from five to 20 wolves, led by the strongest male. Each pack has its own hunting territory of up to 1,000 km² (386 sq miles). The wolves howl loudly to warn other packs to say away from their territory.

Size: body 46–68 cm (18–26½ in);
tail up to 35 cm (13¾ in)
Range: Arctic regions of Europe,
Asia, North America
Habitat: coast, tundra

Arctic fox
Alopex lagopus

The Arctic fox can withstand temperatures as low as -50°C (-58°F) on the icy windswept tundra. It feeds on birds, lemmings and other small rodents. In winter its white coat acts as camouflage against the snow and ice. When the snow melts, its coat turns brown or grey and blends in with the ground.

Size: body 46–86 cm (18–33¾ in);
tail 30.5–55.5 cm (12–21¾ in)
Range: North America, Europe, northern
Africa, northern Asia
Habitat: inhabited areas, farmland,
deciduous forest, temperate

Red fox
Vulpes vulpes

The red fox has adapted to many different environments, from forests and grasslands to mountains, deserts and even towns and cities. Red foxes live and hunt alone and only come together to breed and rear their young. They usually prey on rodents, rabbits and other small animals, but they also eat fruit, vegetables, earthworms and fish.

RACCOONS, BEARS AND PANDAS

Both the bear and raccoon families developed from dog-like ancestors millions of years ago. Bears are the largest flesh-eating land mammals, but they will eat almost anything, including plants and insects. Raccoons – and their relatives the coatis and olingos – are long-tailed carnivores, which like to spend much of their time in trees. There are two different types of pandas: the giant pandas are classified with the bears and the red pandas are now classified in a family of their own.

Northern raccoon
Procyon lotor

Size: body 41–60 cm (16–23½ in); tail 20–40 cm (7¾–15¾ in)
Range: southern Canada, USA, Central America
Habitat: deciduous forest, temperate grassland, tropical grassland

The raccoon runs and climbs well, and swims if necessary. It is most active at night. As well as catching prey such as frogs, fish, mice and birds, it often raids rubbish bins, searching for edible items with its long, sensitive fingers. It has a peculiar habit of washing food before eating it. Its thick fur keeps it warm during winter.

South American coati
Nasua nasua

Size: body 43–67 cm (17–26¼ in); tail 43–68 cm (17–26¾ in)
Range: tropical South America
Habitat: forest, mountain

With its long nose, the coati probes into holes and cracks in the ground, searching for insects, spiders and small animals to eat. Groups of up to 40 animals hunt both day and night, resting during the hottest part of the day. After mating, the female goes off alone to give birth to a litter of between two and seven young in a cave or a tree nest.

Size: body 51–63.5 cm (20–25 in); tail 28–48.5 cm (11–19 in)
Range: Himalayas, from Nepal to Burma (Myanmar), southwestern China
Habitat: tropical evergreen forest

Red panda
Ailurus fulgens

The red panda looks more like a raccoon than a giant panda. It sleeps during the day, curled up on a branch with its tail over its eyes or its head tucked into its chest. It feeds during the night, mainly on bamboo shoots, although it will also eat grass, roots, fruit, acorns, mice, birds and birds' eggs.

Size: body 2.2–2.5 m (7¼–8 ft); tail 7.5–12.5 cm (3–5 in)
Range: ice sheets and coastal waters of Arctic Ocean
Habitat: polar

Size: body 1.1–1.4 m (3½–4½ ft); no tail
Range: Southeast Asia
Habitat: tropical evergreen forest, high ground

Sun bear
Helarctos malayanus

The sun bear spends the day sleeping and sunbathing. It searches for food at night, using its long tongue to lick honey out of bees' nests and termites from their mounds. With its curved claws it hooks fruit from branches and tears off tree bark to uncover tasty grubs.

Polar bear
Ursus maritimus

With a thick layer of fat beneath its skin to keep it warm, a polar bear is perfectly comfortable roaming across the Arctic ice in freezing temperatures. Cubs are born in dens dug by their mother in deep snow. They stay with her for about 28 months, learning how to hunt seals and fight.

Size: body 1.5–2.5 m (5–8 ft); small tail
Range: Europe, Asia, North America
Habitat: northern forest, tundra

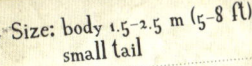

Brown bear
Ursus arctos

Also known as the "grizzly", this bear mostly eats leaves, berries, fruit, nuts, roots and sometimes insects, rodents and fish. It also hunts large mammals such as moose and musk oxen. The bear may hide the dead prey under dirt and leaves until it is ready to consume it.

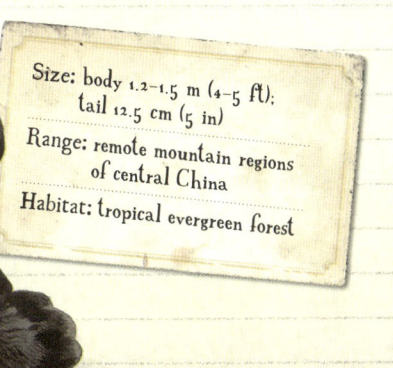

Size: body 1.2–1.5 m (4–5 ft); tail 12.5 cm (5 in)
Range: remote mountain regions of central China
Habitat: tropical evergreen forest

Giant panda
Ailuropoda melanoleuca

The giant panda has to feed for up to 15 hours each day to survive, during which time it consumes up to 20 kg (44 lb) of bamboo. The panda has a thumb-like bone in its hands that allows it to grip its food. Unfortunately, there are only about 1,600 giant pandas left in the wild.

MUSTELIDS, CIVETS AND MONGOOSES

All of these mammals are small- to medium-sized carnivores. Most of the mustelids, which include stoats, badgers, otters, skunks and wolverines, have a long, supple body, short legs and a long tail. There are about 56 species of mustelid living throughout most of the world except Australia and Madagascar. The 34 or so species of civet are tree-dwelling hunters that are active at night. They live in southern Europe, Africa and Asia. About 34 species of mongooses live in Africa and Asia, and these are fast-moving ground dwellers.

Eurasian otter
Lutra lutra

The slender-bodied otter moves fast both in water and on land. It uses its strong tail to push itself along in water and its short, thick fur keeps its skin warm and dry. Its nostrils and ears can be closed off when it is in water. The otter lives in a burrow in the riverbank. Rarely seen during the day, it comes out at night to find fish, frogs, voles and other water creatures to eat.

Size: body 55–80 cm (21¾–31½ in); tail 30–50 cm (11¾–19¾ in)
Range: Europe, northern Africa, Asia
Habitat: fresh water, coast

African palm civet
Nandinia binotata

This civet has short legs and a long thick tail. It is a skilled climber and spends much of its life in trees, where it rests during the day. It usually hunts at night, catching insects and small creatures such as lizards and birds. It also eats many kinds of fruit and leaves. The female gives birth to litters of two or three young at any time of year.

Size: body 43–60 cm (17–23½ in); tail 48–62 cm (19–24½ in)
Range: Central Africa
Habitat: tropical evergreen forest, tropical grassland, deciduous forest, inhabited areas, farmland

Sea otter
Enhydra lutris

This otter feeds on shellfish and uses rocks as tools to help it open the hard shells. The otter lies on its back in the water and places a rock on its chest. It bangs its prey against the rock until the shell breaks, revealing the soft flesh inside.

Size: body 1–1.2 m (3¼–4 ft); tail 25–37 cm (9¾–14¼ in)
Range: northern Pacific coast: Bering Sea and from Vancouver to California
Habitat: coast

Size: body 28–38 cm (11–15 in); tail 18–25 cm (7–9¾ in)
Range: North America
Habitat: deciduous forest, temperate grassland, inhabited areas, farmland water

Meerkat
Suricata suricatta

Meerkats are a type of mongoose. They are sociable animals and several families may live together. During the day, while most of the group forages for food such as insects, lizards, birds and fruit, some meerkats watch out for birds of prey. They give a shrill call to alert the others to any danger.

Striped skunk
Mephitis mephitis

Skunks are well known for the foul-smelling fluid they spray when threatened. The fluid comes from glands near the tail. The strong smell makes it difficult for an enemy to breathe and irritates its eyes. The striped skunk is active at night, when it searches for food.

Size: body 25–30 cm (9¾–11¾ in); tail 19–24 cm (7½–9½ in)
Range: southern Africa
Habitat: temperate grassland, tropical grassland

Size: body 56–81 cm (22–32 in); tail 11–20 cm (4¼–7¾ in)
Range: Europe, Asia
Habitat: deciduous forest, temperate grassland

Eurasian badger
Meles meles

Families of Eurasian badgers live in huge burrows called setts. These burrows have several entrances and networks of underground passages and chambers. Badgers are generally active at night, coming out of the sett around dusk. They eat large quantities of earthworms as well as other small animals, plants, fruit and nuts.

Indian mongoose
Herpestes javanicus

The mongoose eats almost any food it can catch, including snakes, scorpions and insects. It is popular among humans because it hunts pests such as rats and mice. As a result, the mongoose has been introduced into areas outside its normal range.

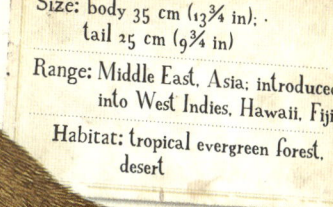

Size: body 35 cm (13¾ in); tail 25 cm (9¾ in)
Range: Middle East, Asia; introduced into West Indies, Hawaii, Fiji
Habitat: tropical evergreen forest, desert

CATS AND HYENAS

Cats are ruthless hunters. Their strong legs enable them to catch their prey in a brief, rapid chase or with a lightning-quick pounce. They have bendy backbones that allow them to twist and turn easily when chasing prey. When they pounce, their claws extend and grip their victim's flesh, but when a cat is walking or running, the claws retract into the toes so they are not damaged. Most cats have coats patterned with spots or stripes to camouflage them as they stalk prey. There are 36 species of wild cat, from big cats such as lions and tigers, to smaller ones such as the lynx.

Wild cat
Felis silvestris

The wild cat looks similar to a domestic cat, but it is larger and has a shorter, thicker tail. It is a good tree-climber, but stalks most of its prey on the ground, catching small rodents and birds.

Size: body 50–65 cm (19¾–25½ in); tail 25–38 cm (9¾–15 in)
Range: Europe, Africa, Middle East, India, Central Asia
Habitat: deciduous forest, temperate grassland, tropical grassland, high ground

Eurasian lynx
Lynx lynx

The lynx lives alone in forests and woodland and hunts hares, rabbits, rodents, small deer and birds such as grouse. The lynx has excellent eyesight – it can spot a mouse 75 m (250 ft) away.

Size: body 80 cm–1.3 m (31½ in–4¼ ft); tail 4–8 cm (1½–3 in)
Range: Europe, Asia
Habitat: northern forest

Striped hyena
Hyaena hyaena

Although hyenas have a dog-like body, they are more closely related to cats. They specialize in feeding on carrion (dead animals) and the scraps left by big cats such as lions. They also prey on young sheep and goats, small mammals, birds, lizards, snakes and insects.

Size: body 1–1.2 m (3¼–4 ft); tail 25–35 cm (9¾–13¾ in)
Range: northern and eastern Africa, through Middle East to India
Habitat: temperate grassland, tropical grassland, desert

Jaguar
Panthera onca

The largest South American cat, the jaguar cannot run fast for very long, so it relies on getting close to its prey to make a successful kill. It is a good swimmer, and feeds on fish and turtles, as well as on deer and other land animals.

Size: body 1.5–1.8 m (5–6 ft); tail 70–91 cm (27½–36 in)
Range: southern USA, Central and South America
Habitat: deciduous forest, tropical evergreen forest, tropical grassland

Children's Animal Encyclopedia

Size: body 1.3–1.9 m (4¼–6¼ ft); tail 1.1–1.4 m (3½–4½ ft)
Range: Africa, Middle East, southern and Southeast Asia
Habitat: deciduous and tropical evergreen forest, temperate and tropical grassland, desert

Leopard
Panthera pardus

The leopard hauls the bodies of large prey up into trees and out of reach of scavenging hyenas and jackals. Its stunning coat is dappled with spots to camouflage it among the leaves of the trees and the long grass below. It will sometimes leap straight out of a tree onto passing prey.

Snow leopard
Uncia uncia

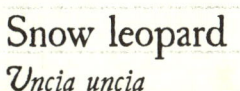

Size: body 1.2–1.5 m (4–5 ft); tail about 91 cm (36 in)
Range: Himalayas in central Asia
Habitat: mountain forest, high grassland

The solitary snow leopard feeds mainly on wild sheep and goats. Its broad, furry feet stop it sinking in the snow on high mountain slopes. It can make huge leaps between rocky crags, using its tail for balance.

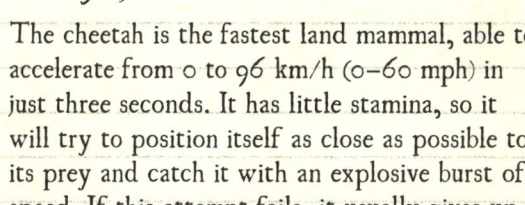

Size: body 1.1–1.4 m (3½–4½ ft); tail 65–80 cm (25½–31½ in)
Range: Africa, south of the Sahara; Iran
Habitat: temperate grassland, tropical grassland

Cheetah
Acinonyx jubatus

The cheetah is the fastest land mammal, able to accelerate from 0 to 96 km/h (0–60 mph) in just three seconds. It has little stamina, so it will try to position itself as close as possible to its prey and catch it with an explosive burst of speed. If this attempt fails, it usually gives up.

Lion
Panthera leo

Lions live in family groups called prides. A pride normally contains up to three males, 15 females and their young. The females do most of the hunting, often stalking antelopes and zebras in pairs or larger groups. The male's role is to defend the pride's territory.

Size: body 1.4–2 m (4½–6½ ft); tail 67–100 cm (26¼ in–39½ in)
Range: Africa, south of the Sahara; northwestern India
Habitat: tropical grassland

33

TIGERS

The tiger is the biggest and strongest of all the wild cats. At the beginning of the 20th century, there were hundreds of thousands of tigers living throughout the forests of Asia. Hunting and the destruction of forests have had such a devastating effect on their numbers that there are now just 4,000 wild tigers left, mainly living in parts of India, China, Indonesia and Siberia. Tigers live alone, roaring loudly to tell other tigers to keep away from their territory, which they mark out with scent, droppings and scratches on tree trunks. They hunt large mammals, usually at night, and sometimes travel up to 20 km (12 miles) in search of food. As few as one in every ten hunts may be successful, so when they do make a kill they gorge themselves on as much meat as they can eat. Despite stories of "man-eating" tigers, they rarely attack humans.

TIGER CUBS

Tigers are born in litters of between two and six cubs. They are blind for the first 10 days and their mother suckles the cubs for up to eight weeks. Not until they are about 18 months old do they hunt for themselves, and they stay with their mother for two to three years. The father takes no part in their rearing.

HUNTING

At dusk, tigers set out to hunt buffalo, deer, wild pigs and other forest animals. They can only run fast for short distances, so they rely on their cunning and stealth to catch their prey. Their striped coat camouflages them against the background of trees and long grass, enabling them to sneak up on their victims without being seen. When they are close enough, they sprint forwards and pounce on the unsuspecting animal.

Children's Animal Encyclopedia

Unlike domestic cats, tigers like to be near water, and (like this Bengal tiger) will take a dip to cool off on a hot day. They are good swimmers, and may cross rivers or swim between islands in search of their prey. Tigers can also be seen climbing trees occasionally.

TIGER TYPES

A century ago, there were nine types, or subspecies, of tiger, but the Bali, Javan and Caspian tigers are now extinct. The Bengal tiger is the most numerous but it and the Siberian, South China, Indo-Chinese, Malayan and Sumatran tigers are all endangered. The largest of all is the Siberian tiger, weighing up to 384 kg (847 lb).

Siberian tiger Also known as the Amur tiger, this is one of the largest cats in history.

Indo-Chinese tiger It is thought that only 350 of these tigers survive.

Caspian tiger This tiger was last seen in the wild in the 1970s.

Sumatran tiger This is the smallest and darkest tiger, and is critically endangered.

Seals, whales and dolphins

SEALS, WHALES AND DOLPHINS

Marine mammals are well adapted to life in the water, with sleek and streamlined bodies and paddle-shaped flippers. Under their skin, these marine mammals have a thick layer of fat called blubber to keep them warm. They spend much of their time underwater, often diving to great depths in search of food. But because they have lungs, and not gills like fish, they have to surface regularly to breathe air.

SEALS, SEA LIONS AND WALRUSES

With their torpedo-like bodies, these marine mammals are skilful swimmers and divers. Their heart beat slows during dives, to enable them to stay underwater for long periods. Unlike whales and dolphins, they come ashore to have their babies. Seals and walruses swim by pushing themselves through the water with their tail-like hind flippers, but sea lions use their long front flippers.

Walrus
Odobenus rosmarus

Walruses live in the Arctic, where they feed on shellfish. They have sharp tusks which they use to drag themselves out of the water, and for fighting. Walruses are excellent swimmers, but on land they move with great difficulty.

Size: 2.2–3.5 m (7¼–11½ ft)
Range: Arctic Ocean, occasionally northern Atlantic Ocean
Habitat: coastal waters, polar

Size: 1.4–1.8 m (4½–6 ft)
Range: southern Pacific and Atlantic oceans
Habitat: coastal waters

South American fur seal
Arctocephalus australis

This seal eats fish, squid, penguins and small marine creatures. The female gives birth to a single pup. She stays with it for 12 days, then goes off to sea to feed, returning regularly to suckle her young pup.

Size: 1.7–2.2 m (5½–7¼ ft)
Range: Pacific coasts, from Canada to Mexico
Habitat: coastal waters

California sea lion
Zalophus californianus

This is the fastest swimmer of all the seals and sea lions, reaching speeds of 40 km/h (25 mph). It can also move fast on land by tucking its back flippers under its body. Huge colonies gather to breed on the rocky southwestern shores of the USA.

Children's Animal Encyclopedia

Size: 2.4–2.8 m (7¾–9¼ ft)
Range: northern Pacific Ocean
Habitat: coastal waters

Harbour seal
Phoca vitulina

Like all seals, the harbour seal spends most of its life in water, coming to land only to mate and give birth. Harbour seal pups are well developed when they are born. They can swim from birth, and can dive for up to two minutes when just two or three days old. The harbour seal feeds on fish and squid.

Size: 1.4–1.8 m (4½–6 ft)
Range: North Atlantic and northern Pacific oceans
Habitat: polar, coastal waters

Steller sea lion
Eumetopias jubatus

This is the largest of the sea lions. It catches fish, squid and octopus. A large male may even eat smaller seals. The beaches where it breeds can be so crowded that young pups are crushed. A seal mother often goes to sea to find food for herself and her pup. When she comes back, she calls to nearby pups, and then smells and touches them until she finds the one that belongs to her.

Harp seal
Pagophilus groenlandicus

The harp seal has a grey body with a black head and stripe across its back. In the breeding season, rival males fight over females. After mating, the females form groups on the ice to give birth. The pups grow rapidly as they feed on their mothers' nourishing, fat-rich milk.

Size: 1.6–1.9 m (5¼–6¼ ft)
Range: North Atlantic Ocean and Arctic Ocean
Habitat: polar

Leopard seal
Hydrurga leptonyx

The leopard seal is the fiercest hunter of all seals, with large, tooth-studded jaws for grasping prey and tearing it apart. The leopard seal preys on penguins by catching them underwater just as they launch themselves off the ice. It also hunts other smaller seals, as well as fish, squid and shellfish.

Size: 3–3.5 m (10–11½ ft)
Range: Southern Ocean
Habitat: coastal waters, polar

ANTARCTIC SEALS

The world's coldest continent is Antarctica, most of which is permanently covered in thick ice. With wind speeds sometimes exceeding 320 km/h (200 mph) and temperatures plunging as low as -89°C (-128°F), few animals can survive. Even the surrounding seas freeze over, but they are rich in food and support many animals, including seals. There are six species of Antarctic seal: southern elephant, Ross, leopard, crabeater, Weddell and southern fur seals. The southern elephant seal is the world's largest seal, with males weighing up to 4,000 kg (8,800 lb). Born in late winter, by late spring seal pups are strong enough to find their own food in the Antarctic waters.

CRABEATER SEAL

Surprisingly, crabeater seals do not eat crabs. They actually feed on small, shrimp-like creatures called krill, which they filter from the water through their teeth. They detect nearby krill with their long, downward-curving whiskers. On land, crabeater seals can move as fast as 25 km/h (16 mph), but they are often attacked by killer whales.

ELEPHANT SEAL

In the breeding season, a male southern elephant seal guards a group of 40–50 females, with whom he mates. If a rival male challenges him, he takes up a threatening pose and roars loudly. The skin bag on his nose inflates to amplify the sound. If the challenger does not back off, a bloody battle occurs. A female elephant seal gives birth to a single pup, which she suckles for about a month. During this period she herself does not eat but lives off the energy already stored in her blubber.

Puppy fat

At birth, a Weddell seal pup weighs about 25 kg (55 lb) but it grows quickly, nourished by its mother's rich milk. It first enters the water when about six weeks old to start learning to find its own food.

Children's Animal Encyclopedia

ROSS SEAL

The smallest of the Antarctic seals, the Ross seal is uniformly grey along its back and sides, and silvery-grey to white underneath. It has a small head, needle-like incisor teeth and long flippers. It feeds on squid, fish and krill.

WEDDELL SEAL

The Weddell seal makes longer, deeper dives than any other seal, often reaching depths of 300–400 m (980–1,300 ft) to feed on Antarctic cod. One Weddell seal was recorded as diving to 600 m (2,000 ft) for 73 minutes. In summer, these large gentle seals spend many hours asleep on the ice. In winter, they tend to stay underwater to avoid the harsh conditions, breathing through holes that they make in the ice.

39

Whales, dolphins and porpoises

WHALES, DOLPHINS AND PORPOISES

Whales are the largest sea mammals. There are two kinds of whales: toothed and baleen. Baleen whales have bristly plates in their mouths instead of teeth. When they feed, they take gulps of water. Baleen plates act like filters, so the water drains away but the fish, krill and plankton stay in the whale's mouth. Toothed whales can locate other sea creatures by echolocation. They send out high-pitched clicking sounds and detect the echoes as they bounce back from objects. Dolphins and porpoises are small-toothed whales. Whales swim with up-and-down strokes of their tails, using their flippers to steer.

Size: 1.8–2.3 m (6–7½ ft)
Range: northern Pacific Ocean
Habitat: coastal waters, oceanic

Dall's porpoise
Phocoenides dalli

Dall's porpoise is larger and heavier than most porpoises, and inhabits deeper waters. It lives in groups of up to 15 porpoises. Schools of 100 or more porpoises may gather to migrate north in summer and south in winter. Mothers suckle their calves for as long as two years.

Harbour porpoise
Phocoena phocoena

Size: 1.4–1.8 m (4½–6 ft)
Range: northern Atlantic and Pacific oceans, Black and Mediterranean Seas
Habitat: coastal waters, oceanic

These porpoises feed on fish such as herring and mackerel. They dive for up to six minutes when hunting prey, which they pinpoint using echolocation clicks. Before breeding, they perform long courtship rituals, caressing one another as they swim side by side. Calves are born 11 months after mating. While a mother suckles her calf, she lies on her side at the water's surface, so the calf can breathe easily.

Killer whale
Orcinus orca

The largest of the dolphin family, the killer whale is a fierce hunter that feeds on fish, squid, sea lions, birds and even other whales. It sometimes snatches seals from the shore or tips them off floating ice into its mouth. It lives and hunts in travelling family groups of up to 40 animals.

Size: 7–9.7 m (23–32 ft)
Range: worldwide, especially cooler seas
Habitat: coastal waters, oceanic, polar

Children's Animal Encyclopedia

Ganges dolphin
Platanista gangetica

One of only five species of freshwater dolphin, the Ganges dolphin lives in muddy rivers in India. It is blind and uses radar-like echolocation signals to find its prey of fish and shrimps.

Size: 1.5–2.4 m (5–8 ft)
Range: India: Ganges and Brahmaputra river systems
Habitat: fresh water

Common dolphin
Delphinus delphis

Also known as the short-beaked dolphin, this mammal has pointed flippers, a curved dorsal fin and a long beak. It lives in groups of between 20 and 100 dolphins. Curious and playful, they are often seen swimming alongside ships, leaping and rolling in the water.

Size: 2.1–2.6 m (7–8½ ft)
Range: warm and tropical oceans worldwide
Habitat: coastal waters, oceanic

Blue whale
Balaenoptera musculus

The world's largest mammal, the blue whale can weigh 145 tonnes (tons) and measure 32 m (105 ft). This giant feeds on huge quantities of tiny, shrimp-like creatures called krill, consuming up to 4 tonnes (tons) each day in the summer. The blue whale is in danger of extinction, as there are only 10,000–25,000 left.

Size: 25–32 m (82–105 ft)
Range: all oceans
Habitat: oceanic

Atlantic bottle-nosed dolphin
Tursiops truncatus

The curving line of this dolphin's mouth makes it look as if it is always smiling. It feeds mainly on bottom-dwelling fish, and is a skilful echolocator, producing up to 1,000 clicking noises a second.

Size: 3–4.2 m (10–14 ft)
Range: warm and tropical oceans worldwide
Habitat: coastal waters, oceanic

41

Whales, dolphins and porpoises

Size: 11–20 m (36–66 ft)
Range: all oceans
Habitat: oceanic, polar

Sperm whale
Physeter macrocephalus

The sperm whale has as a huge head filled with a waxy substance called spermaceti. The spermaceti helps the whale to alter its buoyancy – its ability to float. This enables it to reach depths of more than 1,000 m (3,280 ft) in search of squid to eat.

White whale
Delphinapterus leucas

White whales, also called belugas, often live together in small groups called pods. They communicate with a variety of sounds, such as whistles, clicks, clangs, twitters and moos. Polar bears prey on belugas that get trapped by the Arctic ice. In winter, big herds of belugas migrate south.

Size: 4–6.1 m (13–20 ft)
Range: Arctic Ocean and subarctic waters
Habitat: coastal waters, oceanic

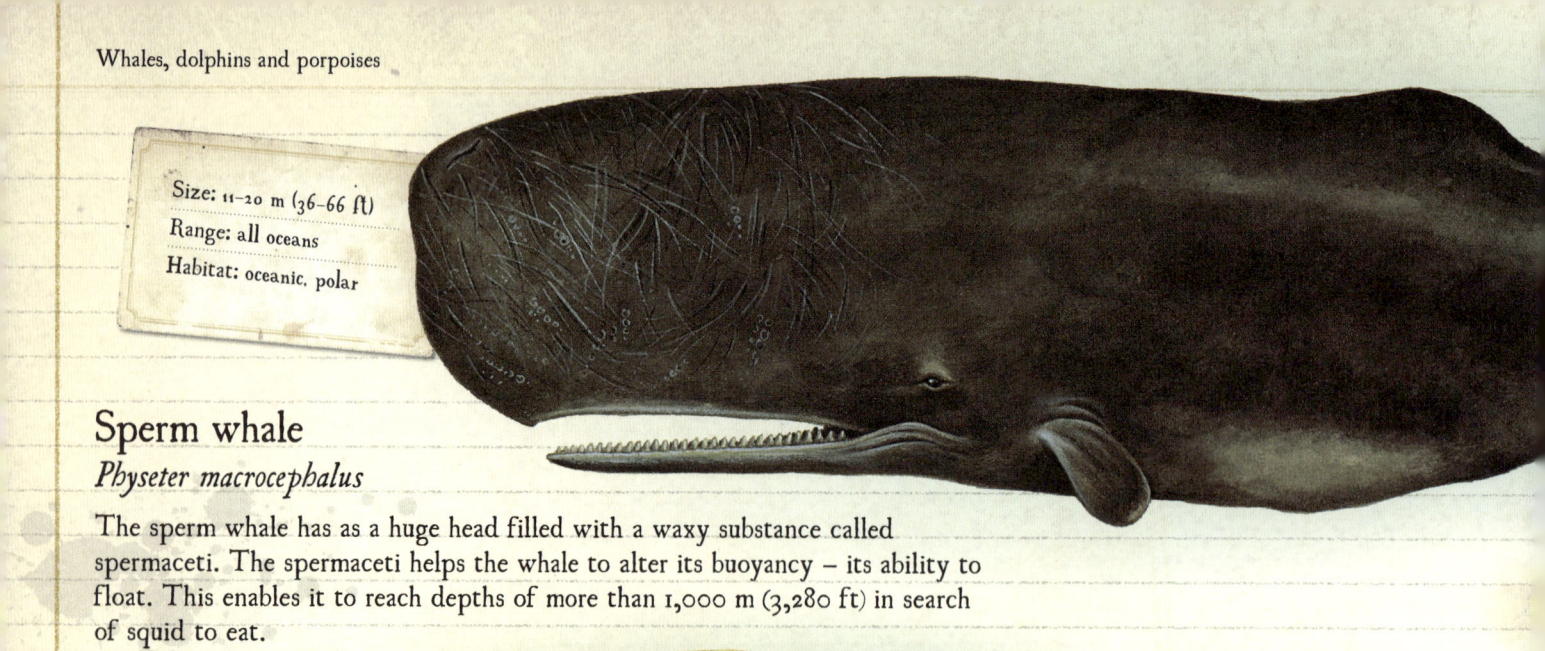

Narwhal
Monodon monoceros

The narwhal is related to the white whale, but has only two teeth. One of the male's teeth grows into a spiral tusk up to 2.7 m (8¾ ft) long, which sticks through its top lip. The tusk is probably used to impress females and fight rivals in the breeding season. Females sometimes have a short tusk.

Size: 4–6.1 m (13–20 ft)
Range: high Arctic Ocean
Habitat: oceanic, polar

Cuvier's beaked whale
Ziphius cavirostris

This whale dives deeper and for longer than any other mammal. A dive can extend to nearly 3,000 m (10,000 ft) and can last for more than two hours. A whale undertakes these long journeys in search of squid and fish.

Size: 6.4–7 m (21–23 ft)
Range: all oceans, temperate and tropical waters
Habitat: oceanic

Children's Animal Encyclopedia

Size: up to 3 m (10 ft)
Range: east African coast, Arabian Gulf, Indian Ocean, Red Sea to northern Australia
Habitat: coastal waters

Dugong
Dugong dugon

Surprisingly, dugongs are related to elephants. The dugong is fleshy and streamlined, with a crescent-shaped tail. It is shy and solitary, spending much of its life on the seabed, feeding on seaweed and seagrass. A female dugong gives birth to a single baby in the water and helps it to the surface.

Humpback whale
Megaptera novaeangliae

The humpback whale is famous for the amazingly complex songs it sings to keep in touch with other whales and to attract mates. It often sings for hours on end, only pausing to take a breath of air. These songs travel great distances through the water.

Size: 14.6–19 m (48–62½ ft)
Range: all oceans
Habitat: coastal waters, oceanic, polar

Grey whale
Eschrichtius robustus

This whale stirs up the seabed with its snout and uses its baleen plates to filter tiny creatures to eat. It makes a round trip of 20,000 km (12,428 miles) between its summer feeding waters off Alaska and the warmer waters off the coast of Mexico, where it breeds in winter.

Size: 12.2–15.3 m (40–50 ft)
Range: northeast and northwest Pacific Ocean
Habitat: coastal waters, oceanic

Minke whale
Balaenoptera acutorostrata

The minke whale is a pint-sized relative of the humpback and blue whales. Like them, it has distinctive grooves along its throat. In polar regions, the minke feeds mainly on plankton, but in warmer waters it eats fish and squid as well.

Size: 8–10 m (26–33 ft)
Range: all oceans, temperate and polar waters
Habitat: coastal waters, oceanic

43

ELEPHANTS

Weighing as much as 5,900 kg (13,000 lb) and standing up to 4 m (13 ft) tall at the shoulder, the elephant is the largest land mammal. There are three elephant species: two live in Africa, the other in India and Southeast Asia. An elephant's flexible trunk – a long nose fixed to its upper lip – contains up to 100,000 muscles, and is used for smelling, feeling, breathing, feeding and making loud trumpeting calls. The elephant uses its tusks for fighting, stripping bark off trees and digging for water. Elephants live on grassy plains and desert scrubland, and in river valleys and swamps. They can reach the age of 78. Females and young elephants live in family herds, while mature males roam alone.

A baby elephant does not need to forage for food, because it drinks its mother's milk for at least two years. Sometimes, other adult females in the herd also suckle it.

SHOWERS AND MUD BATHS

As well as releasing heat through their large flappy ears, elephants also keep cool by giving themselves a shower. They suck up water with their trunks and spray it over their bodies. An elephant can reach every part of its body by swinging its trunk and blowing at just the right moment. Elephants sometimes wallow in mud, too, or throw dust over themselves, which coats their skin and protects them against insects and sunburn. It also stops moisture evaporating from their skin.

Children's Animal Encyclopedia

THREE SPECIES

The African bush elephant is larger and heavier than its Asian cousin, with bigger, more rounded ears. It has two finger-like projections on the end of its trunk, while the Asian has one. The African forest elephant is the smallest of the three species. Poachers are a major threat to African elephants, killing thousands every year for their ivory tusks.

African

Asian

BIG APPETITE

An African elephant eats about 150 kg (330 lb) of grass, leaves, twigs, bark, roots and fruit every day. In order to consume such a large amount, it has to spend three-quarters of its time feeding.

ELEPHANTS AT WORK

For thousands of years, humans have trained elephants to lift, push and drag heavy objects. In forestry work, Asian elephants are sometimes taught to use their tusks to raise heavy logs like a fork-lift truck.

45

HOOFED MAMMALS

Some mammals have toes that end in hard coverings called hooves. Hooves are made of keratin – the same substance as nails and claws. Long ago, all hoofed mammals had five toes. As they evolved, they lost the use of some toes to enable them to run faster. Hoofed mammals are classified according to whether their feet have an odd number (one or three) or an even number (two or four) of working toes.

Pygmy hippopotamus
Choeropsis liberiensis

This small hippopotamus lives around swamps, but spends most of its time on dry land. This pygmy hippo is in severe danger of becoming extinct as its forest habitat is cut down. They are also at risk from hunters, who kill the animal for its meat.

Size: body 1.7–1.9 m (5½–6¼ ft); tail 15–21 cm (6–8¼ in)
Range: western Africa: Liberia, Ivory Coast, Sierra Leone, Guinea
Habitat: tropical evergreen forest, fresh water

PIGS, PECCARIES AND HIPPOPOTAMUSES

A pig is easily recognized by its long, muscular snout, which ends in a round, flat disc. The pig-like peccary lives only in the Americas, while the hippo, the larger cousin of pigs and peccaries, is found in Africa. Pigs, peccaries and hippos are even-toed hoofed mammals, with four toes on their feet (peccaries have only three on their hind feet). They have simpler stomachs than other even-toed hoofed mammals.

Warthog
Phacochoerus africanus

The warthog is not a pretty sight. It has long legs, curving tusks and a long, broad head with two pairs of large wart-like protuberances. It lives in small family groups on the African savanna and on treeless plains, where it feeds on short grasses and herbs. In the hottest part of the day, it shelters in its burrow, which is often the disused burrow of an aardvark. Its main enemies are lions and leopards.

Size: body 1.1–1.4 m (3½–4½ ft); tail 35–50 cm (13¾–19¾ in)
Range: central and southern Africa
Habitat: tropical grassland, desert

Collared peccary
Pecari tajacu

Size: body 75-90 cm (29½-3½ in); tail 1.5-3 cm (⅝-1¼ in)
Range: southwestern USA, Mexico, Central and South America
Habitat: deciduous forest, tropical evergreen forest, desert

A light neckband gives collared peccaries their name. They live in groups of up to 15 animals, marking their territory with scent produced by musk glands on their backs. They eat roots, herbs, grass, fruit, worms and insect larvae. They can run fast enough to escape from predators such as jaguars and pumas.

Wild boar
Sus scrofa

Size: body 1.1-1.3 m (3½-4¼ ft); tail 15-20 cm (6-7¾ in)
Range: all continents except Antarctica
Habitat: deciduous and tropical forest, temperate and tropical grassland, inhabited areas, farmland

The wild boar is the ancestor of the farmyard pig. With its long snout it roots around the woodland floor for plants and insects to eat. It also digs up bulbs and tubers. Young boars have stripey coats that blend in with the trees and hide them from predators.

Western bearded pig
Sus barbatus

Size: body 1.2-1.5 m (4-5 ft); tail 20-30 cm (7¾-11¾ in)
Range: Malaysia, Sumatra, Borneo
Habitat: tropical evergreen forest

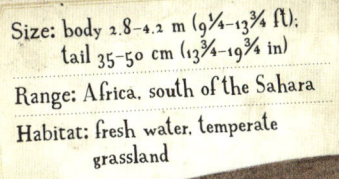

While some bearded pigs have bristles all over their snouts, others have a line of whiskers along their jaws and cheeks. The bearded pig lives in rainforests, but it is also found on beaches and around swamps. Fallen fruit, rats and insect larvae are this pig's main foods. It often follows monkeys to pick up any fruit that they might have dropped.

Hippopotamus
Hippopotamus amphibius

Size: body 2.8-4.2 m (9¼-13¾ ft); tail 35-50 cm (13¾-19¾ in)
Range: Africa, south of the Sahara
Habitat: fresh water, temperate grassland

The hippo is one of the world's largest land mammals – only rhinos and elephants weigh more. It lives near rivers and lakes, and spends up to 16 hours each day in the water to keep cool. It emerges at sunset to graze on riverside plants and eat fallen fruit. It can swim well, but often prefers to walk along the river bottom.

Camels

CAMELS

The camel family consists of the dromedary, the bactrian camel, the vicuña and the guanaco. They are cud-chewing animals, and their feet have just two toes on each foot. The desert-dwelling dromedary and bactrian camels have broad, flat pads under each foot to help them walk over the soft, sandy soil. Vicuñas and guanacos can breathe the thin air on high mountain pastures, and their thick, woolly coats enable them to endure the chilly temperatures at high altitude.

Size: body 2.2–3.4 m (7¼–11 ft); tail 50 cm (19¾ in)
Range: northern Africa, Middle East; introduced into Australia
Habitat: temperate and tropical grassland, desert

Vicuña
Vicugna vicugna

Size: body 1.4–1.6 m (4½–5¼ ft); tail 15 cm (6 in)
Range: Andes, from Peru to northern Chile
Habitat: tropical grassland, high ground

Vicuñas are humpless camels. They live in small family herds in the Andes Mountains of South America, where they feed on grass and small plants. Each herd is guarded by an adult male. He warns the rest of the herd of danger by whistling loudly to them.

Dromedary
Camelus dromedarius

Dromedaries are well suited to life in the desert. Their ears and nostrils can close to keep out sand, while their tough lips enable them to eat thorny desert plants without being injured. They use their humps to store fat, which their bodies break down into water and energy when food and drink become scarce.

Size: body about 1 m (3¼ ft); tail 4–5 cm (1½–2 in)
Range: Himalayas to central China
Habitat: deciduous forest, high ground, desert

DEER, GIRAFFES, PRONGHORNS AND BOVIDS

This group of even-toed hoofed animals all chew the cud, which means that they have complex stomachs. When they eat, they briefly chew leaves and grasses and swallow them. The animal then brings the partly digested food back up into its mouth and chews it properly. Giraffes, pronghorns and bovids (cattle, antelopes, sheep and goats) have horns on their heads, while deer have antlers. Horns are permanent growths, but antlers drop off and grow again each year.

Alpine musk deer
Moschus chrysogaster

A male musk deer has a scent gland which oozes a strong-smelling liquid called musk. The male uses this to send signals to females in the breeding season. The musk deer has a coat of long, thick, bristly hairs and two tusk-like teeth. It feeds on lichens, shoots, buds, grass, moss and twigs.

Children's Animal Encyclopedia

Size: body 1.6–2.5 m (5¼–8 ft); tail 12–25 cm (4¾–9¾ in)
Range: northern Africa, Europe, Asia, North America; introduced into New Zealand
Habitat: deciduous forest, high ground, temperate grassland

Red deer
Cervus elaphus

Male and female red deer live in separate herds. The male's antlers drop off each spring, and are replaced by a new, larger set. In the breeding season, males use their antlers to fight each other for the right to mate with the females. The older males usually win.

Size: body 2.5–3 m (8–10 ft); tail 5–12 cm (2–4¾ in)
Range: northernmost parts of Europe, Asia, North America
Habitat: northern forest, fresh water

Moose
Alces alces

The moose (also known as the elk) is the largest of all the deer species. It has massive antlers, a broad, overhanging muzzle and a flap of skin that dangles from its throat. In winter, the moose eats pine cones, and shovels away the snow with its hooves to find mosses and lichens too. It swims well, and in summer it will often wade into lakes and rivers to feed on water plants. Males bellow to attract the females.

Size: body 1.2–2.2 m (4–7¼ ft); tail 10–21 cm (4–8¼ in)
Range: northern Europe, northern Asia, Greenland, northern North America
Habitat: northern forest, tundra

Caribou
Rangifer tarandus

The caribou, or reindeer, is the only deer species in which both males and females have antlers (it is usually only the males). The caribou feeds mainly on mosses, lichens and fungi in winter. In summer it travels north to feed on the rich grass and plants of the tundra, migrating up to 1,200 km (750 miles) each way. The females and young live in herds, but adult males often live alone.

49

Deer, giraffes, pronghorns and bovids

Size: body 1.2–2 m (4–6½ ft); tail 30–40 cm (11¾–16½ ft)
Range: Democratic Republic of Congo (Zaire)
Habitat: tropical evergreen forest

Size: body 3–4 m (10–13 ft); tail 90–110 cm (35½–43½ in)
Range: Africa, south of the Sahara
Habitat: tropical grassland

Giraffe
Giraffa camelopardalis

The giraffe lives on Africa's savanna. With its amazingly long legs and neck, it stands nearly 6 m (19½ ft) tall, making it the tallest living mammal. Its great height enables it to feed on leaves and buds at the tops of trees, and to spot approaching danger.

Okapi
Okapia johnstoni

The African okapi feeds on the leaves and shoots of rainforest trees. It pulls them off the branches with its tongue, which is so long that the okapi can even use it to clean its eyes and eyelids. Its leg stripes are a good camouflage. It lives alone and meets other okapis only in the breeding season. Males have short horns, like those of a giraffe.

Pronghorn
Antilocapra americana

One of North America's fastest mammals, the pronghorn can run at 80 km/h (50 mph). Both males and females have horns with short, forward-pointing prongs. Pronghorns travel far in the winter in search of food.

Size: body 1.1–1.3 m (3½–4¼ ft); tail 10–15 cm (4–6 in)
Range: eastern South America, south of the Amazon
Habitat: temperate grassland

Pampas deer
Ozotoceros bezoarticus

This deer lives among the tall grasses of the South American grasslands – a habitat called 'pampas'. As the pampas has been turned to farmland, this species has lost much of its natural habitat. The pampas deer lives in groups of up to six animals.

Size: body 1–1.15 m (3¼–5 ft); tail 7.5–10 cm (3–4 in)
Range: central Canada, western USA, Mexico
Habitat: temperate grassland, desert

50

Blue wildebeest
Connochaetes taurinus

In the dry season, huge herds of these large, cow-like antelopes walk very great distances across the African savanna in search of fresh grass and watering holes. Young wildebeest calves are born during the wet season, when the herds split up and food is more plentiful.

Size: body 1.7–2.4 m (5½–7¾ ft); tail 60–100 cm (23½–35½ in)
Range: southern Africa
Habitat: tropical grassland

Size: body 2.5–3 m (8¼–10 ft); tail 60–100 cm (23½–35½ in)
Range: India; Southeast Asia; introduced into other places
Habitat: tropical grassland, tropical evergreen forest, fresh water

Asian water buffalo
Bubalus bubalis

Water buffalo feed early and late in the day on grass and other vegetation growing near lakes and rivers. They spend much of the rest of the time wallowing in mud or submerged in the water, with only their muzzles showing. They use their long, curved horns to defend themselves against tigers.

Wild yak
Bos mutus

Despite its size, the yak is surprisingly sure-footed as it grazes on remote mountain slopes. Its long, thick, ragged hair almost reaches to the ground. It also has a woolly undercoat to help protect it against freezing temperatures.

Size: body up to 3.25 m (10½ ft); tail 50–80 cm (19¾–31½ in)
Range: Himalaya mountains of central Asia
Habitat: high ground, tundra

Size: body 1.7–2.5 m (5½–8¼ ft); tail 45–65 cm (17¾–25½ in)
Range: central and western Africa
Habitat: deciduous forest, tropical evergreen forest, high ground

Bongo
Tragelaphus eurycerus

The shy, forest-dwelling bongo hides among the bushes and trees during the daytime. At dawn and dusk it comes out to feed on leaves, bark and fruit. When it runs, the bongo tilts its head so that its horns lie along its back, to prevent them catching on branches.

51

HORSES AND TAPIRS

Along with rhinoceroses, horses and tapirs make up a group of odd-toed, hoofed mammals. Animals in the horse family, including zebras and asses, live in herds and feed mainly on grass. Their feet have only one toe with a single hoof on the end. This enables them to run fast. Tapirs are short stocky creatures with four toes on the front feet and three on the hind feet. Rhinoceroses have three toes on each foot, short legs, large heads and heavy bones.

Size: body 2.5 m (8 ft); tail 5–10 cm (2–4 in)
Range: Southeast Asia: Indonesia, Malaysia, Burma, Thailand
Habitat: tropical evergreen forest, fresh water

Malayan Tapir
Tapirus indicus

The Malayan tapir is a shy, solitary animal that lives in humid swampy forests. It swims well and rushes into the water to hide when it feels threatened. The Malayan tapir prefers to feed on aquatic vegetation, but also eats the leaves, buds and fruit of some land plants.

Size: body 3–3.6 m (10–12 ft); tail 60–70 cm (23½–27½ in)
Range: eastern and southern Africa
Habitat: tropical evergreen forest, tropical grassland, desert

Black rhinoceros
Diceros bicornis

The black rhino's hook-like upper lip helps it to grab leaves, buds and shoots from small trees and bushes. It has poor eyesight but good senses of hearing and smell. If it feels threatened, it will charge. Despite its bulk, it can reach a speed of 48 km/h (30 mph). This is one of five species of rhino, which are all endangered by the illegal trade in rhino horn.

Children's Animal Encyclopedia

Przewalski's horse
Equus ferus przewalskii

This short sturdy horse is the ancestor of all modern horses. It was once common on the dry plains of Mongolia, where it grazed on grass and leaves. It had not been seen in the wild since 1968, but horses have been carefully bred and protected to create a small population that has been re-introduced to Mongolia, where it is living wild.

Size: body 1.8–2.6 m (6–6½ ft); tail 90 cm (35½ in)
Range: Mongolia, western China
Habitat: temperate grassland

Sumatran rhinoceros
Dicerorhinus sumatrensis

This is the smallest and hairiest of the rhinoceros family. There are only a few hundred wild Sumatran rhinos left. It is hunted for its horns, which are used in traditional medicine, and the forests where it lives are being chopped down.

Size: body 2.5–2.8 m (8–9¼ ft); tail about 60 cm (23½ in)
Range: Southeast Asia: Sumatra, Borneo, possibly Malaysia
Habitat: tropical evergreen forest, fresh water

Grevy's zebra
Equus grevyi

Herds of grazing zebras roam Africa's savanna. Zebras need to drink frequently, so they spend most of their time near water holes. Grevy's zebra is the largest zebra – the others are the plains zebra and the mountain zebra – and each species has a different pattern of stripes. The stripes may confuse predators and help individuals to recognize each other.

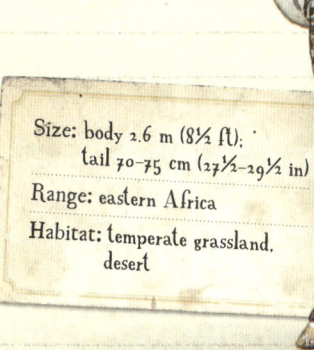

Size: body 2.6 m (8½ ft); tail 70–75 cm (27½–29½ in)
Range: eastern Africa
Habitat: temperate grassland, desert

RODENTS AND RABBITS

Rodents are a large group of small- to medium-sized mammals, which include such groups as squirrels, rats and beavers. There are more than 2,000 species of rodent, found all over the world in every kind of habitat. Most feed on plants and they have a single pair of sharp incisor teeth, which allow them to chew through the toughest of food. Pikas, rabbits and hares are another successful group of plant-eating mammals called lagomorphs. They also have sharp incisors for chewing plant food.

PIKAS, RABBITS AND HARES

Pikas are smaller than rabbits and have short rounded ears and no tail. There are about 30 species, most of which live in north and central Asia, although two species also live in North America. Rabbits and hares are common on every continent apart from Antarctica. There are about 60 species in all, and most of these fast-moving rabbits and hares have long, narrow ears, small fluffy tails and well-developed back legs.

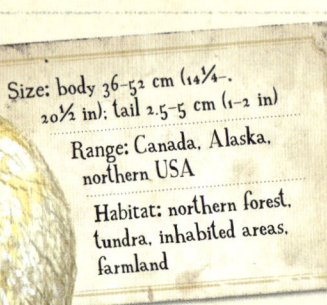

Size: body 20–25 cm (7¾–9¾ in)
Range: northern Asia
Habitat: northern forest, high ground

Northern pika
Ochotona alpina

The pika lives in family groups, which shelter in dens among rocks or tree roots. Grass and juicy plant stems are its main food. In summer it gathers extra food which it piles up in little haystacks to keep for the winter months. The pika can tunnel through snow to reach its food stores.

Size: body 36–52 cm (14¼–20½ in); tail 2.5–5 cm (1–2 in)
Range: Canada, Alaska, northern USA
Habitat: northern forest, tundra, inhabited areas, farmland

Snowshoe hare
Lepus americanus

The snowshoe hare is dark brown in summer but turns white in winter. Its light coat helps it to hide from enemies in its snowy home. Usually active at night and in the early morning, the snowshoe hare eats grass in summer and twigs and buds in winter.

European rabbit
Oryctolagus cuniculus

Rabbits live in burrows which they dig near to one another. There may be a couple of hundred rabbits in a colony, called a warren. Grass and leafy plants are their main food, but they also eat grain and can damage young trees. Females have several litters a year.

Size: body 36–46 cm (14¼–18 in); tail 4–7 cm (1½–2¾ in)
Range: Europe, northwestern Africa; introduced into Australia, New Zealand, Chile
Habitat: inhabited areas, farmland, coast, deciduous forest, temperate grassland

SQUIRRELS, BEAVERS, POCKET GOPHERS, POCKET MICE AND SPRINGHARES

These animals are all rodents. The squirrel family includes animals such as woodchucks, prairie dogs and chipmunks. Pocket gophers live in North America and spend most of their lives underground. Pocket mice are found in North and South America. Some live in dense forest, others bound across arid plains on long hind legs. The springhare can also leap like a kangaroo. Beavers spend much of their lives in water.

Woodchuck
Marmota monax

Size: body 45–61 cm (17¾–24 in); tail 18–25 cm (7–9¾ in)
Range: North America
Habitat: deciduous forest, northern forest, inhabited areas

The woodchuck, or ground hog as it is sometimes known, eats plenty of plant food in summer and gets fat. At the first sign of frost it goes into its burrow and sleeps through the winter, living on its store of body fat.

Indian palm squirrel
Funambulus palmarum

Size: body 11.5–18 cm (4½–7 in); tail 11.5–18 cm (4½–7 in)
Range: India, Sri Lanka
Habitat: temperate grassland, deciduous forest, inhabited areas, farmland

These active little squirrels leap about in palm trees during the day, feeding on palm nuts, flowers and buds. Rival males fight for females but after mating have nothing further to do with females or young. The females produce about three litters a year, each containing about three young.

Black-tailed prairie dog
Cynomys ludovicianus

Size: body 28–33 cm (11–13 in); tail 7.5–10 cm (3–4 in)
Range: central USA
Habitat: temperate grassland

Prairie dogs live in huge underground burrows, called towns. A town may house several thousand animals. They come out during the day to feed on grass and other plants and warn each other of any danger with sharp dog-like barks.

European red squirrel
Sciurus vulgaris

Size: body 20–24 cm (7¾–9½ in); tail 15–20 cm (6–7¾ in)
Range: Europe, Asia
Habitat: deciduous forest

Red squirrels use their sharp teeth to feed on conifer cones in winter, but in summer they also eat mushrooms and fruit. Where food is plentiful, females may have two litters of about three young a year. The young are born in a tree nest called a drey.

Rodents and rabbits

Springhare
Pedetes capensis

Size: body 35–43 cm (13¾–17 in); tail 36–47 cm (14¼–18½ in)
Range: southern Africa
Habitat: tropical grassland

When alarmed or travelling a long way, the springhare bounces along on its long back legs like a kangaroo. When feeding, it moves on all fours. The springhare spends much of the day in its burrow and comes out at night to forage for bulbs, roots and grain as well as some insects.

Plains pocket gopher
Geomys bursarius

This gopher's name comes from its two deep fur-lined cheek pouches. These can be crammed full of food (mostly roots) to carry back to the nest. Gophers spend most of their lives underground in burrows, which they dig with their sharp front teeth and strong paws.

Size: body 18–24 cm (7–9½ in); tail 10–12.5 cm (4–5 in)
Range: central USA
Habitat: temperate grassland

Desert kangaroo rat
Dipodomys deserti

Size: body 12–16.5 cm (4¾–6½ in); tail 18–20 cm (7–7¾ in)
Range: western USA
Habitat: temperate grassland, desert

Kangaroo rats belong to the pocket mouse family. This desert species spends the day in a burrow and comes out at night to find food such as seeds. It is well adapted to dry areas and may live its whole life without ever drinking. It can carry food in cheek pouches.

American beaver
Castor canadensis

One of the largest rodents, the American beaver weighs up to 27 kg (60 lb). Beavers eat leaves, bark and twigs and always live near water. They build a dam across a stream with branches and mud, which creates a lake. A shelter, or lodge, is also made of branches and used to store food.

Size: body 70–100 cm (28–39 in); tail 20–30 cm (8–12 in)
Range: North America
Habitat: fresh water

NEW WORLD RATS AND MICE

There are at least 430 species in this group of rodents, found in all kinds of habitats throughout the Americas. They adapt well to different conditions – fish-eating rats which live near rivers and lakes even have partially webbed feet. Most New World rats and mice are small – the largest, the giant water rat, measures 30 cm (11¾ in). Plant material is their main food, although some also feed on insects.

Deer mouse
Peromyscus maniculatus

Agile little mice, deer mice run and hop through grass and dense vegetation. They build nests underground or in tree holes and feed on insects as well as seeds, nuts and acorns. Young deer mice start to breed at only seven weeks old. They may have several litters a year, each containing up to nine young.

Size: body 12–22 cm (4¾–8¾ in); tail 8–18 cm (3¼–7 in)
Range: Canada to Mexico
Habitat: deciduous forest, Northern forest, desert

Arizona cotton rat
Sigmodon arizonae

Cotton rats sometimes occur in such numbers that they are considered pests. They feed on plants and small insects but may also take the eggs and chicks of bobwhite quails as well as crayfish and crabs. The female has her first litter of up to 12 young when just 10 weeks old.

Size: body 12.5–20 cm (5–7¾ in); tail 7.5–12.5 cm (3–5 in)
Range: USA
Habitat: temperate grassland, deciduous forest, inhabited areas, farmland

HAMSTERS AND MOLE-RATS

Hamsters and mole-rats are both burrowing rodents. Hamsters are found from Europe across the Middle East to central Asia. There are about 18 species, all with a rounded body and short tail. They have large cheek pouches, which they use for carrying food back to the burrow. There are two groups of mole-rats: one group includes two species of East African mole-rats and four species of bamboo rats from Southeast Asia. All are plant-eating. The other group includes eight species, which all live in Africa. The most unusual is the virtually hairless naked mole-rat.

Size: body 22–30 cm (8¾–11¾ in); tail 3–6 cm (1¼–2¼ in)
Range: western Europe, central Asia
Habitat: inhabited areas, farmland, temperate grassland

Common hamster
Cricetus cricetus

The hamster lives in a burrow with separate areas for sleeping and storing food. It feeds mainly on seeds, grain, roots, green plants and insect larvae. In late summer, it gathers extra food to store for the winter. From October to March or April, the hamster hibernates, waking from time to time to feed on its food stores.

Hamsters and mole-rats

Naked mole-rat
Heterocephalus glaber

This little rodent has a lifestyle more like an insect than a mammal. It lives in a colony of up to 200 animals, ruled by one female, or queen. She is the only one to breed. Worker mole-rats dig burrows and gather food such as roots for the whole colony to eat. A few non-workers tend the queen.

Size: body 8–9 cm (3¼–3½ in); tail 4 cm (1½ in)
Range: eastern Africa
Habitat: tropical grassland, desert

Bamboo rat
Rhizomys sumatrensis

This rat has a heavy body, short legs and a short, almost hairless tail. Its front teeth are large and strong and it uses these and its claws for digging. It burrows underground near clumps of bamboo. Bamboo roots are its main food, but it also eats other plants, seeds and fruit.

Size: body 36–48 cm (14½–19 in); tail 10–15 cm (4–6 in)
Range: Southeast Asia
Habitat: tropical grassland

VLEI RATS, GERBILS, LEMMINGS AND VOLES

Africa's vlei rats do not always live near water or swampy areas, but they are all good swimmers. Lemmings and voles are plump-bodied rodents which live in North America and northern Europe and Asia. All feed mainly on plants and they usually live in large groups or colonies. There are about 120 species. Gerbils live in Africa and in central and western Asia. All are well adapted to desert conditions and are able to survive with very little water. Their long hind legs and feet help keep their bodies well away from hot sand.

South African vlei rat
Otomys irroratus

This plump, active rat feeds on seeds, berries, shoots and grasses. It often goes into water and even dives to escape enemies – many larger creatures feed on these rats. It usually makes a nest of leaves and twigs above ground but may sometimes shelter in a burrow left by another animal.

Size: body 13–20 cm (5–7¾ in); tail 5–17 cm (2–6¾ in)
Range: southern Africa
Habitat: temperate grassland, fresh water

Norway lemming
Lemmus lemmus

The Norway lemming is busy day and night, feeding on grass, leaves and moss. In winter it clears pathways under the snow so it can still run around foraging for food. Lemmings start to breed in spring under the snow and may produce as many as eight litters of six young each during the summer.

Size: body 13–15 cm (5–6 in); tail 2 cm (¾ in)
Range: Scandinavia
Habitat: temperate grassland, tundra

58

Size: body 16–20 cm (6¼–7¾ in);
tail 13–16 cm (5–6¼ in)
Range: Middle East and Asia
Habitat: desert

Great gerbil
Rhombomys opimus

This gerbil manages to survive in the Gobi Desert, with its hot summers and icy winters. During the summer, it builds up stores of 60 kg (130 lb) or more of plant material in its burrow so that it has plenty of food for the winter months.

Size: body 9–12.5 cm (3½–5 in);
tail 3.5–6.5 cm (1¼–2½ in)
Range: North America
Habitat: deciduous forest, northern forest, temperate grassland, fresh water

Meadow vole
Microtus pennsylvanicus

The meadow vole manages to live in many kinds of habitat. Grass, seeds, roots and bark are its main food and it moves along runways which it clears and keeps trimmed in the grass. It makes a nest on the ground or a burrow under the runways.

OLD WORLD RATS AND MICE

This large group of almost 500 species of rodent contains some of the world's most common and widespread mammals. Rodents such as the brown rat and house mouse have adapted to life all over the world in many different kinds of conditions and will eat a wide range of foods. Many of this group are considered pests by humans because they damage grain and root crops as well as stored food. Some such as the brown rat also carry diseases such as salmonella.

Brown rat
Rattus norvegicus

This rat is a serious pest. It has followed humans all over the world and lives wherever people settle. An extremely adaptable animal, it eats any scraps of waste food. It breeds all year round and produces about eight litters of eight to ten young each in a year.

Size: body 25–30 cm (9¾–11¾ in);
tail 25–32 cm (9¾–12½ in)
Range: worldwide
Habitat: inhabited areas, farmland, temperate grassland, fresh water

Size: body 8–13 cm (3¼–5¼ in);
tail 7–9.5 cm (2¾–3¾ in)
Range: Europe, Asia, northern Africa
Habitat: deciduous forest, northern forest, temperate grassland

Wood mouse
Apodemus sylvaticus

The wood mouse is one of the most common small rodents in Europe. It comes out of its nest under the roots of trees in the evening and forages for seeds, insects and berries. The female usually produces young between April and November, but may breed through the winter if there is plenty of food.

Dormice and jerboas

DORMICE AND JERBOAS

There are about 26 species of dormouse living in Africa, Europe and northern Asia. In autumn most dormice eat extra food to build up reserves of fat in the body. They then hibernate – sleep through the winter – living on their fat but waking from time to time to feed on stored food. Jerboas are small rodents with long back legs used for jumping. There are about 33 species of jerboa, living in North America, eastern Europe and Asia.

Desert dormouse
Selevinia betpakdalensis

This dormouse is active at night, catching insects to eat. It also feeds on plants and makes stores of plant food for the winter months. It digs a burrow in which it shelters during the day, and it may also use it for hibernation.

Size: body 7–8.5 cm (2¾–3¼ in); tail 7–9.5 cm (2¾–3¾ in)
Range: central Asia: Kazakhstan
Habitat: desert

Size: body 9–15 cm (3½–6 in); tail 16–22 cm (6¼–8¾ in)
Range: northern Asia
Habitat: temperate grassland, desert

Great jerboa
Allactaga major

This lively rodent leaps through the desert on its long back legs. At night, it searches for seeds and insects to eat, which it finds by combing through the sand with the long slender claws on its front feet. During the day the jerboa shelters in a burrow.

PORCUPINES, CHINCHILLAS, GUINEA PIGS, CAPYBARA AND HUTIAS

These widely varied animals belong to small families of medium to large rodents. Porcupines have long sharp spines. There are two families: one in Africa and Asia, the other in North and South America. Chinchillas and guinea pigs are all ground-living rodents which live in South America, as does the capybara. Hutia live in the West Indies.

Size: body 20–40 cm (7¾–15¾ in); no visible tail
Range: Peru to Argentina
Habitat: temperate grassland

Montane guinea pig
Cavia tschudii

The wild guinea pig has a chunky body, short legs and small ears. It lives in family groups, which may join together to form colonies of up to 40 animals. At dawn and dusk, guinea pigs come out of their burrows to eat grass and leaves.

Size: body 22–38 cm (8½–15 in); tail 7.5–15 cm (3–6 in)
Range: northern Chile
Habitat: high ground

Common chinchilla
Chinchilla lanigera

With its large eyes, long ears and bushy tail, the chinchilla is an appealing animal. It lives in colonies of 100 or more and feeds on plants. It usually sits up to eat, holding its food in its front paws. Female chinchillas are larger than males. They breed in winter and have two litters of up to six young.

60

Children's Animal Encyclopedia

Capybara
Hydrochoerus hydrochaeris

The largest rodent, the capybara spends much of its time in water and is an expert swimmer and diver. Its feet are partially webbed and when swimming only its eyes, ears and nostrils show above the water. It eats mainly plants, including water plants.

Size: body 1–1.3 m (3¼–4¼ ft)
Range: Colombia and Venezuela to Argentina
Habitat: flooded grassland, marsh, forest

Bahamian hutia
Geocapromys ingrahami

The hutia feeds mostly on fruit and leaves, but it also eats some insects and small reptiles. It is a good climber and may search for food in trees. Active during the night, it shelters in a burrow or rock crevice at day.

Size: body 30–50 cm (11¾–19¾ in); tail 15–30 (6–11¾ in)
Range: Caribbean: Bahamas
Habitat: tropical forest, scrub

Tree porcupine
Coendou prehensilis

The body of the tree porcupine is covered with short, thick spines. Its tail is prehensile, which means it can grip easily, acting like an extra limb. Tree porcupines usually feed at night on leaves, plant stems and fruit.

Size: body 30–61 cm (11¾–24 in); tail 33–45 cm (13–17¾ in)
Range: Bolivia, Brazil, Venezuela
Habitat: tropical evergreen forest, tropical grassland

Crested porcupine
Hystrix cristata

The spines on the back of this rodent are up to 30 cm (12 in) long. If threatened, it charges backwards, driving these sharp spines, which detach easily, into its enemy. It feeds at night and shelters in its burrow by day.

Size: body 71–84 cm (28–33 in); tail up to 2.5 cm (1 in)
Range: northern Africa
Habitat: tropical evergreen forest, high ground

WHY DO ZEBRAS HAVE STRIPES?

A zebra's stripes, the humps on a camel's back, the "fishing rod" on the head of an angler fish and the leaf-like wings of an insect may seem extraordinary features, but they all make the animals that have them better able to survive in their environment. These types of features are called adaptations. They include the special markings or colours, known as camouflage, that allow creatures to hide from predators or prey. Other features help animals to survive in extreme conditions such as hot deserts or freezing polar lands.

Insect wings

LEAF INSECT

Some insects look remarkably like the leaves of the trees and bushes they live among, and are very hard for their enemies to spot. The bright green, leaf-like wings of this leaf insect have vein-like markings and edges which look as if they have been nibbled by other insects.

BACTRIAN CAMEL

This is one of the biggest animals in the desert and it has special features to help it cope with life there. Wide flat feet stop it from sinking into soft sand. Large humps store fat to help it survive food shortages. When it gets the chance, the camel can drink a huge quantity of water at one go.

Angler fish

Glowing light

ANGLER FISH

The long thin fin like a fishing rod on this deep-sea angler fish's head is topped with a special light that glows in the darkness. Other fish come near to investigate what could be a morsel of food. The angler opens its huge mouth and swallows the prey.

ZEBRA

The bold black and white stripes of the zebra make the animal very obvious in the grasslands of Africa, but in a herd the mass of stripes makes it difficult for a predator to pick on one zebra to attack. Because the pattern of the stripes is slightly different in each individual, experts think that they enable the zebras to recognise their own family group. This helps keep them together and so safer from predators.

BIRDS

There are about 10,200 species of birds, ranging in size from tiny hummingbirds to huge eagles and fast-running ostriches. Birds are among the most successful of all the world's animals, and have conquered air, land and water. They are found all over the world, including the icy lands of Antarctica and the remotest islands. Despite their differences, all birds lay eggs. The baby bird is protected inside a hard-shelled egg, which is usually kept warm, or incubated, by the parents in a nest.

Children's Animal Encyclopedia

What is a bird?

WHAT IS A BIRD?

A typical bird has a strong but light body, two legs and a pair of wings. All birds are covered with feathers – and are the only creatures to have feathers. The feathers are made of keratin, a protein that also makes up the scales on reptiles and the hair and nails of humans and other mammals.

Ostrich
Not all birds fly. The largest bird, the ostrich, is too heavy to take to the air. Instead it runs fast on its long legs.

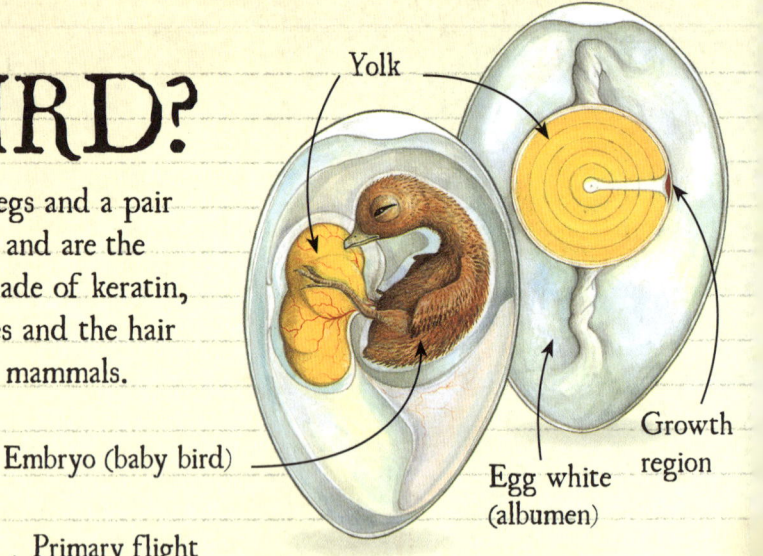

Albatross
Swift
Hummingbird
Swallow
Hawk
Vulture
Pheasant

WINGS

A bird's wings are shaped for different kinds of flight. The long broad wings of hawks and vultures allow these birds to soar for hours on air currents over land. The long wings of the albatross are suited to the different wind conditions over oceans. Agile, fast-flying birds such as swifts and swallows have slender pointed wings. The hummingbird's wings can move in almost any direction while the pheasant's wings are for slower, flapping flight.

Yolk
Embryo (baby bird)
Egg white (albumen)
Growth region

A baby bird grows inside an egg. The yolk is its food supply and the egg white protects it from sudden movements or changes in temperature. The hard shell protects the whole structure.

Primary flight feathers
Secondary flight feathers
Wing coverts (small feathers)
Beak
Eye
Breast
Toes
Talons
Tail feathers

BIRD ANATOMY

Here is a powerful martial eagle poised to snatch its prey. Its strong wings keep its body in the air and its tail feathers are spread to help it steer during flight. Its strong talons are held ready to crush its prey, which it will then tear apart with its hooked beak. All birds have wings, beaks and claws that are shaped for their particular life-style.

Children's Animal Encyclopedia

ALL TYPES OF FEET

Perching birds, such as crows, all have four-toed feet, three toes facing forwards and one backwards. Seabirds, such as the cormorant, have webbed feet. The ostrich's two-toed foot is suited to running and the eagle's strong toes and claws are used for killing prey.

Ostrich

Great cormorant

Harpy eagle

Carrion crow

Wings

Feathers

Contour feather

Bristle feather

Filoplume

Flight feather

Feathers keep a bird warm and streamline its body. Colourful or specially shaped feathers, such as filoplumes and bristles, help to attract mates. The largest strongest feathers are usually the flight and tail feathers. Softer contour feathers cover the body and down feathers beneath these add warmth.

Giant hummingbird

Warbler

Toucan

BEAKS

Beaks vary widely in shape depending on the bird's diet. The hummingbird probes long tube-like flowers to reach the nectar deep inside. The toucan reaches berries at the end of slender branches it is too heavy to sit on. Parrots crack open hard nuts, while finches feed on tough seeds. Warblers need thin sharp beaks to snatch insects. Birds of prey, such as eagles, use large hooked beaks to tear flesh. Waders such as the redshank probe sand for small prey. Most ducks crop grass at the water's edge and dabble in mud for plant seeds, but the merganser snatches slippery fish.

Finch

Mallard duck

Red-breasted merganser

Common redshank

Parrot

67

GAME BIRDS AND GROUND BIRDS

Not all birds are high fliers. Many spend most of their life on the ground, where they scratch around to find food. The ratites, or running birds, includes species such as the ostrich, rhea and emu. None of these birds can fly, because their wings are too small to be used for flight. The ratites feed on seeds, leaves and shoots. Game birds, too, spend most of their time on the ground, but they can fly when necessary and often roost in trees at night.

GAME BIRDS

This large and varied group includes more than 260 different species – birds such as pheasants, grouse, guineafowl and malleefowl. Most have plump bodies and short strong legs. They are known as "game birds" because certain species have long been hunted and shot in some parts of the world. Pheasants and other game birds scratch around for seeds and berries. They usually make simple nests on the ground.

Size: male 2.2 m (7¼ ft) with train; female 86 cm (33¾ in)
Range: Pakistan, India, Nepal, Bhutan, Sri Lanka
Habitat: tropical evergreen forest, tropical and temperate grassland, inhabited areas, farmland

Indian peafowl
Pavo cristatus

The male peafowl (peacock) is one of the most magnificent birds of all. It has colourful feathers, and it spreads its glittering train, adorned with "eyespot" markings, by raising the tail beneath. With his train fanned out, the male struts around to attract the female (peahen). She is plainer, with brown and green feathers and a small crest. In the wild, peafowl feed on seeds, berries, leaves and insects. They have been introduced into parks and gardens all over the world.

California quail
Callipepla californica

These quail move and feed in flocks, eating leaves, berries, seeds and some insects. Both males and females have an unusual head plume, but only the male has black and white markings on the face.

Size: 24–28 cm (9½–11 in)
Range: western USA, Chile, Argentina
Habitat: temperate grassland, farmland

Temminck's tragopan
Tragopan temminckii

The favourite home of this beautiful bird is cool mountain forest. The male is striking and colourful, while the female has brownish feathers. At the start of the breeding season, the male bird courts the female by displaying his brilliant plumage. She lays three to six eggs. Tragopans eat seeds, buds, leaves, berries and insects.

Size: 64 cm (25¼ in)
Range: China, Southeast Asia
Habitat: tropical evergreen forest, high ground

Children's Animal Encyclopedia

Ring-necked pheasant
Phasianus colchicus

Pheasants came originally from Asia but have now been introduced into many other countries. The female is plainer than the male, with brown plumage. Wild pheasants eat seeds, buds and berries.

Size: male 76–89 cm (30–35 in); female 53–64 cm (20¾–25⅕ in)
Range: China, east Asia; introduced to Europe and North America
Habitat: tropical evergreen grassland, temperate grassland, fresh water, farmland

Red junglefowl
Gallus gallus

The junglefowl is the ancestor of domestic chickens. The female is smaller than the colourful male and has brown and chestnut feathers. Junglefowl move in flocks of about 50 birds, searching for grain, grass, seeds and insects to eat. In the breeding season the female scrapes a shallow nest in the ground near a bush and lines it with leaves. She lays five or six eggs.

Size: male 63–75 cm (24¾–29½ in); female 40–45 cm (15¾–17¾ in)
Range: Southeast Asia
Habitat: farmland, deciduous forest, desert

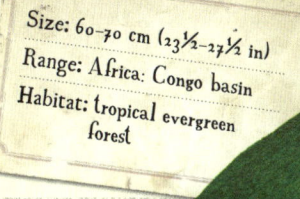

Congo peafowl
Afropavo congensis

Size: 60–70 cm (23½–27½ in)
Range: Africa: Congo basin
Habitat: tropical evergreen forest

This shy, rare bird lives so deep in the African rainforest that scientists did not actually discover it until 1936. Even now, little is known about its life, but it is thought to roost in trees and feed mainly on grain and fruit.

Rock ptarmigan
Lagopus muta

In summer, the ptarmigan has mottled brown and grey feathers. But in winter, the ptarmigan moults and grows plumage that is pure white, except for its tail feathers. This white winter coat helps the ptarmigan hide from its enemies in its snowy Arctic home.

Size: 33–39 cm (13–15½ in)
Range: Arctic and northernmost parts of Europe, Asia and North America
Habitat: tundra, high ground

Game birds and ground birds

Greater prairie chicken
Tympanuchus cupido

Prairie chickens feed mainly on leaves, fruit and grain. In the summer they also catch insects, particularly grasshoppers. In the breeding season, male birds attract females by blowing out their orange neck pouches and raising their crests. They give booming calls and stamp their feet as they display. Females lay 10 to 12 eggs.

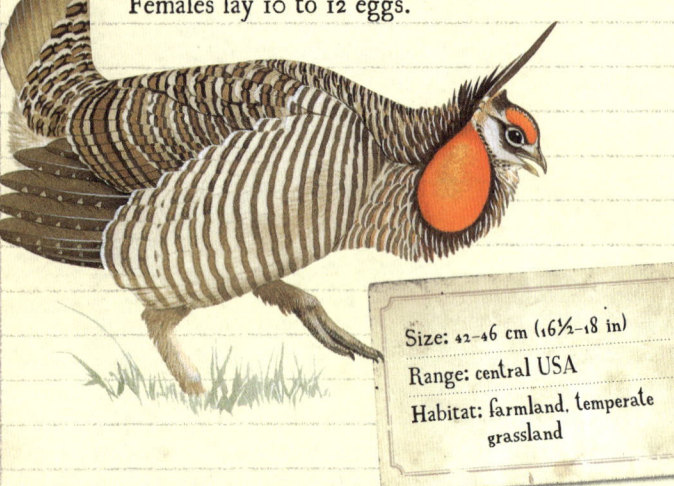

Size: 42-46 cm (16½-18 in)
Range: central USA
Habitat: farmland, temperate grassland

Western capercaillie
Tetrao urogallus

This magnificent turkey-like bird is the biggest of all the grouse. It feeds mainly on pine needles and pine seeds in winter. Its diet changes in summer, when it eats the leaves, stems and juicy fruit of cranberry, bilberry and other forest plants.

Size: male 86 cm (33¾ in); female 58 cm (22¾ in)
Range: northern Europe
Habitat: deciduous forest, Northeren forest

Size: 41-51 cm (16-20 in)
Range: northern Europe, northern Asia
Habitat: scrub, woodland, grassland

Black grouse
Tetrao tetrix

In spring, male black grouse perform a group display, called a lek, to attract female birds. Every morning they gather at a special place to dance, call and spread their beautiful tails before the watching females. The females mate with the best dancers and lay clutches of 6 to 11 eggs.

Size: 91-122 cm (36-48 in)
Range: USA, Mexico
Habitat: forest, field, orchard, marsh

Wild turkey
Meleagris gallopavo

The wild turkey has a lighter, slimmer body and longer legs than domestic farm turkeys. It has bare skin on its head and neck. The turkey can fly well for short distances but finds most of its food on the ground. It eats seeds, nuts and berries and also catches small creatures such as insects and lizards.

GROUND BIRDS

The long-legged running birds, such as ostriches, rheas, cassowaries and emus, live in dry grasslands and semi-desert. They cannot fly and often have to travel far to find food so it is important for them to be fast runners. They also rely on running to escape from danger. Kiwis have shorter legs and move more slowly on the ground, and they cannot fly either. Ground-living birds from other families – such as the curassow, tinamou, great bustard and satin bowerbird – can fly, but spend most of their lives at ground level.

Size: 27–33 cm (10½–13 in)
Range: eastern Australia
Habitat: deciduous forest, tropical evergreen forest

Satin bowerbird
Ptilonorhynchus violaceus

The male bowerbird builds a "bower" (chamber) on the ground to attract females. The bower is made of sticks and decorated with bright blue flowers and berries. If a female comes near, the male dances in his bower, flapping his wings and puffing up his feathers.

Size: 94 cm (37 in)
Range: Mexico to Ecuador
Habitat: tropical evergreen forest

Great curassow
Crax rubra

The great curassow finds food, such as fruit and leaves, on the ground but flies up into the trees to roost. If in danger, it runs away rather than flies.

Size: 46 cm (18 in)
Range: South America
Habitat: tropical evergreen forest

Size: 70 cm (27½ in)
Range: New Zealand: North Island
Habitat: deciduous forest

Brown kiwi
Apteryx mantelli

Using its long sensitive beak, the brown kiwi probes in the undergrowth for insects, worms and berries. Its keen senses of smell and hearing help it find food. Like other kiwis, this bird has tiny wings under its hair-like body feathers and cannot fly.

Great tinamou
Tinamus major

Dense rainforest is the home of the great tinamou. This bird can fly but is weak and clumsy in the air. If in danger it usually remains still, relying on its brownish colouring to keep it hidden. It spends most of its time on the ground, eating berries, seeds and insects. Females lay up to 12 large greenish-blue or violet eggs that are among the most beautiful of all birds' eggs.

Game birds and ground birds

Greater roadrunner
Geococcyx californianus

True to its name, the greater roadrunner runs at speeds of up to 20 km an hour (12 mph) on its big, strong feet. It can fly but does not often do so. This speedy bird eats ground-living insects as well as birds' eggs, lizards and even snakes.

Size: 50-60 cm (19¾-23½ in)
Range: southwestern USA, Mexico
Habitat: desert, scrub, grassland

Size: 70 cm (27½ in)
Range: South America
Habitat: tropical grassland

Red-legged seriema
Cariama cristata

The graceful seriema rarely flies but runs fast to escape from any danger. It kills snakes and lizards with its sharp bill and also feeds on seeds, leaves and insects. The nest is built in a tree and made from sticks. The female lays two or three eggs which the pair take turns to incubate.

Ostrich
Struthio camelus

The world's largest living bird, the ostrich is too big and heavy to fly. Instead it runs fast and can reach speeds of up to 70 km/h (43 mph). Ostriches feed on plants and seeds but also catch small reptiles. Ostrich eggs are larger than any other bird's eggs. Each one weighs about 1.5 kg (3¼ lb).

Size: 1.75-2.75 m (5¾-9 feet) tall
Range: Africa
Habitat: tropical grassland, desert

Size: 1.5 m (5 feet) tall
Range: New Guinea, northern Australia
Habitat: tropical evergreen forest

Common cassowary
Casuarius casuarius

The cassowary lives in the tropical rainforest and cannot fly. It has a large horn casque on the top of its head. No-one is sure if the bird uses this to push through dense undergrowth, or to amplify the sound of its loud booming call. Males and females look similar, but females are slightly larger and have brighter plumage. They both have extremely strong legs with very sharp-toed feet, which they use as weapons if attacked.

Southern ground hornbill
Bucorvus leadbeateri

Most hornbills live in trees, but this bird spends much of its life on the ground. It wanders around in pairs or family groups, searching for insects, reptiles and other small animals to eat.

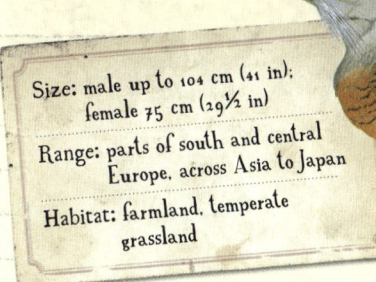

Size: 107 cm (42 in)
Range: parts of Africa south of the equator
Habitat: tropical grassland

Great bustard
Otis tarda

Size: male up to 104 cm (41 in); female 75 cm (29½ in)
Range: parts of south and central Europe, across Asia to Japan
Habitat: farmland, temperate grassland

The great bustard is one of the world's heaviest flying birds. A large male weighs up to 18 kg (40 lb) but can still fly. Females are much lighter – up to 5 kg (11 lb) – and do not have bristly "whiskers". Great bustards move in flocks as they search for plants, seeds and insects to eat. They have strong legs and can run fast.

Emu
Dromaius novaehollandiae

The emu is the second largest bird in the world and, like the ostrich, it cannot fly. It runs at speeds of up to 48 km/h (30 mph) on its long legs as it looks for food in the Australian bush. Fruit, berries and insects are its main foods, and it also eats grass and other crops. The female lays 7 to 10 eggs, which the male keeps warm (incubates).

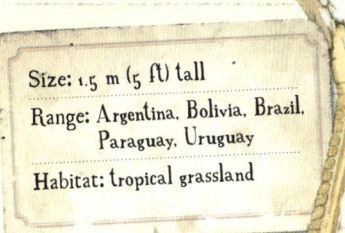

Size: 2 m (6½ ft) tall
Range: Australia
Habitat: deciduous forest, desert

Size: 1.5 m (5 ft) tall
Range: Argentina, Bolivia, Brazil, Paraguay, Uruguay
Habitat: tropical grassland

Greater rhea
Rhea americana

The largest birds in South America, greater rheas are fast runners but cannot fly. They usually live in groups of up to 30 birds. At breeding time the male rhea mates with several females. He makes a shallow nest on the ground and incubates all their eggs together.

Children's Animal Encyclopedia

WADERS, WATERBIRDS, CRANES AND SEABIRDS

A huge variety of birds live in and around water. Wading birds, such as sandpipers, plovers and jacanas, spend much of their lives on seacoasts or by rivers and lakes farther inland. Waterbirds, such as herons, flamingos and ducks, spend more time actually in the water and many are excellent swimmers. Lakes, ponds, rivers and marshlands provide plenty of plant and animal foods and birds can nest among bankside reeds. Seabirds depend on the ocean for their food and many can swim and dive to perfection.

WADERS

Most wading birds, or shorebirds, are small to medium-sized, ranging from the smallest plovers, only 15 cm (6 in) long, to curlews measuring almost 60 cm (23½ in) in length. Wading birds usually feed on the ground and most are fast runners. Their beaks are various lengths and shapes for probing different depths in mud and sand looking for food. All are strong fliers, and many perform long migrations every year between winter feeding areas and the places where they lay eggs and rear young in spring and summer.

Size: 42 cm (16½ in)
Range: Europe, Asia
Habitat: coast, coastal waters, fresh water

Pied avocet
Recurvirostra avosetta

The avocet has an unusual beak that curves upwards. It catches insects and small water creatures by holding its long beak slightly open and sweeping it from side to side at the surface of mud or shallow water. In deeper water it dips its head below the surface to find food.

Size: 30 cm (11¾ in)
Range: Europe, Asia, western and northern Africa
Habitat: farmland, temperate grassland, fresh water

Size: 28 cm (11 in)
Range: Europe, Asia, northern Africa
Habitat: farmland, temperate grassland, fresh water, coast, coastal waters

Lapwing
Vanellus vanellus

The lapwing is also known as the "pee-wit" because of the shrill call it makes during its display flight. A common bird of farmland and other open areas, it eats insects as well as worms, snails and some seeds.

Redshank
Tringa totanus

This common bird lives near almost any kind of water. It breeds on moorland and marshes, but spends the winter on shores, mudflats, meadows and estuaries. Insects are its main food, but it also eats other small creatures such as crabs and snails. It lays its eggs in a grass-lined nest on the ground.

Northern jacana
Jacana spinosa

The jacana is best known for its amazing feet. The toes and claws are very long so that the bird's weight is spread over a large area. This allows the jacana to walk on unsteady surfaces, such as floating lily pads, as it looks for food.

Size: 25 cm (9¾ in)
Range: Central America, West Indies
Habitat: fresh water

American golden plover
Pluvialis dominica

The golden plover is a champion long-distance traveller. It breeds on the Arctic tundra of North America. After breeding, it flies about 13,000 km (8,000 miles) south to spend the winter months in South America. It feeds mainly on insects and other small creatures such as snails.

Size: 23–28 cm (9–11 in)
Range: Arctic North America (summer); South America (winter)
Habitat: temperate grassland, fresh water, tundra

American woodcock
Scolopax minor

Although it is a kind of sandpiper, the American woodcock spends more time inland than other wading birds. It feeds mainly on earthworms, which it finds by probing the soil with its long beak. Females make their nests under trees or bushes and lay up to four eggs.

Children's Animal Encyclopedia

Size: 28–33 cm (11–13 in)
Range: northern Canada, Alaska
Habitat: coastal water

Eskimo curlew
Numenius borealis

Huge flocks of eskimo curlews used to migrate every year from the northern tundra to South America where they spent the winter months. Today, the bird is almost extinct because so many have been shot by hunters. Shooting is now banned, but it is probably too late to save the eskimo curlew.

Size: 46 cm (18 in)
Range: Europe, coastal Africa, coastal Asia north of the equator
Habitat: farmland, coast, coastal water

Eurasian oystercatcher
Haematopus ostralegus

The oystercatcher has a long, blunt beak that it uses to prise shellfish such as cockles and mussels off seashore rocks and to chisel open their hard shells. It also eats insects and worms, which it finds on farmland.

Size: 28 cm (11 in)
Range: North America, east of the Rockies
Habitat: temperate forest, farmland

75

WATERBIRDS AND CRANES

Waterbirds such as egrets, storks, ibises and flamingos are all large birds with long necks and legs. They stand in water while feeding and take food with their beaks. Ducks, geese and swans swim on the water as they look for food, and some dive beneath the surface. Most have strong legs and webbed feet to help them swim. Other birds found in fresh water include cranes, grebes and divers, or loons. Cranes are long-legged birds that wade in shallow water to find food. Fast-swimming grebes and divers feed mainly on fish, which they chase and catch under the water with their pointed beaks.

Size: 43-51 cm (17-20 in)
Range: eastern Asia, China, Japan, introduced worldwide
Habitat: fresh water

Mandarin duck
Aix galericulata

The colourful mandarin duck is most active at dawn and dusk when it feeds on seeds, acorns and rice as well as insects, snails and small fish. Mated pairs stay together year after year. They perform elaborate courtship displays using the sail-like feathers on their sides.

Size: 56-110 cm (22-43½ in).
Range: North America; introduced into Europe and New Zealand
Habitat: farmland, fresh water, tundra

Canada goose
Branta canadensis

This goose breeds in the north and migrates south in autumn. Birds use the same routes year after year and tend to return to their birthplace to breed. The female lays about five eggs in a shallow nest scraped on the ground. Her mate stays nearby while she incubates the eggs for 25 to 30 days. Canada geese feed on water and land plants.

Size: 55-65 cm (21½-25½ in)
Range: Central America, Africa, Europe, Asia, Australasia
Habitat: coast, fresh water

Size: 41-66 cm (16¼-26 in)
Range: Northern Hemisphere
Habitat: fresh water, inhabited areas, coast

Mallard
Anas platyrhynchos

The mallard is the ancestor of most domestic ducks. It has been introduced into Australia and New Zealand and can even live on ponds in city areas. It eats plants as well as insects and other small creatures and is often seen feeding tail-up in shallow water.

Glossy ibis
Plegadis falcinellus

The beautiful glossy ibis lives around lakes and marshes and eats insects and water creatures, which it picks from the mud with its long bill. It breeds in colonies, sometimes of thousands of birds. The female lays three or four eggs in a nest in a tree or reed bed. Both parents incubate the eggs and care for the young once they hatch.

Children's Animal Encyclopedia

Common crane
Grus grus

The common crane is famous for its dancing display. The birds walk in circles, bowing, bobbing and tossing small objects over their heads. Cranes nest on the ground or in shallow water. After breeding they fly south to spend the winter in northern Africa, India or Southeast Asia.

Size: 1.1–1.2 m (3½–4 ft)
Range: Europe, Asia
Habitat: farmland, temperate grassland, fresh water

Sunbittern
Eurypyga helias

In its courtship display, the sunbittern spreads its wings and fans its tail to reveal colourful feathers. It spends most of its life searching shallow water for prey, such as insects and fish, which it seizes in its sharp beak.

Size: 46 cm (18 in)
Range: southern Mexico to Bolivia and Brazil
Habitat: temperate grassland, fresh water

Tundra swan
Cygnus columbianus

This swan lays eggs and rears its young on the Arctic tundra. In autumn, it flies south, usually returning to the same place year after year. Tundra swans feed on plants in shallow water.

Size: 51 cm (20 in)
Range: Europe, Asia, Africa, Australia, New Zealand
Habitat: fresh water

Great crested grebe
Podiceps cristatus

This beautiful bird does not often fly and is rarely seen on land, where it moves awkwardly. Before mating, great crested grebes perform an elegant courtship dance on the water. During the dance they wag their heads and present one another with pieces of weed.

Size: 1.1–1.4 m (3½–4½ ft)
Range: North America, northern Europe, Asia
Habitat: tundra, fresh water

Waterbirds and cranes

Size: 71-91 cm (28-36 in)
Range: Colombia, Venezuela
Habitat: fresh water

Northern screamer
Chauna chavaria

Although related to ducks and geese, the northern screamer does not have webbed feet and seldom swims in open water. It has a loud trumpeting call which it uses to warn others of danger. This noisy bird lives in the rivers and swamps of a small area of northern South America. It walks around over floating leaves, its long toes helping to spread its weight. Females lay four to six eggs in a nest made of plants.

Size: 90-120 cm (35½-47 in)
Range: worldwide except cold northerly places
Habitat: fresh water, coastal waters

Red-throated diver
Gavia stellata

This graceful bird has a slender beak and a red patch on its throat. It flies well and is an expert swimmer and diver. It feeds on fish, which it catches under water. It makes a variety of calls, including growling sounds and high-pitched wails. The female lays two eggs in a nest on the ground.

Size: 53-69 cm (20¾-27¼ in)
Range: North America, northern Asia, northern Europe
Habitat: fresh water, tundra, coastal waters

Common eider
Somateria mollissima

Like most ducks, the common eider lines her nest with downy feathers plucked from her breast. Eider down is particularly warm and soft. It has long been collected for making items such as duvets and sleeping bags. Eiders live mainly on shellfish and other small creatures

Size: 56-71 cm (22-28 in)
Range: North Pole
Habitat: coast, coastal waters

Great egret
Casmerodius albus

This egret, also known as the American egret, lives in marshy areas and eats fish, insects and other small creatures. It finds its food either by waiting in the water until it spots something or by slowly stalking its prey. In the breeding season adults have a mostly black beak. The rest of the year it is yellow. Breeding pairs make a nest in a tree or clump of reeds. The female lays two to five eggs and both parents take it in turns to incubate the clutch.

Children's Animal Encyclopedia

Limpkin
Aramus guarauna

This long-legged waterbird uses its curved beak to probe for snails and mussels in muddy swamps. It also eats seeds, insects and even reptiles. It is called the limpkin because it seems to limp when it walks. Limpkins can fly but rarely do so and spend most of their lives on the ground.

Size: 59–71 cm (23¼–28 in)
Range: USA, Mexico, Caribbean, Central America
Habitat: fresh water

Size: 1.25–1.45 cm (4¼–4¾ ft)
Range: southern Europe, parts of Asia and Africa
Habitat: fresh water, coast

Greater flamingo
Phoenicopterus roseus

The flamingo's long legs allow it to wade into deeper water than most other birds when looking for food. It feeds by sucking water and mud in at the front of its beak and then pumping it out again at the sides, where bristly plates trap small water creatures. The flamingo builds a nest of mud and lays one or two eggs.

Whooping crane
Grus americana

These cranes are very rare in the wild and are now strictly protected. To increase numbers, birds are being bred in captivity for release into the wild. Whooping cranes eat grain and plants as well as insects, frogs and other small animals.

Size: 1.2–1.4 cm (4–4½ ft)
Range: northern Canada, southern USA
Habitat: temperate grassland, fresh water, coastal water

Size: 71–79 cm (28–31 in)
Range: Morocco
Habitat: desert, high ground, fresh water

Hermit ibis
Geronticus eremita

This peculiar, bald-headed bird used to be much more widespread, but it does not cope well with the changes in its habitat and food supply caused by farming. Last seen in Turkey in 1989, it now breeds only in Morocco, in a rather dry, rocky area where there is not much farming.

Seabirds

SEABIRDS

Life at sea is harsh and demanding for birds. Many seabirds, such as albatrosses, terns and gannets, are powerful fliers. They cover long distances over the open ocean as they search for food. Some spend almost the whole year in the air, only coming to land to breed, lay eggs and raise their chicks. There are some seabirds, though, that cannot fly at all. Penguins are the best-known examples. They are expert swimmers and divers.

Size: 39 cm (15½ in)
Range: Antarctic coasts and South Atlantic islands, Chile, Argentina
Habitat: coast

Snowy sheathbill
Chionis albus

These birds are eager scavengers of any food they can find. They haunt penguin colonies to seize eggs and chicks, and search the rubbish tips of Antarctic research stations. They also feed on fish and shellfish. They swim well and can fly, but spend most of their time on the ground.

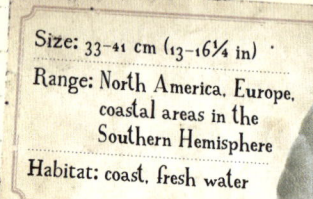

Size: 80–100 cm (31½–39½ in)
Range: every continent except Antarctica and South America
Habitat: coast, fresh water

Great cormorant
Phalacrocorax carbo

The cormorant swims by using its webbed feet to push itself along. It eats mainly fish and catches prey during underwater dives that may last a minute or more. The cormorant usually brings fish to the surface and tosses them in the air so they can be swallowed headfirst. The cormorant makes a nest in trees or on the ground. The female lays three or four eggs and both parents care for the chicks.

Size: 33–41 cm (13–16¼ in)
Range: North America, Europe, coastal areas in the Southern Hemisphere
Habitat: coast, fresh water

Common tern
Sterna hirundo

A coastal bird, this tern feeds on shrimps and other small sea creatures. It catches its food by hovering above the sea until it spots something, then diving rapidly into the water to seize the prey in its sharp beak. Terns nest in large colonies on islands and cliffs. The female lays two or three eggs in a nest scraped in the ground.

Children's Animal Encyclopedia

Great skua
Stercorarius skua

A strong bird with a hooked bill, the great skua is a fierce hunter. It not only attacks other birds to steal their prey, but also kills and eats puffins, kittiwakes and gulls, and preys on their eggs and young. It also eats unwanted fish thrown overboard from fishing boats.

Size: 51–56 cm (20–22 in)
Range: North Atlantic Ocean to the Equator, Mediterranean Sea
Habitat: coastal waters, oceanic

Size: 1.3 m (4½ ft)
Range: Pacific coast from California to Chile, warm western Atlantic coasts
Habitat: coast, coastal waters

Brown pelican
Pelecanus occidentalis

The brown pelican is the smallest pelican. It is a seabird and feeds by diving for fish, making high-speed plunges into the water from heights of more than 9 m (30 ft). Once in the water it opens its mouth and catches the fish in the pouch below its beak, then returns to the surface to eat. This bird lays two or three eggs in a nest on the ground.

Great black-backed gull
Larus marinus

One of the largest gulls, this bird is a fierce hunter which spends more time at sea than other types of gull. It chases and kills other seabirds, such as puffins, and takes their eggs and young. It also eats fish and scavenges on waste. The young of these gulls have speckled brown feathers.

Size: 71–79 cm (28–31 in)
Range: Atlantic coasts of North America and Europe
Habitat: coast, temperate grassland, fresh water

Size: 55–66 cm (21¾–26 in)
Range: most of Northern Hemisphere
Habitat: coastal water

Herring gull
Larus argentatus

The herring gull is the most common gull on North American and European sea coasts. It catches small fish, steals eggs and young from other birds and scavenges on waste. It also flies inland to find worms and other creatures on farmland. Herring gulls nest on cliffs, islands or beaches. They make nests of weeds and grass in a hollow in the ground or in a tree. The female lays two or three eggs which are cared for by both parents.

Seabirds

Size: 87–100 cm (34¼–39½ in)
Range: north Atlantic Ocean
Habitat: coast, coastal water

Jackass penguin
Spheniscus demersus

Also known as the African penguin, the jackass penguin lives in a warmer climate than most other penguins. It comes to land to breed and nests in a burrow or under rocks to avoid the hot African sun.

Size: 69 cm (27 in) tall
Range: coasts of southern Africa
Habitat: coast, coastal waters

Northern gannet
Morus bassanus

A sturdily built seabird with a strong beak, the northern gannet soars over the ocean, searching for fish and squid. When it spots prey, the gannet will plunge 30 m (100 ft) or more into the water to seize the catch and bring it to the surface.

Red-tailed tropicbird
Phaethon rubricauda

This elegant seabird is an expert in the air, but it moves awkwardly on land. It usually nests on ledges or cliffs in a position that allows for easy take-off. Fish and squid are its main foods. Females lay a single egg on the ground. Both parents incubate the egg and care for the chick.

Size: 86–100 cm (33¾–39½ in)
Range: Indian and Pacific oceans
Habitat: coast, oceanic

Size: 90–100 cm (35½–39½ in including tail)
Range: Indian and Pacific oceans
Habitat: coast, oceanic

Great frigatebird
Fregata minor

This large seabird has a wingspan of more than 1.8 m (6 ft) and a big, hooked beak. It spends most of its life in the air and does not often land on the water. It catches food by snatching prey from the surface of the water or by threatening other seabirds until they drop their meals. Large colonies nest together on oceanic islands.

Children's Animal Encyclopedia

Little penguin
Eudyptula minor

The smallest of all the penguins, the little penguin lives around coasts and islands, looking for small fish and other food in shallow waters. It nests in a crevice or burrow. The female lays two eggs which both parents take turns to incubate for between 33 and 40 days.

Size: 40 cm (15¾ in) tall
Range: Australia, New Zealand
Habitat: coast, coastal waters

Size: 1.1–1.35 m (3½–4½ ft)
Range: southern oceans
Habitat: coast, oceanic

Wandering albatross
Diomedea exulans

This seabird has the longest wingspan of any bird – up to 3.4 m (11 ft). It spends most of its life soaring over the open ocean, sometimes flying up to 500 km (300 miles) in a day.

Galápagos penguin
Spheniscus mendiculus

This is the only penguin to live near the equator. The Galápagos Islands are bathed by a cool current, making the area suitable for a cold-loving penguin. The Galápagos penguin feeds mainly on small fish. It nests in small groups and females lay two eggs in a cave or a hole in volcanic rock.

Size: 50 cm (19¾ in) tall
Range: Galápagos Islands
Habitat: coast, coastal waters

Size: 29–36 cm (11½–14¼ in)
Range: North Atlantic and Arctic oceans
Habitat: coast, oceanic

Atlantic puffin
Fratercula arctica

This puffin uses its colourful beak to catch fish and can hold as many as a dozen fish at a time. An expert swimmer and diver, the puffin can also fly well. Its short legs are set well back on the body and it waddles clumsily when it comes to land to nest. The female puffin lays one egg, sometimes two, in an old burrow or in a hole it digs itself.

83

PENGUINS

Penguins cannot fly but are better suited to life in the sea than any other bird. Expert swimmers and divers, they use their strong flippers to push themselves through the water. Most penguins live around the Antarctic and on islands near the Antarctic Circle and have to survive in freezing conditions. They have a dense covering of glossy waterproof feathers, which keep them both warm and dry. A thick layer of fat beneath the feathers also helps to keep out the cold. There are about 17 different kinds of penguin. The smallest is the little, or fairy, penguin, which measures about 40 cm (15 in). The biggest is the emperor penguin, which stands about 115 cm (45 in) high.

TAKING CARE OF YOUNG

At the beginning of winter, the female emperor penguin lays one egg on land. Her partner then incubates the egg on his feet for about 64 days. When the chick hatches he keeps its warm on his feet, wrapped in a fold of skin.

UNDERWATER HUNTER

The king penguin dives deep to catch prey and often plunges to 45 m (150 ft) or more. The deepest recorded dive is almost 320 m (1,050 ft). The penguin uses its webbed feet and tail for steering as it dives.

Fish is the main food for penguins, but they also catch squid and crustaceans. Smaller penguins such as gentoos and chinstraps catch much smaller prey as well, such as shrimp-like krill.

Squid

FRIENDLY BEHAVIOUR

Penguins are sociable birds and usually live in huge colonies on land and in the sea. Penguins usually keep the same mate for several years. When a breeding pair meets, they rub their heads in greeting. They also preen each other's feathers.

Children's Animal Encyclopedia

Adélie penguins nest in large colonies around the Antarctic coasts. Eggs are laid in late November and incubated first by the male and then by the female for a total of 35 days.

TOBOGGANING

Not at their best on land, penguins slip and slide as they waddle over the frozen ground. Often the birds lie down on their bellies and toboggan over the ice – an easier way to move. Once in the water, most penguins swim at speeds of 5–10 km/h (3–6 mph).

85

OWLS AND BIRDS OF PREY

Most birds of prey hunt and kill other creatures to eat. They are among the most interesting of all birds and include species such as eagles, hawks and buzzards. This is a varied group of birds, ranging from tiny falcons to huge condors, but they all have features in common. These include keen vision, strong feet with sharp claws, and a hooked beak for tearing prey apart. Owls, too, kill other animals to eat but, unlike hawks and eagles, they usually hunt at night.

OWLS

There are 202 or so kinds of owl found over most of the world, except on a few islands. Most look similar, with large, disc-like faces and huge eyes. Typically, an owl sits on a branch watching and listening for the slightest movement of prey. When it hears something, it pinpoints the direction of the prey with its incredibly acute hearing before flying down to pounce. The edges of an owl's feathers are soft and fluffy – not hard like those of most birds. This cuts down the noise of flight so the hunter can fly almost silently in the darkness.

Size: 52-65 cm (20½-25½ in)
Range: Arctic to northern USA, Europe and Asia
Habitat: coast, tundra, fresh water

Long-eared owl
Asio otus

The tufts on the head of this owl are feathers not ears. But this bird does have excellent hearing, which helps it catch prey such as voles and mice. This owl lays its eggs in a nest abandoned by a bird such as a crow.

Size: 33-40.5 cm (13-16 in)
Range: North America, Europe, northwest Africa, Asia
Habitat: farmland, deciduous forest

Barn owl
Tyto alba

The barn owl is easily recognised by its pale, heart-shaped face. During the day it roosts in a sheltered spot. At dusk it comes out to hunt for food, usually small creatures, such as rats and mice.

Size: 34 cm (13½ in)
Range: worldwide, except temperate Asia and many Pacific islands
Habitat: farmland, deciduous forest, temperate grassland

Snowy owl
Bubo scandiaca

The snowy owl has long dense feathers right down to its toes to protect against the cold. It hunts by day as well as by night, for birds and for mammals such as mice, hares and lemmings. The female owl is bigger than the male and has dark markings on her mainly white feathers. She lays 4 to 15 eggs.

BIRDS OF PREY

Birds of prey hunt in a variety of ways. Some, such as goshawks and sparrowhawks, live mainly in forests and woodlands. They move from one leafy perch to the next, ready to dash out to snatch their prey in a sudden attack. Others, such as buzzards and eagles, soar over open country, watching for victims. Not all birds of prey are killers. Vultures are scavengers – they eat carrion, the bodies of creatures that are already dead.

Size: 61–66 cm (24–26 in)
Range: Europe, Middle East, northern Africa
Habitat: deciduous forest, temperate grassland

Red kite
Milvus milvus

This large bird of prey has long wings and a forked tail. It hunts in woodland and open country and often hovers briefly as it searches for prey, such as rats, birds and reptiles. Like vultures, it also eats carrion. The red kite nests in a tree and the female lays up to five eggs.

Northern goshawk
Accipiter gentilis

A powerful, fast-moving hunter, the northern goshawk can catch creatures such as hares and pheasants. It flies through the forest, weaving in and out of trees as it chases prey. It kills its victims with its strong sharp talons and eats them on the ground.

Size: 1.1–1.15 m (3¼–3¾ ft)
Range: parts of Africa, Saudi Arabia, Yemen, Oman
Habitat: desert, high ground, tropical grassland

Size: 51–66 cm (20–26 in)
Range: North America, Europe, northern Asia
Habitat: deciduous forest

Lappet-faced vulture
Torgos tracheliotus

Like all vultures, this bird feeds mostly on carrion. It has huge wings on which it soars long distances searching for food, and a powerful hooked beak, which cuts easily into the flesh of dead animals. This vulture lays one egg in a nest at the top of a tree.

Size: 46–61 cm (18–24 in)
Range: North and Central America, West Indies
Habitat: deciduous and tropical evergreen forest, desert, farmland

Red-tailed hawk
Buteo jamaicensis

A powerful, aggressive bird, this hawk can live anywhere from forest to desert. It hunts other birds in the air or swoops down on rabbits, snakes and lizards from a high perch. It nests high in a tree or cactus plant. The female lays one to four eggs. Both parents take turns to incubate the eggs.

Birds of prey

Rough-legged buzzard
Buteo lagopus

The rough-legged buzzard hovers over the tundra as it hunts for prey, such as lemmings and voles. It nests in the far north, laying up to four eggs in a nest of twigs made in a tree or on a rocky ledge. After the breeding season, this buzzard flies south for the winter.

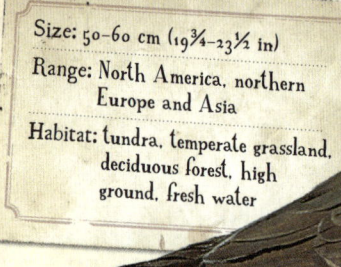

Size: 50-60 cm (19¾-23½ in)
Range: North America, northern Europe and Asia
Habitat: tundra, temperate grassland, deciduous forest, high ground, fresh water

Madagascar fish eagle
Haliaeetus vociferoides

With a population of less than 120 breeding pairs, this fish eagle is one of the rarest of all birds. It usually hunts around shallow estuaries and coastal swamps where it plunges down to catch fish with its strong feet.

Size: 68-79 cm (26¾-31 in)
Range: western and southern Madagascar
Habitat: coast, coastal waters

Bald eagle
Haliaeetus leucocephalus

Once rare, the national bird of the United States is now thriving in many places. Fish is one of its main foods, and eagles gather around Alaskan rivers to catch exhausted salmon as they migrate up river. Made of sticks, the eagle's nest is one of the largest of all birds' nests.

Size: 81-102 cm (32-40 in)
Range: North America
Habitat: coast, coastal waters, deciduous forest, tropical evergreen forest

Size: 76-89 cm (30-35 in)
Range: North America, Europe, northern Asia and Africa
Habitat: Northern forest, high ground, temperate grassland

Golden eagle
Aquila chrysaetos

The magnificent golden eagle has a hooked beak, extremely sharp eyesight and strong feet with long curved claws. When hunting, the eagle soars over land, searching for food. Once it spots prey, it dives down and kills its victim on the ground.

Osprey
Pandion haliaetus

This bird of prey flies above water looking for fish to catch. When the bird catches sight of prey, it plunges down, holding its feet out to seize the fish. The soles of the osprey's feet are studded with small spines to help it grip its slippery catch.

Size: 53-62 cm (20¾-24½ in)
Range: almost worldwide
Habitat: coast, fresh water, farmland

Secretary bird
Sagittarius serpentarius

This long-legged bird spends much of its life on the ground where it may walk 30 km (20 miles) or so every day. It runs to catch prey such as small mammals, birds, insects and reptiles. Pairs make a nest of sticks and turf on top of a tree. The nest is lined with grass and leaves. The female lays two or three eggs.

Size: 1.5 m (5 ft) tall
Range: Africa, south of the Sahara
Habitat: tropical grassland

Size: 79 cm (31 in)
Range: Mexico, Central and South America
Habitat: tropical grassland, tropical evergreen forest

King vulture
Sarcoramphus papa

With its brightly patterned, bare-skinned head, the king vulture is one of the most colourful of all birds of prey. Although it may occasionally kill some prey for itself, it feeds mostly on carrion – animals that are already dead. The king vulture is one of the few birds that uses its sense of smell to find food.

Size: 38-51 cm (15-20 in)
Range: almost worldwide
Habitat: coast, temperate grassland, tundra, high ground

Peregrine falcon
Falco peregrinus

One of the fastest flying of all birds, the peregrine is an expert hunter that preys on other birds. It makes a spectacular high-speed dive towards its prey, often a pigeon or a dove, and seizes it in mid-air. It kills the prey with its powerful talons and takes it to the ground to eat.

EAGLES

Eagles are large birds of prey with strong, hooked beaks, sharp talons and big, golden eyes. There are about 60 kinds of eagle living all over the world. Typically, a hunting eagle soars over the land for long periods, searching for food. With its keen eyesight, an eagle spots prey from a great distance, and then makes a rapid dive to the ground to seize and kill the animal with its talons. But some eagles hunt in a different way. Harpy eagles chase their prey through the trees, and sea eagles seize fish from the water. Eagles usually build their nests in trees or on cliffs. The nests are made of sticks and branches and may be used year after year. All look very similar, with black or grey feathers on the back and white on the belly.

A SNAKE HUNTER

Like other snake eagles, the crested serpent eagle feeds mostly on snakes and other reptiles. It generally hunts by perching in a tree to watch for prey, then dropping down on to it. The eagle's short strong toes have a rough surface that helps it to grip its wriggling catch.

FISH-EATING EAGLE

Fish is the main food of the sea eagle. The bird soars over the ocean looking for prey. It then swoops down to the water surface to seize a fish in its talons. Sea eagles also catch other creatures and rob smaller birds of their prey. They may also dive repeatedly at swimming birds such as ducks until they are exhausted and easy to catch. There are several different types of sea eagles. The largest is the Steller's sea eagle which lives on Siberian coasts.

Children's Animal Encyclopedia

RAINFOREST EAGLE

The world's biggest and most powerful eagle, the harpy, lives in the South American rainforest. Instead of soaring high in the air, this eagle makes short flights from tree to tree, looking for prey. The harpy preys mostly on monkeys, sloths and tree porcupines. When it spots a victim, such as a monkey, the harpy chases it through the trees at high speed until it is close enough to catch the monkey in its strong talons.

BIRDS OF THE TREES AND MASTERS OF THE AIR

One of the many advantages of flight is that it allows birds to fly up into trees. Up among the branches, they find havens from ground-living hunters, and safe places to roost and nest. Many birds also gather much of their food in trees. Pigeons and parrots feed mostly on seeds, nuts and fruits. Others, such as woodpeckers and cuckoos, eat insects. Some birds are more skilful fliers than others. Hummingbirds, for example, are true masters of the air and perform extraordinary aerial acrobatics. Swifts are so used to life in the air that they rarely, if ever, walk on land.

Crested treeswift
Hemiprocne coronata

This swift catches insects in the air to eat. It makes a tiny cup-shaped nest from thin flakes of bark, glued together with spit. There is just room for one egg, which both parents take turns to incubate.

Size: 20.5 cm (8 in)
Range: Southeast Asia
Habitat: tropical evergreen forest

Grey potoo
Nyctibius griseus

The potoo feeds by night, flying out from a perch to capture insects in its large beak. By day, it sits upright and very still on a broken branch or stump. With its head and beak pointing upwards, the potoo looks like part of the tree and so is hidden from its enemies. It lays its single egg on top of a tree stump.

Nightjar
Caprimulgus europaeus

The nightjar becomes active at sunset, when it takes to the air to dart after moths and other night-flying insects. The nightjar's tiny beak opens very wide and is fringed with bristles that help it to trap its prey.

Size: 26 cm (10 ¼ in)
Range: Europe, Asia, northern Africa
Habitat: deciduous forest, tropical evergreen forest, temperate grassland, desert

Size: 41 cm (16 ¼ in)
Range: West Indies, Central America, tropical South America
Habitat: deciduous forest, tropical evergreen forest

Children's Animal Encyclopedia

Sand martin
Riparia riparia

The sand martin is also known as the bank swallow. A lively bird, it darts in the air as it chases and snaps up insects. It lives in a burrow which it digs into sand banks near water, using its beak and feet. Martins lays up to eight eggs in a nest at the end of the burrow.

Size: 12-14 cm (4¾-5½ in)
Range: parts of Europe, Asia and North America; winters in South America, Africa and Southeast Asia
Habitat: farmland, fresh water, tropical grassland

Ruby-throated hummingbird
Archilochus colubris

Like all hummingbirds, the ruby-throated bird plunges its beak deep inside flowers to feed on nectar. After breeding in Canada and the eastern United States, this amazing small bird travels some 800 km (500 miles) to winter in Central America and the West Indies.

Size: 9 cm (3½ in)
Range: North America; winters in Central America and West Indies
Habitat: farmland, deciduous and tropical evergreen forest

Barn swallow
Hirundo rustica

The barn swallow eats insects, which it catches in the air or snatches from the surface of water. Both male and female help to make a nest of mud and grass on the wall of a building. The female lays four or five eggs.

Size: 19.5 cm (7¾ in)
Range: almost worldwide
Habitat: inhabited areas, farmland, fresh water

Size: 18-21.5 cm (7-8½ in)
Range: North America
Habitat: high ground, desert, tropical grassland, temperate grassland

Poorwill
Phalaenoptilus nuttallii

Named after its call, which sounds like "poor-will", this bird hunts insects at night. It is the only bird known to hibernate and each autumn it finds a rock crevice in which to spend the winter. Its body temperature falls and heart and breathing rates slow down, so that it uses as little energy as possible.

White-throated swift
Aeronautes saxatalis

Swifts are fast and expert fliers. They catch insects, eat, drink and even mate in the air. Their legs and feet are tiny, and they rarely walk. The white-throated swift makes a cup-shaped nest from feathers and grass, glued together with spit. The nest is built in a crack or crevice in a cliff or mountainside. The female lays four or five eggs.

Size: 15-18 cm (6-7 in)
Range: western USA, Central America
Habitat: high ground, desert

Birds of the trees and masters of the air

Resplendent quetzal
Pharomachrus mocinno

The beautiful male quetzal has a train of long tail feathers that wave and flutter as he flies and performs courtship displays. These feathers are shed after each breeding season and are then regrown. The ancient Mayan and Aztec peoples of Central America and Mexico believed the quetzal was a sacred bird, and its feathers were highly prized.

Size: 30 cm (11¾ in); tail feathers 61 cm (24 in)
Range: Mexico, Central America
Habitat: tropical evergreen forest, high ground

Size: 28 cm (11 in)
Range: Europe, Asia, Africa
Habitat: inhabited areas, farmland, temperate grassland, deciduous forest, tropical evergreen forest

Hoopoe
Upupa epops

This bird catches insects and other small creatures in trees and on the ground. It makes a nest in a hole in a tree or wall or on the ground. The female lays two to nine eggs and is fed by her mate as she incubates them for 16 to 19 days.

Size: 23-28 cm (9-11 in)
Range: Mexico, Central and South America
Habitat: tropical evergreen forest, fresh water

Rufous-tailed jacamar
Galbula ruficauda

This brightly plumaged long-billed bird sits on a branch, watching for insects. When it spots something, it darts after the prey and snaps it up in mid-air. Then it flies to a perch and to eat it. The female jacamar digs a breeding tunnel in the ground and lays two to four eggs. Both parents incubate the eggs for 19 to 23 days and then feed and care for their young until they can fly, at about three weeks old.

Size: 23 cm (9 in)
Range: Africa
Habitat: farmland, tropical evergreen forest, tropical grassland

Double-toothed barbet
Lybius bidentatus

This barbet has two sharp tooth-like structures on its beak. It perches in trees and bushes, feeding on figs, bananas and other fruits, and also darts out to catch flying termites.

Pileated woodpecker
Dryocopus pileatus

Ants and termites are the main foods of this woodpecker. Clinging tightly to a tree trunk with its sharp claws, the bird hammers into the bark with its strong beak to find prey. It also feeds on fruit. The female bird lays four eggs in a tree hole nest.

Size: 38-48 cm (15-19 in)
Range: North America, Mexico
Habitat: deciduous forest

Size: 58.5-73.5 cm (23-29 in)
Range: Indonesia, New Guinea, Biak and Yapen islands
Habitat: coast, fresh water, tropical evergreen forest

Victoria crowned pigeon
Goura victoria

The world's largest pigeon, the Victoria crowned pigeon has been hunted heavily and is now rare. This beautiful bird usually feeds on the ground, eating fallen fruit, seeds and berries. If disturbed, it flies off to perch in a tree.

Size: 38-41 cm (15-16¼ in)
Range: Mexico, Central and South America
Habitat: farmland, tropical evergreen forest

Blue-crowned motmot
Momotus momota

This bird has an unusual tail which has two long central feathers with racquet-shaped tips. With its tail swinging from side to side like a pendulum, the motmot sits on a branch, watching for prey. It darts out from its perch to catch insects, spiders and lizards and returns to eat them.

Belted kingfisher
Megaceryle alcyon

This kingfisher is an agile flier. It watches for prey from a tree overhanging a river or stream, then dives down to seize a fish or frog from the water. A breeding pair digs a long nesting tunnel in a riverbank. The female lays five to eight eggs in a nest made at the end of the tunnel.

Size: 28-35.5 cm (11-14 in)
Range: North America
Habitat: coast, fresh water

Birds of the trees and masters of the air

Red-crested turaco
Tauraco erythrolophus

A fruit-eating bird, the red-crested turaco lives in trees and does not often come down to the ground. A poor flier, it runs, hops and climbs well among the branches. It also eats insects.

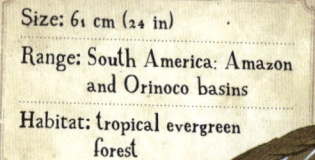

Size: 40.5 cm (16 in)
Range: Angola
Habitat: tropical evergreen forest

Size: 61 cm (24 in)
Range: South America: Amazon and Orinoco basins
Habitat: tropical evergreen forest

Hoatzin
Opisthocomus hoazin

Although it lives in trees, the hoatzin is a poor flier. It clambers along branches, feeding on fruit, buds and leaves.

Common cuckoo
Cuculus canorus

The cuckoo does not make a nest but lays her eggs in the nests of other birds. She usually lays 8 to 12 eggs, all in different nests. The young cuckoos hatch in about 12 days and are bigger and stronger than the host's young, which they eject from the nest so they get all the food.

Size: 33 cm (13 in)
Range: Europe, northern Africa, Asia
Habitat: deciduous forest, temperate grassland

Size: 26 cm (33½ in)
Range: Mexico, Central America, northern South America
Habitat: tropical evergreen forest

Size: 1.5 m (5 feet)
Range: India, Southeast Asia
Habitat: tropical evergreen forest

Scarlet macaw
Ara macao

These spectacular birds are usually seen in pairs or flocks of up to 20 birds. At sunrise the birds fly, screeching noisily, from their roost sites to feeding areas. There they feast on seeds, fruit and leaves high in the trees. At dusk they return to their roosts.

Great hornbill
Buceros bicornis

This hornbill lives high in the rainforest, eating fruit and catching small animals. A female lays up to three eggs in a hole in a tree and she uses her own droppings to seal the entrance. A small slit is left for the male to pass food to the mother and her chicks. She stays walled up until the young are hatched and old enough to leave the nest.

Children's Animal Encyclopedia

Toco toucan
Ramphastos toco

Although the toucan's colourful beak is up to 18 cm (7 in) long, it is not solid, so it is not as heavy as it looks. The toucan feeds on fruit. It picks up food in the tip of its bill, then tosses the morsel into its mouth.

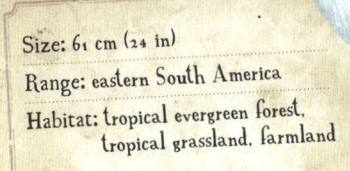

Size: 61 cm (24 in)
Range: eastern South America
Habitat: tropical evergreen forest, tropical grassland, farmland

Rainbow lorikeet
Trichoglossus haematodus

Screeching, chattering flocks of up to 100 lorikeets fly among the branches, eating fruit, insects, pollen and nectar. The brightly coloured feather patterns vary slightly from bird to bird.

Size: 26 cm (10¼ in)
Range: Indonesia, New Guinea, Australia
Habitat: inhabited areas, farmland, deciduous and tropical evergreen forest

Budgerigar
Melopsittacus undulatus

Best known as cage birds with many colour variations, these small fast-moving parrots usually have mainly green feathers in the wild. Flocks of budgerigars search the ground for grass seeds.

Size: 18 cm (7 in)
Range: Australia; introduced into USA
Habitat: farmland, desert, forest, grassland, scrub

Eclectus parrot
Eclectus roratus

The male eclectus parrot has mostly green feathers, while the female is bright red with a blue belly. Both feed mainly on fruit, nuts, flowers and nectar. They usually make a nest in a hole high in a tree. The female lays two eggs and incubates them for about 26 days.

Size: 35 cm (13¾ in)
Range: New Guinea, northeast Australia
Habitat: tropical evergreen forest

Sulphur-crested cockatoo
Cacatua galerita

This noisy parrot gathers in huge flocks to feed on seeds, fruits, palm hearts and insects. In the breeding season the cockatoos separate into pairs or family groups. A pair makes a nest in a tree and both parents incubate the two or three eggs.

Size: 50 cm (19¾ in)
Range: Australia, New Zealand, New Guinea, Indonesia, Palau
Habitat: tropical evergreen forest, tropical grassland, farmland

97

HUMMINGBIRDS

Beautiful hummingbirds are more agile in the air than any other group of birds. They are named after the humming sound made by the rapid beating of their wings. They hover in front of the flowers as they feed, and can fly upwards, sideways, downwards and even backwards. They live only in the Americas, mostly in the warmest parts. They measure from just over 5 cm (2 in) to about 20 cm (7 in) long, but the tail feathers make up as much as half of this length. Females usually have duller plumage than males. The sweet nectar contained in flowers is the main food of hummingbirds. Most have long beaks, which they plunge deep into flowers to get to the nectar.

A COLOURFUL HUMMINGBIRD

The male crimson topaz has colourful plumage and long curving tail feathers. It takes nectar from a wide range of flowers and also catches insects. The female bird has mostly green feathers.

WHITE-TIPPED SICKLEBILL

The long, strongly curved beak of the white-tipped sicklebill is perfect for taking nectar from deep flowers such as heliconias.

THE LONGEST BEAK

The sword-billed hummingbird has a longer beak than any other hummingbird. The beak allows the bird to reach nectar inside the deepest tube-shaped flowers. This bird also eats insects, which it catches in the air.

Children's Animal Encyclopedia

COURTSHIP DISPLAY

This hummingbird, known as the marvellous spatuletail, has only four full-grown tail feathers, two of which have a long, bare shaft ending in a broad wedge shape, or spatule. During courtship displays the male shows off these decorative feathers as he flies to and fro in front of the female.

Spatule

A male violet sabrewing hummingbird hovers on rapidly beating wings as he feeds on nectar from a ginger flower. Like many hummingbirds, this bird has shimmering feathers.

THE SMALLEST BIRD

The bee hummingbird is the world's tiniest bird. The male is only about 5 cm (2 in) long, including its beak and tail. Females are about half a centimetre (⅕ in) longer.

99

SONGBIRDS

About half of all the kinds of bird in the world are included in the group known as songbirds. There are more than 6,000 kinds, found all over the world except at the poles. Not all sing as sweetly as the lark or the nightingale, but the males of most species do sing sequences of musical notes, when courting mates or defending their territory. Female singers are rare, apart from a few species such as song sparrows and robins. Songbirds are also called passerines, or perching birds, and have feet adapted for perching on trees and posts. Their feet have four toes – three that point forwards and one backwards – and are ideally shaped for holding on to twigs, reeds and even wires.

Size: 16.5–19 cm (6½–7½ in)
Range: North America: east of Rockies and into Central America
Habitat: inhabited areas, farmland, deciduous and tropical evergreen forest

Eastern bluebird
Sialia sialis

The eastern bluebird feeds mainly on insects and berries. The male performs acrobatic flight displays to court his mate. Both birds then build a nest of grass and twigs in a hole in a tree. Eastern bluebirds lay between three to seven eggs. Both parents feed the young chicks for up to 20 days after they hatch.

Size: 16 cm (6¼ in)
Range: Europe, Asia, northern Africa; winters in tropical Africa
Habitat: farmland, deciduous forest, tropical evergreen forest

Nightingale
Luscinia megarhynchos

Best known for its beautiful song, the nightingale sings night and day. It eats insects such as ants and beetles, which it finds in undergrowth and on the ground. In summer, it also eats berries and fruit. The female makes a nest of leaves on or close to the ground and lays four or five eggs.

Size: 14 cm (5½ in)
Range: Europe, northern Africa, Asia
Habitat: inhabited areas, deciduous forest

Starling
Sturnus vulgaris

Starlings are common in both country and city areas and have been introduced into countries outside their natural range. Only a century ago, 60 birds were released in New York. Now, the starling is one of the most common birds in North America. Starlings eat insects, worms, snails, fruit, berries and seeds.

Size: 21.5 cm (8½ in)
Range: Europe, Asia; introduced almost worldwide
Habitat: inhabited areas, farmland, temperate grassland, deciduous forest

European robin
Erithacus rubecula

In many areas the robin is a shy forest bird, but in Britain and parts of Europe it lives in gardens and is often quite tame. Insects, spiders, worms and snails are the robin's main food, but it also eats berries, small fruit and scraps of food put out by humans.

Children's Animal Encyclopedia

American robin
Turdus migratorius

This bird lives in urban areas and feeds on insects, earthworms, fruit and berries. In the breeding season, the male has a black head and tail and a reddish breast, while the female is duller, with a grey head and tail.

Size: 10 cm (4 in)
Range: Trinidad, South America
Habitat: farmland, tropical evergreen forest

Purple honeycreeper
Cyanerpes caeruleus

Groups of purple honeycreepers feed on fruit, especially bananas, and insects in trees. They also perch by flowers and suck nectar from them with their long curved beaks. The female honeycreeper builds a neat cup-shaped nest in the fork of a tree or bush. She lays two eggs, which she incubates for 12 to 14 days.

Size: 23-28 cm (9-11 in)
Range: North America, Mexico, West Indies
Habitat: inhabited areas, deciduous forest

Northern cardinal
Cardinalis cardinalis

Only the male cardinal has brilliant red plumage. The female is mainly brown, with a red beak. Cardinals eat foods such as insects, fruits, seeds and buds. They also visit bird feeders in gardens.

Size: 20-23 cm (7¾-9 in)
Range: North America, east and south of the Rockies; Mexico
Habitat: inhabited areas, deciduous forest, fresh water

Winter wren
Troglodytes troglodytes

The tiny northern wren has a plump body and a short tail, which it nearly always holds cocked up. Its main foods are insects and spiders, which it finds on low plants. In spring, the wren makes a nest in a hollow tree stump or among tree roots. The female lays five to eight eggs, which she incubates.

Size: 23-28 cm (9-11 in)
Range: North America
Habitat: inhabited areas, deciduous forest

Size: 8 cm (3¼ in)
Range: North America, Europe, northern Africa, Asia
Habitat: inhabited areas, deciduous forest

Northern mockingbird
Mimus polyglottos

One of the best-known American songbirds, the mockingbird is the state bird of five US states. The male sings night and day and often mimics other birds and sounds. Mockingbirds feed mainly on insects such as grasshoppers and beetles, and also eat spiders, snails, small reptiles and fruit. They lay three to six eggs at a time.

Songbirds

Size: 16 cm (6¼ in)
Range: Arctic region, northern Europe, northern Asia, North America
Habitat: coast, tundra, high ground, temperate grassland

Snow bunting
Plectrophenax nivalis

The snow bunting breeds farther north than any other land bird. To escape the cold it sometimes burrows in the snow. After breeding, it flies south for the winter. Seeds, insects and grasses are its main foods.

Scarlet tanager
Piranga olivacea

The scarlet tanager usually nests in woodlands, where it eats bees, wasps and other insects and their larvae, as well as fruit. After breeding, male tanagers moult their scarlet feathers and become olive green like the female birds.

Size: 19 cm (7½ in)
Range: eastern North America
Habitat: deciduous forest, Northern forest

Size: 20.5 cm (8 in)
Range: Southeast Asia; introduced into USA, Middle East and Australia
Habitat: tropical evergreen forest, inhabited areas, farmland, fresh water

Northern parula
Parula americana

This little warbler feeds mainly on caterpillars and other insects that it finds in trees. It creeps over the branches and hops from perch to perch as it looks for prey. It makes its nest in hanging tree lichen or Spanish moss. The female usually lays four or five eggs, which she incubates for 12 to 14 days. Both parents feed and care for the young.

Size: 11 cm (4¼ in)
Range: North and Central America, West Indies
Habitat: deciduous forest, fresh water

Red-whiskered bulbul
Pycnonotus jocosus

This bulbul is named for the tufts of red feathers at each side of its head. Male and female look alike, but young birds have white whiskers. Flocks of these lively, noisy birds gather to feast on fruit trees, where they eat both ripe and unripe fruit. They also eat the insects they come across while feeding. The female lays two to four eggs in a cup-shaped nest made of grass, roots and stalks.

Children's Animal Encyclopedia

Size: 10 cm (4 in)
Range: Central and northwestern South America
Habitat: fresh water, tropical evergreen forest

Pine grosbeak
Pinicola enucleator

A type of finch, the pine grosbeak uses its heavy bill to crush the stones of fruit such as cherries and plums. It also eats seeds, buds and insects. A breeding pair make a nest in a tree and the female lays four eggs.

Size: 20 cm (7¾ in)
Range: northern Europe, northern Asia, North America
Habitat: northern and deciduous forest, farmland

Torrent tyrannulet
Serpophaga cinerea

This bird lives by fast-flowing streams. It often plucks insects from slippery rocks surrounded by foaming water, drenching itself in the process. A breeding pair makes a cup-shaped nest, usually hanging over water. The female lays two eggs. Both parents feed the young on insects.

Size: 20.5-23 cm (8-9 in)
Range: North America
Habitat: inhabited areas, farmland, temperate grassland, deciduous forest

Eastern kingbird
Tyrannus tyrannus

This noisy bird attacks anything that enters its territory, particularly larger birds. It eats many different types of insects, which it catches in the air or on the ground or scoops out of water. It also hovers in the air to pick berries from trees. The female lays three to five eggs.

Size: 35.5 cm (14 in) including bill
Range: northern South America
Habitat: tropical evergreen forest

Size: 12-15 cm (4¾-6 in)
Range: North America
Habitat: deciduous forest, northern forest, inhabited areas

Long-billed woodcreeper
Nasica longirostris

Using its long beak, this woodcreeper searches the leaves of rainforest plants for insects and spiders to eat. It also finds prey under the bark of trees. An expert climber, it uses its stiff tail for support as it clambers around trees. The female lays two eggs in a nest in a tree hole and incubates them for about 14 days.

Black-capped chickadee
Parus atricapillus

This little bird has a call which sounds like "chick-a-dee-dee-dee". It feeds on caterpillars and other insects as well as seeds and berries. The chickadee makes its nest in the soft wood of a dead tree, where it lays five to ten eggs.

Songbirds

Size: 11.5 cm (4 in)
Range: Southeast Asia
Habitat: tropical evergreen forest, tropical grassland, farmland

Crimson sunbird
Aethopyga siparaja

This sunbird eats flower nectar as well as insects. It hovers before tube-shaped flowers and reaches into them with its long tongue. When feeding from big blooms such as hibiscus, it pierces the petals to get the nectar at the base.

Size: male 25.5–30.5 cm (10–12 in); female 14–15 cm (5½–6 in)
Range: Africa
Habitat: high ground, tropical grassland

Red-tufted malachite sunbird
Nectarinia johnstoni

This sunbird lives only on high mountain slopes, where it feeds on the nectar of plants such as giant lobelias and protea flowers. But its main food is insects, particularly flies, which it catches in the air. Both male and female have scarlet tufts at the sides of the breast, but only the male has long central tail feathers.

Size: 30 cm (11¾ in)
Range: North America, Mexico
Habitat: inhabited areas, deciduous forest, tropical evergreen forest, northern forest

Blue jay
Cyanocitta cristata

Noisy groups of blue jays are a familiar sight in gardens. Seeds and nuts are their main foods, and they bury extra supplies to save for the winter. Blue jays also eat insects and even steal eggs and chicks from the nests of other birds. A breeding pair makes its nest in a tree or bush, and the female lays two to six eggs.

American crow
Corvus brachyrhynchos

This large, black bird eats almost anything it can find, including insects, spiders, frogs and birds and their eggs. It also scavenges on waste food. A nest of sticks and twigs is made in a tree or bush. The female lays three to six eggs in it.

Size: 43–53 cm (17–20¾ in)
Range: North America
Habitat: deciduous forest, temperate grassland, farmland, inhabited areas

Children's Animal Encyclopedia

Wire-tailed manakin
Pipra filicauda

Only the male manakin has dramatic black, red and yellow plumage, but both male and female have long wiry tail feathers. The male shows off his bright colours in courtship displays. These birds usually feed alone, searching for insects and fruit in forests and cocoa plantations.

Size: 13 cm (5 in)
Range: islands of Vanuatu, Samoa, Santa Cruz, Solomon, New Caledonia
Habitat: tropical evergreen forest, farmland, fresh water

Size: 11.5 cm (4½ in)
Range: northern South America
Habitat: tropical evergreen forest, farmland, fresh water

Cardinal honeyeater
Myzomela cardinalis

The cardinal honeyeater feeds by sipping nectar from flowers and picking insects from leaves. The female is duller than the colourful male. She has olive grey feathers with red patches. This bird's cup-shaped nest hangs from a forked branch, and the female lays two or three eggs.

Size: 16 cm (6¼ in)
Range: Europe, Asia, North America, northern Africa
Habitat: temperate grassland, desert, tundra, high ground

Shore lark
Eremophila alpestris

Only the male bird has black tufts of feathers on his head. He raises them during courtship displays or when defending territory. Shore larks eat seeds, buds, insects and other small creatures. A simple nest of plant stems, surrounded with pebbles, is made on the ground. The female lays four eggs.

Size: 20.5 cm (8 in)
Range: Africa, south of the Sahara
Habitat: tropical grassland, farmland, fresh water

Size: 44–57 cm (17¼–22½ in)
Range: Europe, northern Africa, Asia, North America
Habitat: inhabited areas, farmland, deciduous and Northern forest, temperate grassland

Yellow-throated longclaw
Macronyx croceus

This bird gets its name from the back claw on each foot which is nearly 5 cm (2 in) long. It is often seen on farmland and feeds on insects which it often finds in grass. In the breeding season, the male makes a special courtship flight, and fans his tail and sings. The female lays three or four eggs in a nest hidden in long grass.

Black-billed magpie
Pica pica

The magpie eats insects, spiders and snails but also snatches young birds from their nests. A breeding pair makes a large nest in a tree or bush. The female lays five to eight eggs and incubates them while the male keeps her supplied with food.

BIRDS OF PARADISE

Birds of paradise are named for their beautiful plumage and are among the most spectacular of all birds. But only the males have the colourful and decorative head and tail feathers for which birds of paradise are famed. The females look quite different, with dull, usually brownish plumage. There are more than 40 species, ranging in size from about 13 to 107 cm (5 to 42 in) long. Most live in the rainforests of New Guinea, but a few birds of paradise are found in the nearby Moluccan Islands and the forests of northeast Australia. Fruit is their main food, but they also catch insects, spiders, and occasionally frogs and lizards.

The striking colours and magnificent tail plumes of the greater bird of paradise are a spectacular sight as it perches on a branch in the rainforest.

Plume

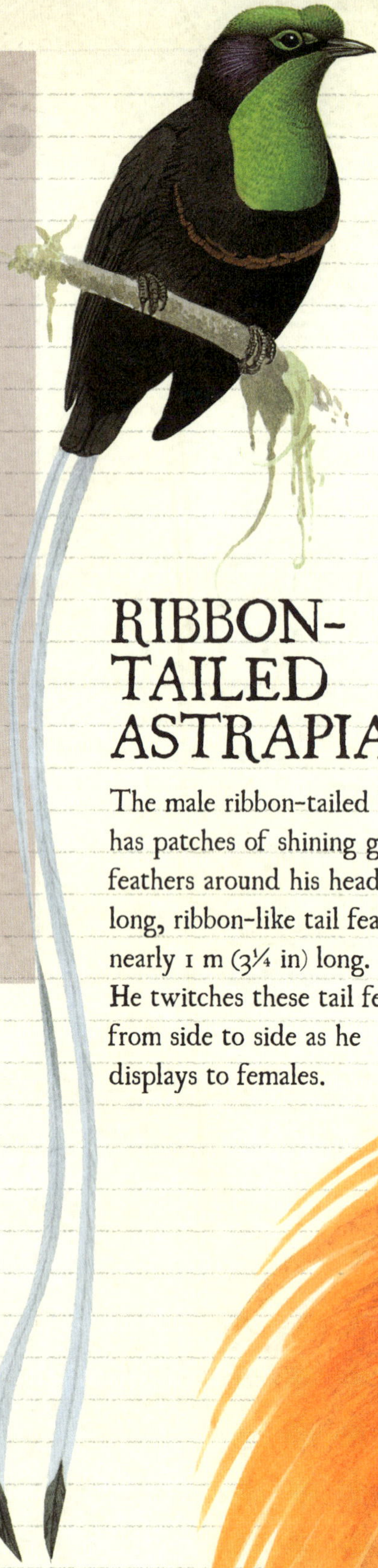

RIBBON-TAILED ASTRAPIA

The male ribbon-tailed bird has patches of shining green feathers around his head and long, ribbon-like tail feathers nearly 1 m (3¼ in) long. He twitches these tail feathers from side to side as he displays to females.

KING OF SAXONY BIRD

Wire-like plumes, up to 50 cm (19¾ in) long, extend from the head of this bird. During courtship, these are held high while the bird bounds up and down, hissing loudly. As the female approaches, the male sweeps his long head feathers down in front of her. He follows her, and they mate.

TAIL PLUMES

Wilson's bird of paradise has two coiled tail feathers. These are held at right angles to the body when the bird displays.

A GROUP DISPLAY

Most birds of paradise display alone, but the Raggianas gather in groups. When females appear, the males hop around, flapping their wings and calling excitedly. Each then tries to outdo the others in showing off his glorious plumage. At the peak of the display, the birds make a series of high-pitched calls.

Birds of paradise

Size: 24 cm (9½ in)
Range: Europe, Asia, northwest Africa
Habitat: inhabited areas, decidous forest, tropical evergreen forest

Size: 16.5 cm (6½ in)
Range: Central and South America
Habitat: tropical evergreen forest

Golden oriole
Oriolus oriolus

Most of the golden oriole's life is spent high in the trees, feeding on insects and fruit with the help of its sharp beak. Its nest is like a tiny hammock made of grass and hung from a forked branch. Golden orioles lay three or four eggs.

Royal flycatcher
Onychorhynchus coronatus

This flycatcher has an amazing crest which normally lies flat but is opened and closed like a fan during courtship displays. Like all flycatchers, it feeds on insects which it snaps up in the air.

Size: 38 cm (15 in)
Range: northern South America
Habitat: tropical evergreen forest, fresh water

Size: 12.5 cm (5 in)
Range: Africa, south of the Sahara
Habitat: farmland, tropical grassland

Cock-of-the-rock
Rupicola peruvianus

In the breeding season, the brilliantly coloured male cocks of the rock perform group displays, competing for the attention of the plainer females. They leap into the air, make noisy calls and flick their wings. These birds feeds mainly on fruit.

Red-billed quelea
Quelea quelea

In huge flocks of thousands of birds, red-billed queleas move like clouds across the sky. They feed on grain crops and can destroy whole fields. Queleas breed in colonies and lay two or three eggs at a time, in a kidney-shaped nest which hangs from a branch and has a side entrance.

Children's Animal Encyclopedia

Size: 14.5 cm (5¾ in)
Range: Europe, Asia; introduced worldwide
Habitat: inhabited areas

Superb lyrebird
Menura novaehollandiae

Only the male lyrebird has a long, lyre-shaped tail. In the breeding season, he displays to the female by spreading his tail feathers over himself and dancing. These birds rarely fly, but hop and flap up into trees to roost at night. They scratch on the ground to find insects to eat.

House sparrow
Passer domesticus

The house sparrow has been introduced worldwide and is an extremely common and adaptable bird. A few birds were taken to New York in 1850 and they have now spread all over North and South America. Seeds are the sparrow's main food, but it also eats insects and scraps put out by humans.

Size: male 80–95 cm (31½–37½ in); female 74–84 cm (29¼–33 in)
Range: southeastern Australia
Habitat: tropical evergreen forest, deciduous forest

Garnet pitta
Pitta granatina

Both male and female garnet pittas have bright feathers, but young birds are a dull brown. This bird spends much of its time on the ground, catching ants, beetles and other insects. It also eats seeds and fruit and does fly short distances.

Size: 9 cm (3½ in)
Range: Australia, Indonesia
Habitat: deciduous forest, temperate grassland, farmland

Size: 15 cm (6 in)
Range: Malaysia, Sumatra, Borneo
Habitat: tropical evergreen forest, fresh water

Zebra finch
Taeniopygia guttata

Large flocks of zebra finches feed on seeds and insects in trees and on the ground. In dry areas these birds wait for rain before breeding. They make a domed nest low in a tree or bush and the female lays four to six eggs.

HOW DO ANIMALS COMMUNICATE?

Almost all animals have some way of keeping in touch with others of their own kind. Many, such as birds, whales, dogs and monkeys, make a wide range of sounds, each with its own meaning. Other animals communicate by smell. They use scents to announce to others that they are ready to mate or that a particular area is their territory. Sight is also important. Courting lizards nod their heads in a special way and the positions of the ears of animals such as dogs and cats show when they are pleased, angry or frightened.

ANTENNAE DETECTION

A male moth's antennae allow him to smell pheromones – chemicals given off by a female of his own kind – from more than a kilometre (half a mile) away. Silk moths live for just a few days, so they need to find a mate fast and lay eggs before they die.

The large feathery antennae of the male silk moth are especially sensitive.

BARKS AND HOWLS

Like all wild dogs the coyote communicates with barks and yaps as well as by using its tail and ears to show its mood. The coyote's howl is a way of signalling its ownership of a particular territory and warning off rival animals.

SONG-FLIGHT

Warblers are well known for their songs. The zitting cisticola sings during its special song-flight to attract mates. It may go up to 30 m (100 ft) or more above the ground, circling over a wide area.

FLASHING SIGNALS

Wingless female fireflies, called glow-worms, signal to males by making a series of flashes. Each species has a different sequence. The flashes are made by a combination of substances in the firefly's abdomen.

WAVING CLAW

One of the front claws of the male fiddler crab is much larger than the other and brightly coloured. The male crab stands outside his burrow on the seashore and waves this claw to attract the attention of females. Each species of fiddler crab has a slightly different pattern of waves.

Male

Female

The fiddler crab also uses his large front claw to fight off rival males and to dig the burrow where the female will lay her eggs.

Children's Animal Encyclopedia

REPTILES

The first reptiles evolved from amphibians about 340 million years ago. In the form of dinosaurs, which first appeared about 230 million years ago, reptiles dominated life on Earth for 165 million years. Today there are more than 9,400 known species of reptiles, including such animals as sea-living turtles, predatory crocodiles, venomous snakes and fast-moving lizards. They live on all continents except Antarctica. Most hunt other animals to eat but there are some plant-eating turtles, tortoises and lizards.

Children's Animal Encyclopedia

WHAT IS A REPTILE?

Reptiles are vertebrate animals – like mammals and birds, they have a backbone made up of small bones called vertebrae. Their bodies are covered in waterproof scales. Most reptiles live on land, but turtles and some snakes live in water, and crocodiles spend time in water and on land.

TYPES OF REPTILE

Four groups of reptiles survive today. Turtles and tortoises have short broad bodies enclosed by a bony shell. Crocodiles and alligators are hunters and the largest living reptiles. The third group includes lizards and snakes. All snakes and most lizards are predators. The last group, the tuataras of New Zealand, has only two living species.

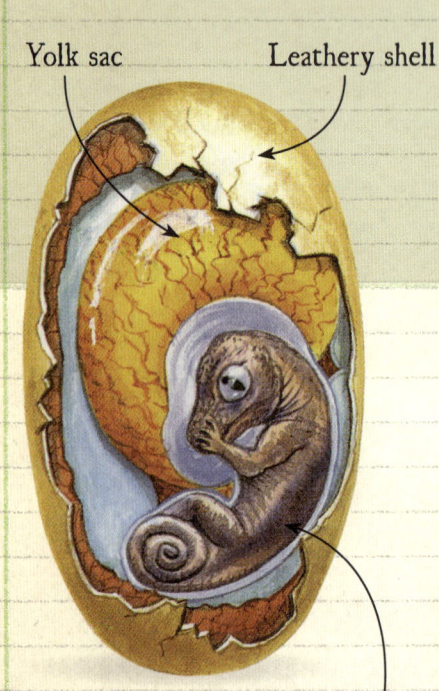

TURTLES AND TORTOISES

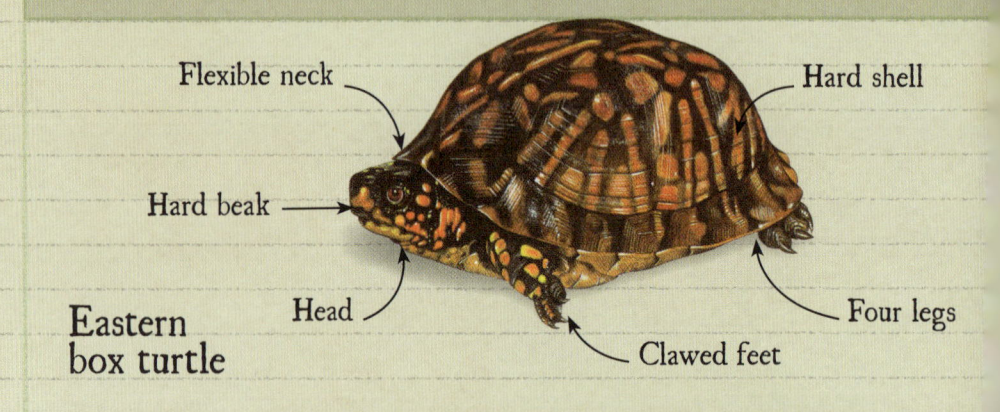

- Flexible neck
- Hard shell
- Hard beak
- Head
- Clawed feet
- Four legs

Eastern box turtle

SNAKES

- Legless body
- Forked tongue

Dark green whipsnake

- Yolk sac
- Leathery shell
- Embryo reptile

EGG-LAYING REPTILES

Most reptiles lay eggs from which their young hatch, although some give birth to live young. The egg is protected by a tough shell. Inside is a yolk sac that provides food for the developing young, or embryo. The embryo grows inside the egg until it is ready to hatch out as a small version of the adult, able to live independently.

Some snakes, such as pythons, curl around their eggs to keep them warm.

Children's Animal Encyclopedia

PREHISTORIC REPTILES

Although not the first reptiles, dinosaurs were the most successful, dominating the Earth for 165 million years. Like reptiles today, they had scale-covered skin and laid eggs. Many, such as *Lambeosaurus*, were plant eaters. Others, such as *Tyrannosaurus rex*, were fierce hunters.

Lambeosaurus with young

LIZARDS

Race runner
- Ear openings
- Long tail
- Slender body
- Four legs

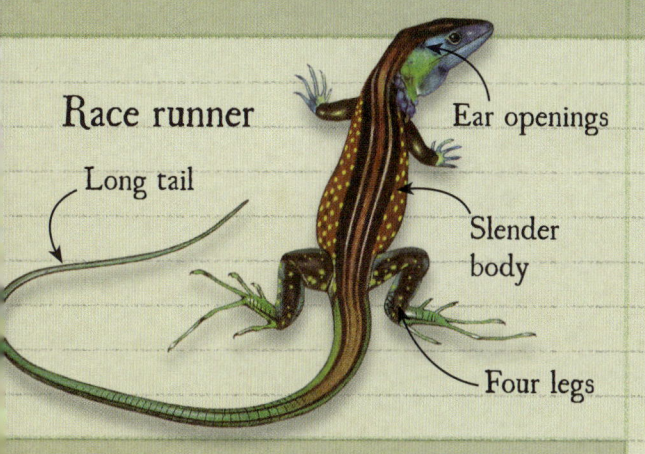

CROCODILES AND ALLIGATORS

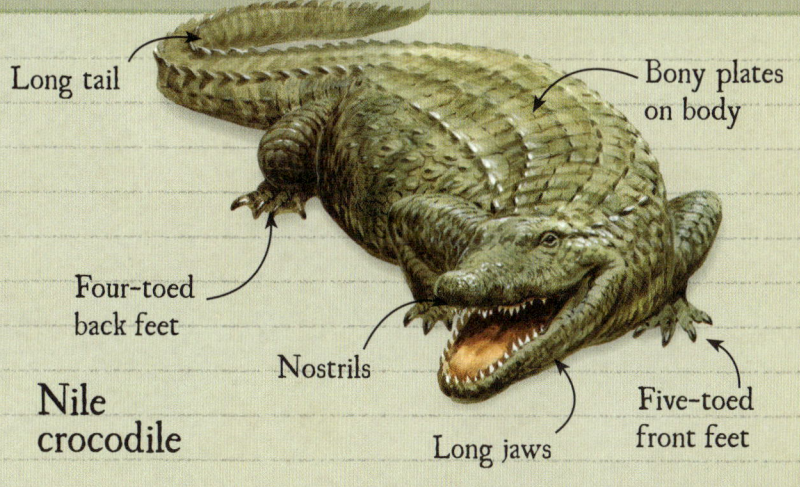

Nile crocodile
- Long tail
- Bony plates on body
- Four-toed back feet
- Nostrils
- Long jaws
- Five-toed front feet

TUATARAS

Tuatara
- Crest on back
- Large head
- Four legs

Nile crocodile skeleton
- Tailbones
- Vertebrae
- Sharp teeth
- Four legs
- Ribs
- Jawbones

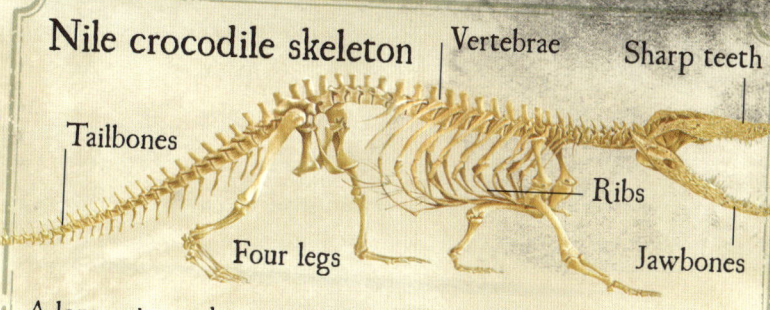

A long spine and a strong tail help the crocodile to move efficiently in the water. Its legs are short but strong, and it has long jaws studded with many sharp teeth.

Most reptiles, such as turtles, simply lay their eggs in a safe place and leave them to hatch by themselves.

COLD-BLOODED

Reptiles are cold-blooded and need the sun's warmth to be active. As a result, most live in warm climates. Reptiles usually switch between basking in the sun to gain heat and moving to shade or burrows to cool down.

Green iguana

CROCODILES, ALLIGATORS, TURTLES AND TORTOISES

All of these kinds of reptile are armoured, but in different ways. A typical turtle or tortoise has a hard shell that protects its soft body. Crocodiles and alligators are covered with hard scales and have thickened bony plates on the back for extra protection. The turtle group includes freshwater turtles, sea turtles and land tortoises. The crocodile group includes three families: crocodiles, alligators and caimans, and the gharial.

CROCODILES AND ALLIGATORS

There are 14 species of crocodiles, eight species of alligators and caimans, and one species of gharial. All are powerful creatures that live on land and in water and hunt a range of other animals. They live in tropical and subtropical areas. Males and females generally look alike, but males tend to grow larger. Both crocodiles and alligators have a pair of large teeth near the front of the lower jaw for grasping prey. In crocodiles, these teeth fit into notches in the upper jaw and can be seen when the jaw is closed. In alligators and caimans, the large teeth fit into bony pits in the upper jaw and cannot be seen when the mouth is closed.

Size: 7 m (23 ft)
Range: India and Nepal
Habitat: fresh water

Gharial
Gavialis gangeticus

The gavial has long jaws studded with about 100 small teeth – ideal equipment for seizing fish and frogs under the water. The most aquatic of all the crocodiles, it moves awkwardly on land and rarely leaves the water. The female hauls herself out onto the shore where she lays 35 to 60 eggs at night in a pit that she digs with her back feet. She stays nearby while the eggs incubate for as long as 94 days. Hunted for its skin, the gharial is now endangered – fewer than 200 survive in the wild.

Size: 5.5 m (up to 18 ft)
Range: southeastern USA
Habitat: coast, fresh water

American alligator
Alligator mississippiensis

At one time American alligators came close to extinction because hunters killed so many for their skins. Efforts to protect the species have been very successful, and it is no longer endangered. These alligators usually mate in spring. The female lays about 50 eggs in a mound of leaves and other plant material and guards the nest while the eggs incubate. The young stay with their mother for up to two years.

Mugger crocodile
Crocodylus palustris

The mugger is a powerful crocodile with a broad, heavy snout. Adults can catch large mammals, such as deer and buffalo, but also feed on frogs, snakes, and turtles. Young muggers eat insects and other small creatures. In the breeding season, the female lays ten to 35 eggs in a hole in the riverbank. She may lay a second clutch later in the season.

Size: 4 m (up to 13 ft)
Range: India
Habitat: fresh water

Spectacled caiman
Caiman crocodilus

Size: 1.5–2 m (5–6½ ft)
Range: Venezuela to southern Amazon basin
Habitat: fresh water, coastal waters

This caiman is extremely adaptable and readily moves into watery habitats made by humans, such as reservoirs and cattle ponds. Smaller caimans feed mostly on insects, crabs, and other invertebrates. Larger animals eat fish and and water snails. In the breeding season, the female makes a nest of earth and leaves and lays up to 40 eggs. In some areas, numbers of this caiman have fallen because so many have been hunted and killed for their skins.

Saltwater crocodile
Crocodylus porosus

This is one of the largest and most dangerous of all crocodiles. It has been known to attack humans. It spends much of its life in the sea, catching fish, but it also preys on land animals such as monkeys, cattle, and buffalo. The female comes to land to lay up to 80 eggs in a mound of plant material.

Size: 9 m (27 ft)
Range: southern India, Indonesia, northern Australia
Habitat: coast, tropical evergreen forest, coastal waters, fresh water

Size: 1.5 m (5 ft)
Range: western Africa south of the Sahara
Habitat: fresh water

West African dwarf crocodile
Osteolaemus tetraspis

This small crocodile has become rare in recent years because of changes to the rivers and lakes it inhabits and because of increased hunting. A slow-moving and not very dangerous animal, it is easy to kill or catch. Little is known about this crocodile's life, but it is thought to be active at night, when it feeds on crabs, frogs, and fish. The female lays 11 to 17 eggs in a mound of leaves and other plant material.

NILE CROCODILES

Unlike most reptiles, the female Nile crocodile is a devoted parent. After mating, the female digs a pit near the river with her back legs and lays 16 to 80 eggs. She covers the nest with soil, then both parents stay close by to guard it while the eggs incubate for six to eight weeks. The female does not leave the nest area even to find food during this time. When they are about to hatch, the baby crocodiles call out to their mother from inside their shells. She uncovers the nest so that the young can get out. The mother may continue to care for her young until they are six months old. By then they are about 45 cm (18 in) long and can find food for themselves.

Nile crocodiles are found along most of the Nile River, and in rivers and lakes all over tropical and southern Africa.

THE CROCODILE'S NEST

The nest is usually made near water on a sandy beach or riverbank and is 20–45 cm (8–18 in) deep. Once she has dug the nest burrow, the female lies over it and deposits her eggs inside.

BEGINNING LIFE

When ready to hatch, the young crocodiles are very sensitive to any movements on the earth above them. When they hear their mother's footsteps they call out. Once she has uncovered the nest, each hatchling uses the sharp egg tooth on its jaw to chip its way out of its shell. The mother may help to pull the babies free.

PROTECTION

Once the hatchlings are out of the eggs they must find shelter from the many predators waiting to catch them. The mother picks the babies up, a few at a time, and carries them to a safe nursery site. She does not close her mouth, and the tiny crocodiles look like prisoners behind the bars of her big, sharp teeth. She releases her babies in a quiet pool and defends them fiercely.

FIERCE HUNTER

The Nile crocodile is a wily hunter. It lurks in the water, often with only its eyes and nostrils above the surface, waiting for prey to come to the riverbank to drink. The crocodile then seizes its prey, drags it into the water and drowns it.

TURTLES AND TORTOISES

There are over 300 species of turtle and tortoise. Typically, they have a hard shell to protect the soft body. The shell is in two parts – the carapace on the back and the plastron underneath. The ribs and most of the vertebrae are attached to the shell, and most turtles and tortoises can pull their head inside the shell for protection. Turtles and tortoises have hard beaks instead of teeth for tearing off pieces of food. All turtles and tortoises lay eggs. Most bury them in sand or earth and leave the hatchlings to make their own way out.

Size: 61-76 cm (24-30 in)
Range: northern South America
Habitat: fresh water

Arrau river turtle
Podocnemis expansa

This is the largest of the turtles known as sidenecks – a sideneck retracts it head by moving it sideways into the shell. Females gather in huge numbers on sandbanks to lay their eggs. When the young hatch, they must make their own way to the water.

Size: 12.5-23 cm (5-9 in)
Range: eastern Canada, northeastern to midwestern USA
Habitat: deciduous forest, temperate grassland, fresh water

River terrapin
Batagur baska

Size: 58 cm (22¾ in)
Range: Bangladesh, Cambodia, India, Indonesia, Malaysia
Habitat: coast, fresh water

A large plant-eating turtle, the river terrapin, or batagur, lives in salt water as well as in rivers. It nests on sandbanks, so it is easy for people to catch and dig up its eggs for food. In Malaysia, to save the river terrapin, eggs are taken to hatcheries where young turtles are kept safe in pools until they are two years old.

Wood turtle
Glyptemys insculpta

This rough-shelled turtle stays near water, but spends most of its life on land. It is a good climber and feeds on fruit, worms, and insects. In May or June females lay six to eight eggs. These may hatch before the autumn, but the eggs of turtles in northern areas usually do not hatch until the next spring.

Yellow-bellied slider turtle
Trachemys scripta

This pond slider rarely moves far from water and often basks on a floating log. Young pond sliders feed mainly on insects, tadpoles, and other small invertebrate animals, but as they grow they also eat plants. In summer, the female pond slider lays up to three clutches of four to 23 eggs each.

Size: 13-30 cm (5-11¾ in)
Range: USA, Central America to Brazil; introduced to Europe, Africa and Asia
Habitat: fresh water

Children's Animal Encyclopedia

Galápagos giant tortoise
Chelonoides nigra

Size: up to 1.2 m (4 ft)
Range: Galápagos Islands
Habitat: tropical evergreen forest, desert

This huge tortoise may weigh more than 215 kg (475 lb) – males are usually larger than females. It lives on land and feeds on almost any plants it can find. Some have a shell that curves up behind the head, allowing the tortoise to reach higher plants. The female digs a pit with her back feet and lays four to ten eggs. She covers the eggs with soil and leaves them to incubate. The young dig themselves out of the pit when they hatch.

Pancake tortoise
Malacochersus tornieri

Size: 15 cm (6 in)
Range: Kenya, Tanzania; introduced to Zimbabwe
Habitat: desert

This remarkable tortoise has a soft flexible shell. If in danger, it crawls into a rocky crevice and breathes in lots of air. Its body expands so much that it becomes stuck tight in the hole and very difficult to pull out. But this does not protect the animal from people, who catch large numbers for the pet trade.

Spur-thighed tortoise
Testudo graeca

Also known as the Greek tortoise, this rare reptile has lost much of its native habitat, which has been built upon or turned into farmland. Millions of these tortoises have been captured and sold as pets, which further damaged the wild population. This species is now regarded as vulnerable to the risk of extinction.

Size: 15 cm (6 in)
Range: Northern Africa, southeastern and southwestern Europe, Middle East
Habitat: inhabited areas, farmland, deciduous forest, temperate grassland, high ground

Eroded hingeback tortoise
Kinixys erosa

Size: 33 cm (13 in)
Range: western and central Africa
Habitat: tropical evergreen forest, fresh water

This tortoise eats some small animals but feeds mainly on plants and spends much of its life hiding among plant debris. Its shell is unique. A hinge allows the rear of the shell to be lowered to protect the animal's hindquarters if it is attacked. Young tortoises do not have a hinge – it develops as they grow.

Turtles and tortoises

Matamata
Chelus fimbriatus

The irregular shape of this turtle keeps it well hidden as it lies among leaves and other debris on the riverbed. Fleshy flaps at the sides of the head wave in water and may attract small fish. When a fish comes close, the turtle opens its large mouth and water rushes in, taking the fish with it. The turtle closes its mouth, leaving only a slit for the water to flow out.

Size: 41 cm (16¼ in)
Range: northern South America
Habitat: fresh water

Hawksbill
Eretmochelys imbricata

Hawksbills have long been hunted for their beautiful shells as well as for their eggs. There are now strict controls on hunting, but numbers are still low. The hawksbill has an unusual diet. As well as eating molluscs and crustaceans, it feeds on sponges. Many of these contain poisons but they do not seem to affect the turtles.

Size: 76-91 cm (30-36 in)
Range: tropical Atlantic, Pacific, and Indian oceans; Caribbean Sea
Habitat: coastal waters, coral reef

Murray River turtle
Emydura macquarii

The shape of the Murray River turtle's shell changes as it develops. Newly hatched young have almost circular shells. As they grow, the shell becomes widest at the back, and adult shells are almost oval. An active turtle, it feeds on frogs, tadpoles and plants. In summer, the female lays between 10 and 15 eggs in a hole dug in the river bank. The eggs hatch after about 10 or 11 weeks.

Size: 30 cm (11¾ in)
Range: southeastern Australia
Habitat: fresh water

Leatherback
Dermochelys coriacea

The world's largest turtle, the leatherback weighs about 360 kg (800 lb). Its shell is not covered with hard plates like those of other turtles but made of a thick leathery material. It has weak scissorlike jaws and feeds mostly on jellyfish. Leatherbacks travel long distances between the areas where they feed and their nesting sites. Most breed only every other year. Newly hatched young have small scales on their shells and skin, but these soon disappear.

Size: 1.5 m (5 ft)
Range: temperate and tropical waters worldwide
Habitat: oceanic, coastal waters

Children's Animal Encyclopedia

Size: 8–13 cm (3–5 in)
Range: North America
Habitat: fresh water

Common musk turtle
Sternotherus odoratus

Also known as the stinkpot, this turtle oozes a strong-smelling fluid from special glands if attacked. It eats insects and molluscs but also feeds on carrion (creatures that are already dead) and small amounts of fish and plants. It rarely strays far from the water.

Loggerhead turtle
Caretta caretta

The loggerhead has a chunky head, which may be as much as 25 cm (10 in) wide, and powerful jaws. It can crush even hard-shelled prey such as clams, but it also eats jellyfish and plants. Its heavy shell is very thick at the back, which may protect it from attack by sharks. Loggerheads usually breed every other year and lay several clutches of about 100 eggs each.

Size: 75–102 cm (30–40 in)
Range: temperate and tropical waters worldwide
Habitat: oceanic, coastal waters

Green turtle
Chelonia mydas

This turtle spends most of its life in water. It may travel huge distances to lay its eggs on the beach where it was born. The female drags herself on to the sand where she digs a pit and lays 100 or more eggs. She covers them with sand and returns to the sea. When the young hatch they must struggle down to the sea.

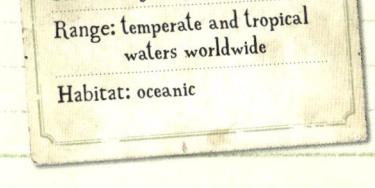

Size: 1–1.25 m (3¼–4 ft)
Range: temperate and tropical waters worldwide
Habitat: oceanic

Size: 15–46 cm (6–18 in)
Range: North America
Habitat: fresh water

Spiny softshell
Apalone spinifera

Softshell turtles have rounded, bendy shells with no hard plates. They can move fast on land and in water but spend most of their lives in water. The spiny softshell feeds on insects, crayfish, and some fish and plants. It breeds in summer when the female lays about 20 eggs.

Alligator snapping turtle
Macrochelys temminckii

This turtle can weigh up to 90 kg (200 lb). It has a lumpy shell that makes it hard to see as it lies on the river bed, watching for prey. It waits with its large mouth open to show a pink fleshy flap on its lower jaw. Passing fish come to try this "bait" and are quickly swallowed or sliced in half by the turtle's strong jaws.

Size: 36–66 cm (14–26 in)
Range: southeastern USA
Habitat: fresh water

LIZARDS AND SNAKES

Lizards and snakes belong to a large group of reptiles, all of which have a body covered with scales. There are at least 5,500 kinds of lizards living over most of the world except the far north and Antarctica. Most live on land or in trees, but the marine iguana spends much of its time in the sea. There are about 3,400 kinds of snakes. Like lizards, they live mainly in warmer parts of the world and there are none in the far north or Antarctica. Most snakes live on land but there are some freshwater and marine species. Tuataras are a separate group.

LIZARDS

Lizards are the largest group of living reptiles. They range from tiny geckos, only 1.6 cm (five-eighths of an inch) long, to the huge Komodo dragon, which measures up to 3 m (10 ft). A typical lizard has four legs, but there are some legless species and others, such as the skinks and snake lizards, that have extremely small limbs. Most have ear openings and movable eyelids. In general, lizards lay eggs in a hole or a safe place under a rock and give them no further attention. But a few types keep their eggs inside their bodies until the young are quite well grown. They hatch almost as soon as the eggs are laid.

Size: 28–42 cm (11–16½ in)
Range: southwestern USA and Mexico
Habitat: desert

Chuckwalla
Sauromalus ater

This plump lizard lies among rocks at night and comes out in the morning to bask in the sun and warm its body. A plant eater, it spends the day feeding on leaves, buds and flowers. If in danger, it hides in a rock crevice and puffs its body up with air so it is almost impossible to move.

Leaf-tailed gecko
Uroplatus fimbriatus

Size: 2.50 cm (8 in)
Range: Madagascar
Habitat: tropical evergreen forest

The spotted pattern on the body of this gecko blends well with tree bark and helps keep it hidden as it lies pressed against a tree trunk. It is usually active at night when it catches insects to eat. After eating, it cleans itself, licking over its whole body with its tongue.

Size: 12.5 cm (5 in)
Range: southwest Africa: Namib Desert
Habitat: desert

Web-footed gecko
Pachydactylus rangei

This rare desert-living gecko has webbed feet that act like snowshoes to help it run over soft sand. It also uses its feet for burrowing into the sand to hide from enemies or the burning sun. It sits in the burrow with its head facing the entrance, waiting to pounce on insects such as termites.

Arabian toad-headed agama
Phrynocephalus arabicus

A burrowing lizard, this agama digs tunnels for shelter or buries itself in the sand. If alarmed, it takes up a defensive position to warn off the enemy – it lifts its tail high, rolls it up, and then unrolls it again.

Size: 13 cm (up to 5 in)
Range: Middle East
Habitat: desert

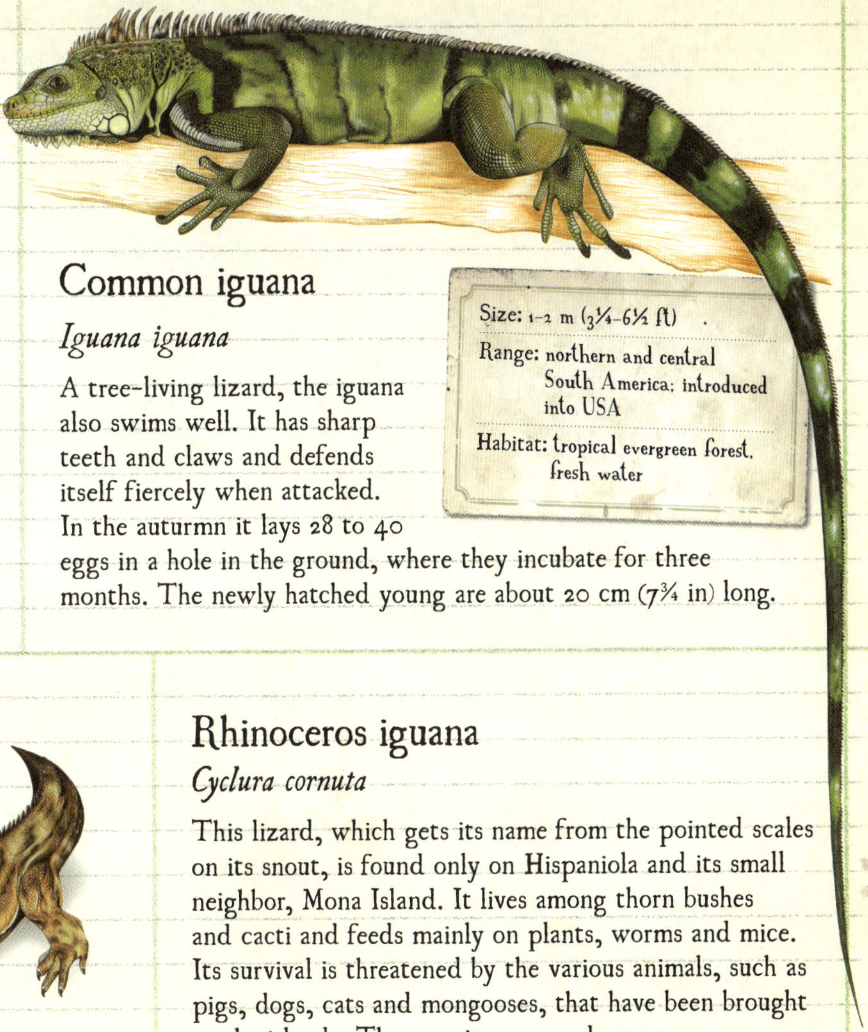

Common iguana
Iguana iguana

A tree-living lizard, the iguana also swims well. It has sharp teeth and claws and defends itself fiercely when attacked. In the autumn it lays 28 to 40 eggs in a hole in the ground, where they incubate for three months. The newly hatched young are about 20 cm (7¾ in) long.

Size: 1–2 m (3¼–6½ ft)
Range: northern and central South America; introduced into USA
Habitat: tropical evergreen forest, fresh water

Rhinoceros iguana
Cyclura cornuta

This lizard, which gets its name from the pointed scales on its snout, is found only on Hispaniola and its small neighbor, Mona Island. It lives among thorn bushes and cacti and feeds mainly on plants, worms and mice. Its survival is threatened by the various animals, such as pigs, dogs, cats and mongooses, that have been brought to the islands. They eat its eggs and young.

Size: 1.2 m (up to 4 ft)
Range: West Indies
Habitat: desert

Tuatara
Sphenodon punctatus

Size: 65 cm (up to 25½ in)
Range: New Zealand
Habitat: deciduous forest, temperate grassland

There are only two kinds of tuatara and although they may look like lizards they actually form their own separate group. The tuatara lives on the ground and shelters in burrows. It eats insects and other small invertebrates as well as small birds and lizards.

Marine iguana
Amblyrhynchus cristatus

Size: 1.2–1.5 m (4–5 ft)
Range: Galápagos Islands
Habitat: coast, coastal waters

The marine iguana is the only lizard that spends most of its life in the sea, swimming and diving as it searches for seaweed, its main food. When in the water, the iguana uses its powerful tail to push itself along. It has to come to the surface to breathe, but when it dives, its heart rate slows so that its body uses less oxygen.

Lizards

Granite night lizard
Xantusia henshawi

This lizard is most active at night or warm winter days. It feeds on spiders, scorpions, insects and eggs. It does not lay eggs itself, but gives birth to one or two live young, which grow inside the mother's body and receive all the nourishment they need from her.

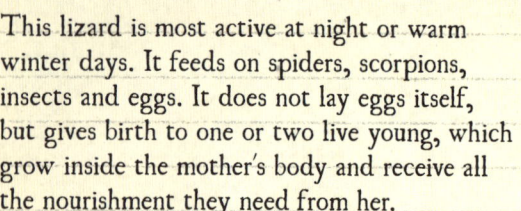

Size: 5–7 cm (2–2¾ in)
Range: southwestern USA to Mexico
Habitat: desert, scrub

Green anole
Anolis carolinensis

The anole's long-toed feet help it climb in trees, where it searches for insects and spiders to eat. The male anole has a flap of pink skin on his throat, which he fans in a display to attract females. After mating, the female lays one egg on the ground among leaves or rocks every two weeks during the breeding season. The eggs hatch in five to seven weeks.

Size: 12–20 cm (4¾–7¾ in)
Range: southern USA
Habitat: inhabited areas, farmland, deciduous forest, temperate and tropical grassland

Gila monster
Heloderma suspectum

Size: 45–60 cm (17¾–24 in)
Range: southwestern USA, Mexico
Habitat: desert

This is one of just a few poisonous lizards. Its venom is made in glands in the lower jaw. When the Gila bites its prey, venom flows into the wound. Birds, mice and other lizards are its main prey. If food is scarce, the Gila can live off fat reserves stored in its tail.

Ground lizard
Ameiva spp.

Size: 6–50 cm (2½–20 in)
Range: Caribbean, Mexico, Central and South America
Habitat: forest, grassland, beach

Ground lizards, or ameivas, are also called jungle runners because they dart around, looking for insects and other bugs. Their colours vary greatly, from dull grey or brown to blues and greens, usually with spots and stripes. Young ground lizards often look different to their parents.

Centralian blue-tongued skink
Tiliqua multifasciata

Skinks have plump bodies, with short necks and legs, and many species have short tails, too. They spend most of their time hiding in burrows, but they emerge to hunt and eat insects and other invertebrates, or even small lizards and rodents.

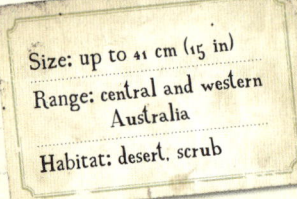

Size: up to 41 cm (15 in)
Range: central and western Australia
Habitat: desert, scrub

Children's Animal Encyclopedia

Size: 3 m (10 ft)
Range: islands of Komodo, Flores, Pintja, and Padar, east of Java
Habitat: tropical grassland, deciduous forest

Size: 35–54 cm (13½–21¼ in)
Range: parts of Europe and Asia, northwestern Africa
Habitat: inhabited areas, farmland, temperate grassland, desert

Slow worm
Anguis fragilis

The slow worm is a smooth long-bodied lizard with no visible legs. It moves like a snake but can shed its tail if seized by an enemy. After spending the night under rocks or logs, it comes out in the morning to hunt for prey such as slugs, worms and insects.

Komodo dragon
Varanus komodoensis

This is the world's heaviest lizard and is strong enough to kill deer, wild boar and pigs. It has a heavy body, a long thick tail, strong legs with talonlike claws – and a venomous bite. Despite its bulk, it is a good climber and moves surprisingly fast. It also swims well and is often found near water.

Size: 66 cm (26 in) including tail
Range: Australia and New Guinea
Habitat: deciduous forest, tropical evergreen forest

Frilled lizard
Chlamydosaurus kingii

This lizard has a collar of skin, which normally lies in folds around its neck. But if disturbed, the lizard's collar stands up like a frill, making it look larger and more frightening than it really is. It eats insects and other creatures that it finds in trees and on the ground.

Size: 40 cm (15¾ in)
Range: South Africa
Habitat: temperate grassland

Transvaal snake lizard
Chamaesaura aenea

With snakelike movements of its long body, this lizard streaks through the grass in search of insects to eat. Its tiny legs are often held off the ground as it moves. The female's two to four eggs develop inside her body. The young break from their shells as they are laid.

Size: 16.5–35 cm (6½–13¾ in)
Range: USA and Mexico
Habitat: temperate grassland, deciduous forest, desert

Great plains skink
Plestidon obsoletus

This lizard is unusual in that the female guards her eggs carefully while they incubate and turns them regularly to make sure they warm evenly. She also helps the young to wriggle free of their shells, and cares for them for about ten days.

127

CHAMELEONS

The amazing chameleon has a tongue like a mobile flypaper, which it shoots out to catch prey such as insects. There are more than 150 species of these tree-living lizards. Most live in Africa and Madagascar, but there are few kinds of chameleon in Asia and one in Europe. A typical chameleon has a flattened body, large eyes and a strong tail that can be used to grip branches tightly. Most chameleons are between 15 and 30 cm (6 and 11¾ in) long, but one Madagascan species grows to 80 cm (31½ in). The colour of its skin helps it to stay hidden from predators and prey – but that colour can suddenly change, too.

CHANGING COLOUR

A chameleon can lighten or darken its skin to help lower or raise its body temperature, or to signal to other members of its species. In the breeding season, when two males compete for territory or for females, the dominant male displays bright coloration while the loser becomes a darker shade of green and hides away.

CATCHING PREY

Once the chameleon is near enough to its prey, it judges its position with its superb eyesight and takes aim. Shooting out its tongue, which may be as long as its body, the chameleon traps the insect on the sticky pad at the tongue's tip and returns it to its mouth. This all happens in less than one-twentieth of a second.

FLAP-NECKED CHAMELEON

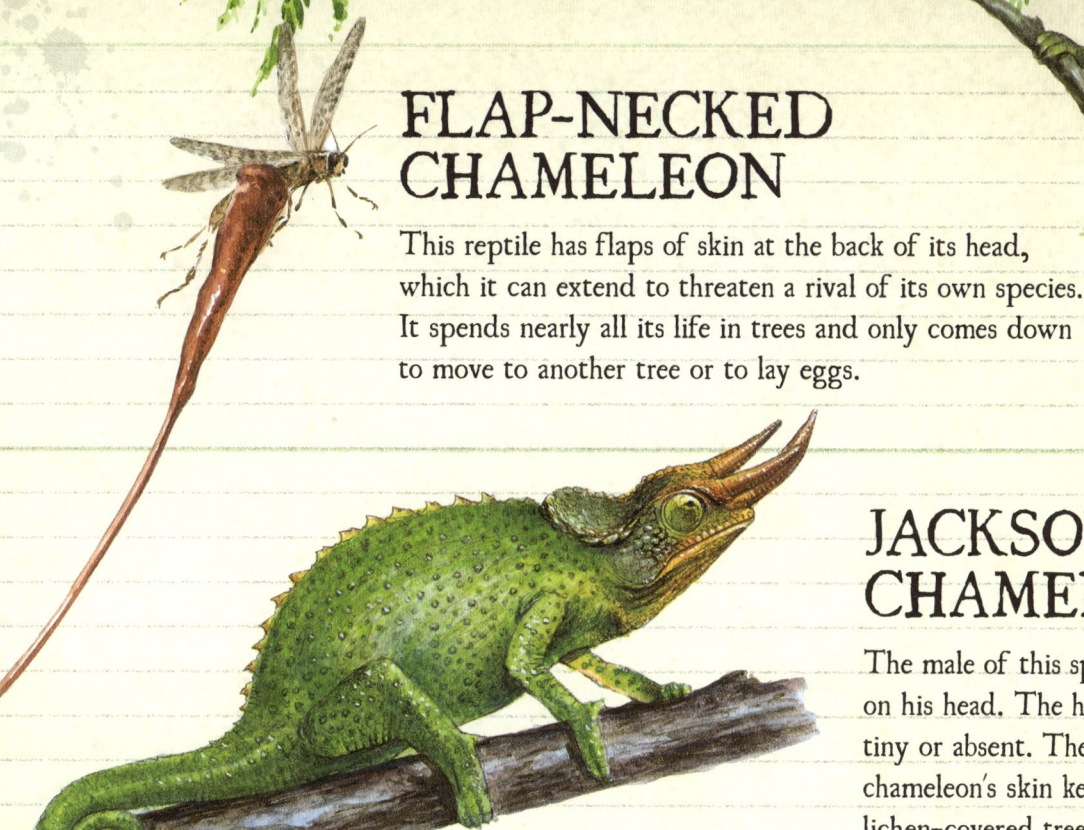

This reptile has flaps of skin at the back of its head, which it can extend to threaten a rival of its own species. It spends nearly all its life in trees and only comes down to move to another tree or to lay eggs.

JACKSON'S CHAMELEON

The male of this species has three large horns on his head. The horns on females are either tiny or absent. The dull green colour of this chameleon's skin keeps it camouflaged on lichen-covered tree bark.

MELLER'S CHAMELEON

The bold markings on this chameleon make it extremely hard to see as it sits motionless on a branch, watching for prey. Meller's chameleon grows up to 58 cm (22¾ inches) long.

Unlike most chameleons, the tiny dwarf chameleon spends its life on the ground and cannot grip with its tail. It looks like the dead leaves it hides among on the forest floor. It even has lines on its body that resemble the veins of a leaf.

129

SNAKES

Snakes have long bodies and no limbs. Even though they have no legs, snakes can still move fast. They wriggle along the ground with wave-like movements of the body, and pointed scales on the underside of the belly help them grip. Snakes range in size from 10 cm (4 in) to about 9 m (30 ft). They all have a long, forked tongue, but they do not have ear openings or movable eyelids. All snakes hunt other animals for food. Some, such as boas, wrap victims in their strong body coils and squeeze them to death. Others, such as vipers, have a venomous bite.

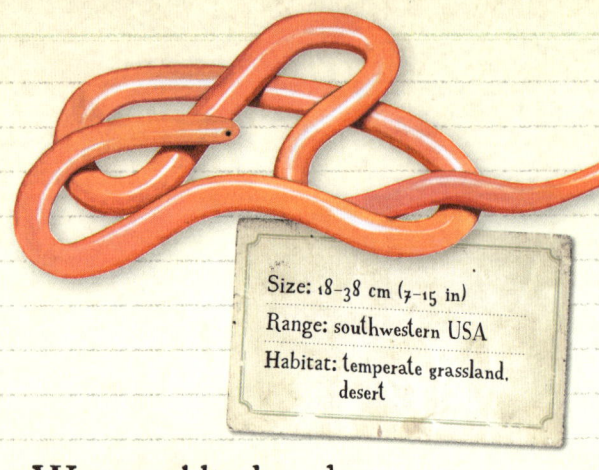

Size: 18–38 cm (7–15 in)
Range: southwestern USA
Habitat: temperate grassland, desert

Western blind snake
Rena humilis

A smooth round-bodied reptile, the western blind snake has a blunt head and tail. It lives where there is sandy or gravelly soil and spends much of its time below ground. It eats ants and termites, which it finds by smell, and its body is so slender that it can slide into their nests.

Size: 5–6 m (17–20 ft)
Range: India, Southeast Asia, Indonesia
Habitat: tropical evergreen forest, fresh water

Indian python
Python molurus

One of the largest snakes in the world, the Indian python basks in the sun by day or rests in a cave or other shelter. At night, it prowls around, searching for prey such as birds, small deer and boar, or waits near a water hole where animals are sure to come. It stalks close to its prey, then grasps it in its body coils and crushes it to death.

Anaconda
Eunectes murinus

One of the longest of all snakes, the anaconda spends much of its life in slow-moving water, watching for prey. When an animal comes to the water's edge to drink, the anaconda seizes the victim in its coils. Female anacondas produce up to 40 live young, each 66 cm (20 in) long.

Boa constrictor
Python molurus

The boa constrictor kills prey, such as birds and mammals, by wrapping the victim in the strong coils of its body until it is suffocated or crushed to death. The boa spends most of its life on the ground, but it does climb trees and can grip branches with its tail.

Size: up to 5.5 m (18 ft)
Range: South America
Habitat: tropical evergreen forest, desert, inhabited areas, farmland, fresh water

Size: 9 m (30 ft)
Range: South America
Habitat: fresh water

Gopher snake
Pituophis catenifer

This large snake is a good climber and burrower. It feeds mostly on mice, small birds and lizards, all of which it kills with its powerful body coils – the victim is squeezed until it suffocates. Gopher snakes mate in spring and the female lays up to 24 eggs in a burrow or under a log. The young hatch in 9 to 11 weeks.

Size: 1.2–2.5 m (4–8¼ ft)
Range: southwestern Canada, USA, Mexico
Habitat: deciduous forest, temperate grassland, desert

Size: up to 2 m (6½ ft)
Range: Africa: central to southern Africa
Habitat: tropical grassland

Boomslang
Dispholidus typus

The active tree-living boomslang is one of the most venomous snakes in Africa. Its venom flows from special glands on to large grooved teeth in the mouth and then enters the victim's body as the snake chews. The snake normally uses its venomous bite on prey such as lizards, frogs and birds but it can even kill humans. It rarely attacks unless disturbed.

Grass snake
Natrix natrix

The grass snake is a strong swimmer. It hunts fish and frogs in woodland rivers as well as mice on land. It is one of the commonest snakes in Europe. In the breeding season, the male courts the female before mating by rubbing his chin over her body. She lays 30 to 40 eggs in a warm spot.

Size: up to 1.2 m (4 ft); occasionally up to 2 m (6½ ft)
Range: from Europe to Mongolia, and northwestern Africa
Habitat: temperate grassland, fresh water

Size: 30–50 cm (11¾–19¾ in)
Range: Indonesia, Malaysia, Singapore
Habitat: fresh water

Spotted water snake
Enhydris punctata

Able to move swiftly both in water and on land, this snake preys on creatures such as fish and frogs. Its small eyes face upward and its nostrils are also on the upper surface of the head. Pads of skin close off the nostrils completely when the snake dives underwater. It is mildly venomous.

Snakes

Bluebanded sea snake
Hydrophis cyanocinctus

This snake spends all its life in the sea. Its body is slightly flattened and its paddle-shaped tail helps it push itself through the water. It breathes air but can stay under water for up to two hours. Like all sea snakes, it eats fish and has a venomous bite.

Size: 2 m (6½ ft)
Range: Indian and Pacific oceans
Habitat: coastal waters

Size: up to 1.2 m (4 ft)
Range: from Burma to Malaysia and the Philippines
Habitat: tropical evergreen forest

Eastern green mamba
Dendroaspis angusticeps

The slender, fast-moving mamba spends much of its life in trees, where it hunts birds and lizards. It has a strong venom. In the breeding season males take part in ritual fights for females. They wrap their bodies around one another and threaten each other with their heads.

Paradise tree snake
Chrysopelea paradisi

This snake is an excellent climber and spends much of its life in trees. Also known as the flying snake, it can launch itself into the air and glide 20 m (65 ft) or more from tree to tree in the rain forest. It does not have much control over its "flight" and cannot glide upward or steer.

Size: 2 m (6½ ft)
Range: eastern and southern Africa
Habitat: tropical evergreen forest

Size: 43–82 cm (17–32¼ in)
Range: southwestern USA and Mexico
Habitat: desert, high ground

Sidewinder
Crotalus cerastes

This venomous snake hides under a bush or in a burrow during the day and comes out at night to hunt for mice, rats and lizards. A desert dweller, the sidewinder has a special way of moving over sand. It presses its tail down, throws the rest of its body to one side, then moves its tail up and repeats the action, moving sideways over the sand.

Children's Animal Encyclopedia

Size: 1–2.4 m (3¼–7¾ ft)
Range: southeastern USA
Habitat: farmland, deciduous forest, coast

Eastern diamondback rattlesnake
Crotalus adamanteus

This is the most dangerous snake in North America, with venom that attacks its victims' blood cells. Like all rattlesnakes, it makes a rattling sound with a series of hard hollow rings of skin at the end of the tail. Each ring was once the tip of the tail, and a new one is left behind each time the snake sheds its skin.

Indian cobra
Naja naja

This large highly venomous cobra feeds on mice, lizards and frogs. It can attack or defend itself from a distance by "spitting" out jets of venom. This can cause severe pain if it reaches the eyes of mammals. To threaten enemies the cobra raises the front of its body and spreads the ribs and loose skin at its neck to form a hood shape. Eye-like markings on the hood confuse the enemy further.

Size: 1.2–2 m (4–6½ ft)
Range: Africa, south of the Sahara
Habitat: tropical evergreen forest

Gaboon viper
Bitis gaponica

The patterns on the Gaboon viper's body help keep it hidden as it lies among dead leaves on the forest floor. It hunts at night, preying on mice, frogs and birds. Its fangs are up to 5 cm (2 in) long, the longest of any viper, and it has powerful venom. The female viper gives birth to litters of up to 30 live young.

Size: up to 75 cm (30 in)
Range: India, Pakistan Sri Lanka and Middle East
Habitat: desert

Saw-scaled viper
Echis carinatus

This snake is one of about 11 species of saw-scaled, or carpet, snakes, which are mostly small and slender. Carpet snakes are found in Asia and Africa. They are deadly reptiles because they are common in places where people live, and their venom is strong and acts quickly.

Size: 1.8–2.2 m (6–7¼ ft)
Range: India, Pakistan, Nepal, Bhutan, Bangladesh, Sri Lanka
Habitat: inhabited areas, farmland, tropical evergreen forest

133

AMPHIBIANS

Amphibians were the first vertebrate animals to live on land. They evolved from fish about 370 million years ago, and today's 6,500 species still spend part of their lives in water. Many also mate and lay their eggs in water. The eggs hatch into water-living larvae that have fins and gills. As they grow, they lose their gills and develop legs and lungs, so that they are able to live on land. Some amphibians such as mudpuppies spend their whole lives in water and keep their feathery gills.

Children's Animal Encyclopedia

WHAT IS AN AMPHIBIAN?

Amphibians are cold-blooded vertebrates. They cannot control their body temperature and must gain heat by basking in the sun. Though most have lungs, they gain most of the oxygen they need through their skin. The skin is not scaly and must be kept moist.

TYPES OF AMPHIBIAN

Caecilians are the least well known of all the amphibians. These wormlike creatures have long, rounded bodies and no legs. They live in burrows and are rarely seen above ground. A typical salamander has a long body and tail and four legs. Although similar to lizards in shape, it does not have scaly skin, claws or ear openings on the outside of the body. Frogs and toads have much shorter bodies than salamanders, and no tails. The well-developed back legs are used for jumping on land and swimming in water.

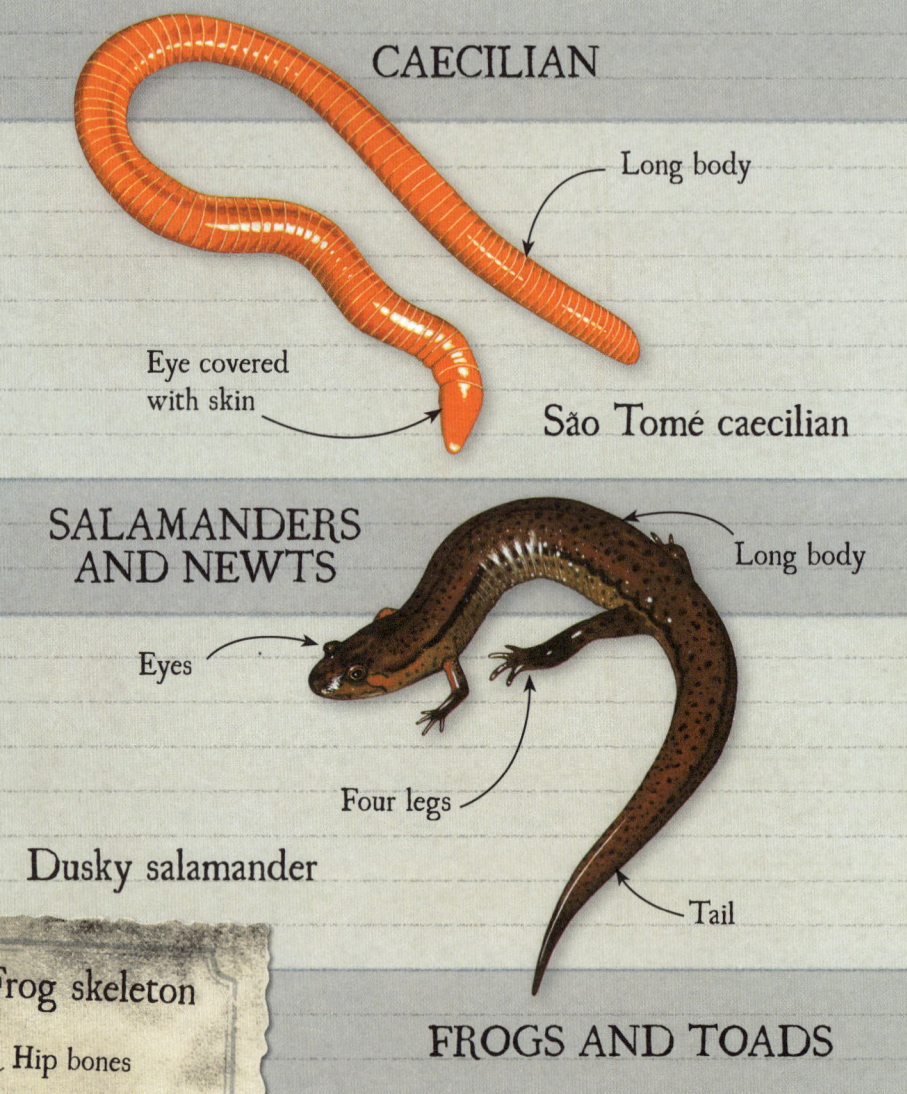

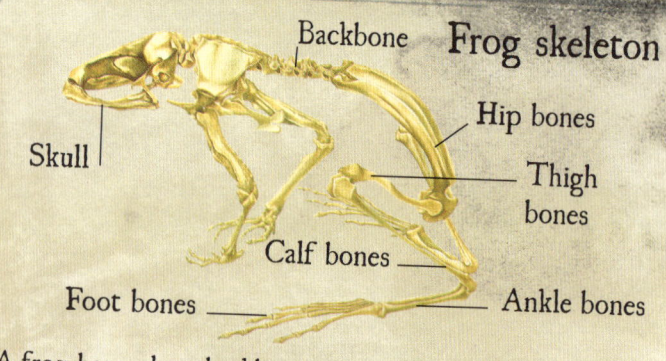

CAECILIAN

- Long body
- Eye covered with skin

São Tomé caecilian

SALAMANDERS AND NEWTS

- Long body
- Eyes
- Four legs
- Tail

Dusky salamander

FROGS AND TOADS

Common frog
- Short body
- Large eyes
- Smaller front legs
- Strong back legs
- Long toes

Frog skeleton

- Backbone
- Hip bones
- Thigh bones
- Skull
- Calf bones
- Foot bones
- Ankle bones

A frog has a short backbone and a rigid hip that helps keep the back straight for jumping. The long muscular rear legs provide power for the jump. The frog has no ribs.

LEAPING FROG

On land, the frog crouches with its long legs folded. The foot, calf and thigh are all about the same length. As the frog leaps, its legs unfold to push it into the air. When stretched out, the frog's back legs are usually longer than its body.

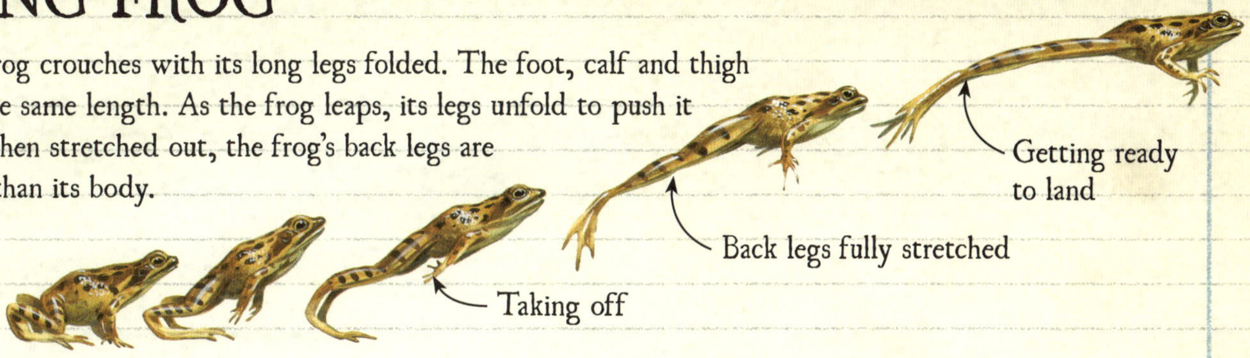

Getting ready to land

Back legs fully stretched

Taking off

BEWARE OF BRIGHT COLOURS

Many amphibians have extremely brightly coloured and patterned skins. This is usually a warning to potential predators that the amphibian's skin contains nasty-tasting secretions. These can cause severe irritation in mammals and some even contain poisons that can kill. The South American false-eyed frog has large eye-like markings on its rear. If attacked, it displays these to fool its enemy into thinking it is larger than it really is.

Arrow-poison frog

Spotted salamander

South American false-eyed frog

Mature frog

Ten weeks old

Five weeks old

Eggs

Lungs develop

Back legs grow

Gills

Two days old

Twelve days old

FROM EGG TO ADULT

This is the life cycle of a typical frog. The eggs, which have a protective jelly-like coating, are laid in water. They hatch into tadpoles, which have a tail and feathery gills. As each tadpole grows, it develops legs and lungs, and the gills disappear. Finally, when it has grown into a miniature version of the adult, the tadpole loses its tail. Not all frogs follow this same cycle — some keep their developing eggs inside their body, and give birth to live young.

PREHISTORIC AMPHIBIANS

Amphibians such as *Ichthyostega* were the first known land animals. *Ichthyostega* was a strongly built creature with four legs. Like its fish ancestors, it had a tail fin and bony scales on its belly and tail.

Ichthyostega

Children's Animal Encyclopedia

NEWTS AND SALAMANDERS

There are about 600 species of newts and salamanders divided into 9 groups, or families. Sirens, congo eels, olms and mudpuppies are all long-bodied water-living amphibians with small, almost useless legs. Many of these creatures keep their feathery gills throughout their adult lives, although most amphibians only have gills when they are larvae.

The lungless salamanders are the largest group of living salamanders. With no lungs, they obtain all their oxygen through their moist skin. There are several other groups of salamanders, most of which have sturdy bodies and well-developed legs. The newt family includes water- and land-living newts, but most stay near water.

Size: 45–115 cm (18–45 in)
Range: eastern USA
Habitat: fresh water

Two-toed congo eel
Amphiuma means

The congo eel has a long body and tiny legs that are almost useless for walking. It usually comes out at night to hunt in water for creatures such as crayfish and frogs. During the day, it may hide in a burrow that it digs in the mud or takes over from another creature. Congo eels mate in water and the female lays about 200 eggs in a beadlike string. She curls around the eggs and protects them until they hatch.

California slender salamander
Batrachoseps attenuatus

True to its name, this salamander has a long, slim body and tail. Its legs and feet are tiny, with four toes on each foot. It generally lives on land and moves by wriggling its body rather than by using its legs. During the day it hides among damp plants, coming out at night to hunt for creatures such as worms and spiders.

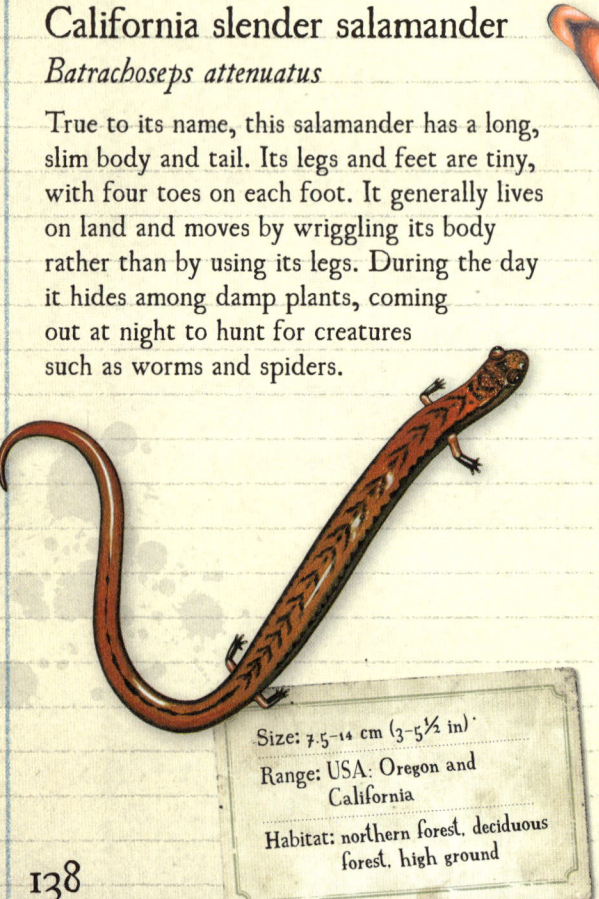

Size: 7.5–14 cm (3–5½ in)
Range: USA: Oregon and California
Habitat: northern forest, deciduous forest, high ground

Size: 20–30 cm (8–12 in)
Range: Balkan Peninsula and Italy
Habitat: fresh water

Olm
Proteus anguinus

This strange salamander has a long body and red feathery gills. Its tail is flattened and it has small, weak legs. It is almost blind and lives in total darkness in underground streams and lakes. There it rummages in the mud to find food such as worms and small crustaceans. Animal collectors have taken so many of these fascinating creatures from the wild that new areas where they have been found are kept secret.

Mudpuppy
Necturus maculosus

The mudpuppy spends all its life in water, so even adults have large feathery gills. It hunts worms, crayfish and insects at night. In the breeding season the female lays up to 190 eggs, each of which is stuck separately to a log or rock.

Size: 20–43 cm (7¾–17 in)
Range: southern Canada and USA
Habitat: fresh water

Greater siren
Siren lacertina

Size: 50–97.5 cm (19¾–39½ in)
Range: USA
Habitat: fresh water

The siren has a long, eel-like body and tiny front legs with four toes on each foot. It has no back legs and swims by fishlike movements of its body. During the day, it hides under rocks or burrows into the muddy riverbed. At night, it catches snails, insect larvae and fish.

Children's Animal Encyclopedia

Size: 9.5–18 cm (3¾–7 in)
Range: eastern USA
Habitat: temperate grassland, fresh water

Red salamander
Pseudotriton ruber

The brilliantly coloured red salamander has a stout body and a short tail and legs. It spends much of its time on land but usually stays near water. Earthworms, insects and smaller salamanders are its main foods. After courting and mating, the female salamander lays between 50 and 100 eggs. The larvae hatch about two months later but do not become adults until they are about two years old.

Size: 9–13.5 cm (3½–5¼ in)
Range: USA: San Marcos, Texas
Habitat: fresh water

Texas blind salamander
Eurycea rathbuni

This salamander lives in water in underground caves. It has a pale body, tiny eyes and red feathery gills that it keeps throughout life. These salamanders eat cave-dwelling invertebrates that feed on the droppings left by the bats that roost in the caves.

Spotted salamander
Ambystoma maculatum

Spotted salamanders spend most of their time well out of sight, burrowing through damp soil, but every spring they gather in crowds around pools to mate and lay eggs in the water. Sadly, this spectacle no longer occurs in many areas because acid rain has polluted breeding pools.

Size: 15–24 cm (6–9½ in)
Range: southeastern Canada, eastern USA
Habitat: deciduous forest, fresh water

139

Newts and salamanders

Tiger salamander
Ambystoma tigrinum

Size: 15–40 cm (6–15¾ in)
Range: North America, Mexico
Habitat: temperate grassland, high ground, deciduous forest, fresh water

The world's largest land-living salamander, the tiger salamander, has a stout body, broad head and small eyes. It lives near water and often hides among leaves or in an abandoned burrow. It feeds on earthworms, insects, mice and even other small amphibians.

Pacific giant salamander
Dicamptodon ensatus

Size: 30 cm (12 in)
Range: North America: west coast
Habitat: fresh water

Most salamanders are silent but this species can make a low-pitched cry. Adults live on land where they hide under logs and rocks. They are usually active at night when they feed on snails, slugs, insects and other small creatures. In spring the female lays about 100 eggs on a branch in water.

Fire salamander
Salamandra salamandra

Bright markings warn that this salamander's body is covered with an unpleasant-tasting slime. This puts off most hunters that might otherwise try to catch it. Although it spends most of its life on land, it usually stays near water and prefers moist areas.
Fire salamanders mate on land. The eggs then develop inside the female's body and about 10 months later she gives birth to up to 50 live young in water.

Size: 15–30 cm (6–12 in)
Range: central and southern Europe; north Africa; Middle East
Habitat: fresh water, deciduous forest

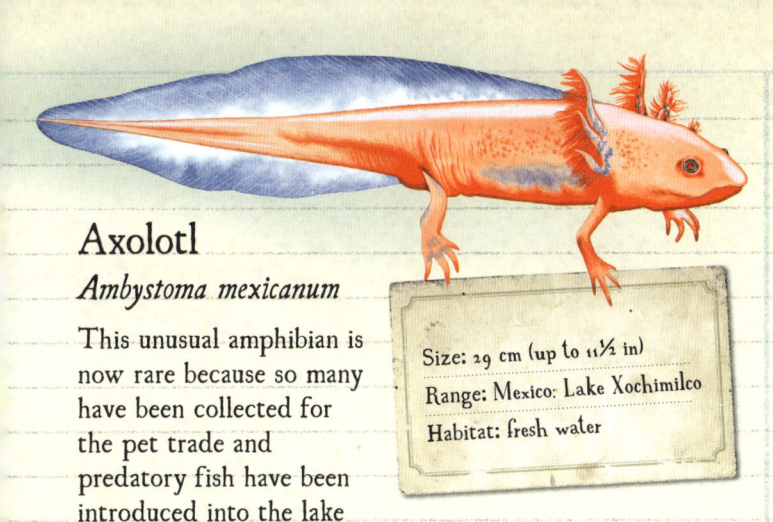

Children's Animal Encyclopedia

Axolotl
Ambystoma mexicanum

Size: 29 cm (up to 11½ in)
Range: Mexico: Lake Xochimilco
Habitat: fresh water

This unusual amphibian is now rare because so many have been collected for the pet trade and predatory fish have been introduced into the lake where it lives. Many axolotls remain as larvae with feathery gills all their lives.

Great crested newt
Triturus cristatus

Size: 10–14 cm (4–5½ in)
Range: parts of Europe
Habitat: deciduous forest, fresh water

A large, rough-skinned newt, the male develops a jagged crest on his back in the breeding season. Females are often larger than males, but they do not develop crests. Great crested newts feed on small invertebrates, small fish and other amphibians and their eggs.

South American caecilian
Siphonops annulatus

Size: 35 cm (13¾ in)
Range: South America, east of the Andes
Habitat: tropical forest, shrub, grassland, farmland

Caecilians are not salamanders but belong to a separate group of blind burrowing amphibians. This caecilian has a short thick body and spends most of its life underground, where it feeds on earthworms.

Eastern newt
Notophthalmus viridescens

Size: 6.5–14 cm (2½–5½ in)
Range: eastern North America
Habitat: fresh water, forest

This newt breeds in early spring. The female lays up to 400 eggs on water plants and larvae hatch two months later. After a few months of feeding and growing, the larvae turn into sub-adults called red efts, shown here. They leave the water and spend up to three years on land, feeding on insects.

Hellbender
Cryptobranchus alleganiensis

Size: 30.5–74 cm (12–29¼ in)
Range: eastern USA
Habitat: fresh water

Despite its fierce name, this large salamander is a harmless creature that hides under rocks in the water during the day. At night it comes out to hunt crayfish, snails, and worms, which it finds by smell and touch rather than sight. In autumn, the female lays up to 450 eggs in a hollow made by the male on the stream bed.

141

FROGS AND TOADS

There are more than 5,850 species of frogs and toads. All are very similar in appearance whatever their lifestyle. Typically, an adult frog or toad has long back legs, webbed toes and no tail. The skin is smooth or warty but always moist. Like all amphibians, frogs and toads are at home both on land and in fresh water and can swim, hop and even climb trees. Most feed on small creatures such as slugs, snails and insects, which they catch with their long sticky tongues.

Frogs and toads usually breed in water, laying eggs that hatch into tailed, swimming young known as tadpoles. The tadpoles live in water, breathing through feathery gills at the sides of the head and eating plants. As the tadpoles grow they lose their gills and tail and grow legs. Some weeks after hatching, they develop into tiny frogs.

Size: up to 3 cm (1¼ in)
Range: northern South America
Habitat: tropical evergreen forest

Glass frog
Sachatamia albomaculata

This delicate little yellow-flecked glass frog lives in small trees and bushes, usually near running water. It has sticky discs on its toes that help it grip when climbing. The female lays her eggs in clusters on the underside of leaves overhanging water. When the tadpoles hatch they drop into the water below, where they complete their development.

Size: up to 6 cm (2½ in)
Range: northeastern South Africa
Habitat: forest, grassland, fresh water

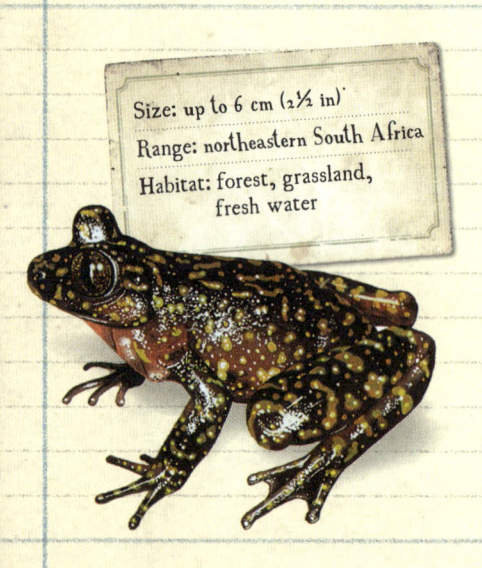

Natal ghost frog
Hadromophryne natalensis

This frog lives in fast-flowing mountain streams. The female lays her eggs in a pool or on wet gravel. Once hatched, the tadpoles move into the streams where they hold on to stones with their sucker-like mouths to stop themselves being swept away.

African clawed toad
Xenopus laevis

Size: 6.5–12.5 cm (2½–5 in)
Range: southern Africa
Habitat: fresh water

This toad moves as fast in the water as any fish and is even able to swim backwards. It uses the claws on its front feet to dig in the mud around pools and streams for food and eats any creatures it can find, even its own tadpoles. The toads mate in water, the male making a soft buzzing sound underwater to attract the female. The eggs are attached to water plants and hatch after seven days.

Western spadefoot
Spea hammondii

An expert burrower, the western spadefoot toad has a hard spike on each back foot that helps it dig. It spends the day in its burrow and comes out at night to feed. The spadefoot waits for rain to fall before mating. Its eggs are laid in a rain-pool, hatching just three to four days later.

Size: 3.5–6.5 cm (1¼–2½ in)
Range: western USA
Habitat: temperate grassland, deciduous forest

Midwife toad
Alytes obstetricans

The midwife toad hides by day under logs or in cracks in walls. At night it feeds on insects and other small creatures. It has unusual breeding habits. After the female has laid her eggs, the male takes them and carries them on his back while they develop. When they are ready to hatch, he places them in shallow water.

Size: up to 5 cm (2 in)
Range: western Europe
Habitat: inhabited areas, farmland, high ground, deciduous forest

Size: 5 cm (2 in)
Range: Siberia, northeastern China, Korea
Habitat: farmland, high ground, fresh water

Oriental fire-bellied toad
Bombina orientalis

The brilliantly coloured rough skin of this toad gives off a milky substance that irritates the mouth and eyes of any attacker. The female fire-bellied toad lays her eggs on the underside of stones in water. The eggs are laid in small clumps of two to eight and are left to hatch by themselves.

Size: 10–24 cm (4–9½ in)
Range: South and Central America, introduced elsewhere
Habitat: inhabited areas, forest, farmland, fresh water

Cane toad
Rhinella marina

One of the largest toads in the world, the cane toad has been introduced to many areas outside its natural range. This is because it feeds on insects that destroy crops, such as sugar, and so helps to control them. In Australia, the cane toad has spread rapidly since being introduced and is now a pest, poisoning local species. Glands at the sides of its body make a poisonous liquid that causes irritation and even death in reptiles and mammals that try to eat it. Eggs are laid in water, hatch into tadpoles up to a week later and grow rapidly.

Frogs and toads

Pumpkin toadlet
Brachycephalus ephippium

This tiny frog often lives among dead leaves on the forest floor but may also hide in cracks in trees or rocks in dry weather. It has a bony shield on its back and may use this to block off the entrance of its hiding place to keep the atmosphere inside moist.

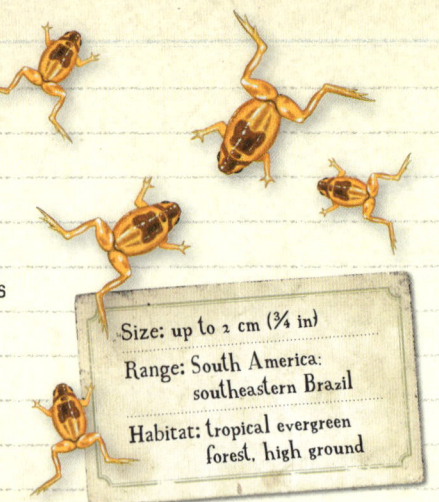

Size: up to 2 cm (¾ in)
Range: South America: southeastern Brazil
Habitat: tropical evergreen forest, high ground

Size: 3 cm (1¼ in)
Range: snowy mountains of southeastern Australia
Habitat: high ground, fresh water

Corroboree frog
Pseudophryne corroboree

This critically endangered frog lives on land near water and shelters under logs or in a burrow that it digs itself. In summer, pairs dig a nesting burrow in a bog. The female lays up to 38 large eggs and one parent usually guards the eggs while they develop. The tadpoles normally stay in the eggs until there is enough rain to wash them into a creek, where they hatch at once.

Size: up to 4 cm (1½ in)
Range: South America
Habitat: tropical evergreen forest, high ground

Marsupial frog
Gastrotheca marsupiata

The marsupial frog has an unusual way of caring for its eggs. As the female lays her eggs, the male helps her to pack them into a skin pouch on her back. A few weeks later, she finds some shallow water to release her brood. She uses the long toe on her back foot to open the pouch and free the tadpoles.

Amazon horned frog
Ceratophrys cornuta

Size: 15 cm (6 in)
Range: northern and central South America
Habitat: forest, grassland, marsh

This horned frog is almost as broad as it is long and has a wide head and a large mouth. It has small eyes, with a lump on each upper eyelid. Even though it spends much of its life half-buried in the ground, its toes are partly webbed. It feeds on snails, small frogs and mice, and probably also eats tadpoles of its own species.

Darwin's frog
Rhinoderma darwinii

This frog has unusual breeding habits. The female lays 20 to 45 eggs on land. Several males stand guard for up to 20 days until the young begin to move around inside the eggs. Each male then gathers up to 19 eggs in his mouth and lets them slide into the large sac under his chin. The tadpoles continue to develop inside the sac. When they have grown into tiny frogs the males let them go in water.

Size: 3 cm (1¼ in)
Range: southern Chile and southern Argentina
Habitat: temperate forest, rainforest

Natterjack toad
Epidalea calamita

The male natterjack has the loudest call of any European toad. His croak carries 2 km (1¼ miles) or more. Natterjacks usually live on land but are often found near the sea and may even breed in salty water. Natterjacks mate at night and the female lays strings of up to 4,000 eggs in shallow water. The eggs hatch into tadpoles in about ten days.

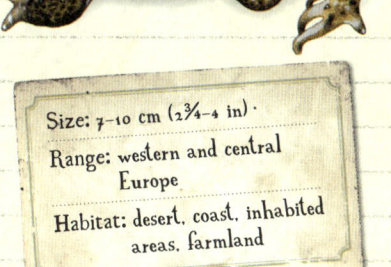

Size: 7–10 cm (2¾–4 in)
Range: western and central Europe
Habitat: desert, coast, inhabited areas, farmland

Arum lily frog
Hyperolius horstockii

Size: up to 4 cm (1½ in)
Range: South Africa
Habitat: fresh water

A good climber, this frog has large, sticky discs on each toe that help it grip. The undersides of its legs are orange but the rest of the body changes colour according to conditions. In bright sun it is light cream and in shade it turns dark brown. Courting males often climb up on to arum lilies to call to females. They mate in water and eggs are laid on plants.

Children's Animal Encyclopedia

Common tree frog
Hyla arborea

Size: up to 5 cm (2 in)
Range: most of Europe
Habitat: deciduous forest, conifer forest, fresh water

This smooth-skinned tree frog spends most of its life in trees. It can change colour with amazing speed, turning from bright green in sunlight to dark grey in shade. The frogs breed in early summer and the female lays up to 2,000 eggs in water.

Spring peeper
Pseudacris crucifer

Size: 2–3 cm (¾–1¼ in)
Range: southeastern Canada, USA
Habitat: deciduous forest, fresh water

This agile frog can climb trees and jump more than 17 times its own body length. It feeds mainly on small spiders and insects, including flying insects, which it leaps into the air to catch. In the breeding season, males sit in trees courting females with their high-pitched whistle calls.

145

Frogs and toads

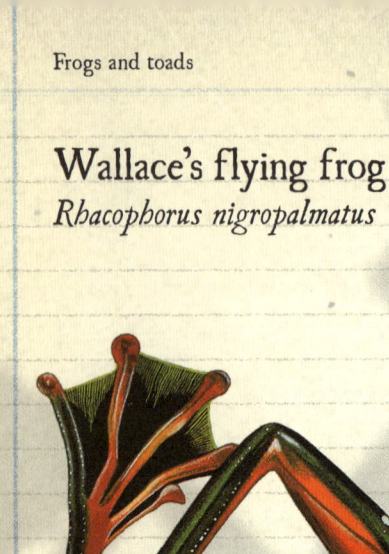

Wallace's flying frog
Rhacophorus nigropalmatus

Size: 10 cm (4 in)
Range: Malaysia, Indonesia, Thailand
Habitat: tropical evergreen forest

This frog does not fly but glides from tree to tree in the forest. The large webbed feet and flaps of skin on its legs act like a parachute to help it float as far as 12 m (40 ft) through the air. It can even steer by changing the position of one or more of its feet. Little is known about this frog's breeding habits, but it is thought to lay its eggs in a mass of foam, which protects them while they incubate.

South African rain frog
Breviceps adspersus

This plump frog has small legs and a sprinkling of warty lumps on its back. It spends much of its life in underground burrows, which it digs with its strong back feet. It comes above ground only during wet weather to hunt insects and other small creatures.

Size: 3 cm (1¼ in)
Range: southern Africa
Habitat: tropical grassland, deciduous forest, gardens

Termite frog
Phrynomerus bifasciatus

Size: 5 cm (2 in)
Range: Africa, south of the Sahara
Habitat: tropical grassland

As its name suggests, termites and ants are the main food of this frog and it digs in burrows or climbs trees to find the insects. Its bright markings warn that its skin contains a nasty-tasting substance that irritates the mouths or skin of predators. Termite frogs breed in shallow pools. The jelly-coated eggs attach to plants or lie at the bottom of the water until they hatch.

Eastern narrow-mouthed toad
Gastrophryne carolinensis

Size: 2–4 cm (¾–1½ in)
Range: southeastern USA
Habitat: woodland, grassland, swamp

An excellent burrower, this small frog can disappear into the earth in a moment. It rests in a burrow during the day and comes out at night to hunt for ants and other insects. It breeds in summer when there is heavy rain.

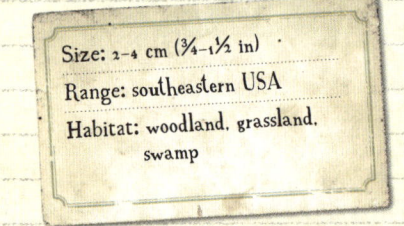

Marsh frog
Pelophylax ridibundus

This noisy frog spends most of its life in water but comes out onto banks or to float on lily pads. It catches small invertebrates and also eats small birds and mammals. Males call night and day, particularly in the breeding season. The female lays thousands of eggs in several large clusters.

Size: up to 15 cm (6 in)
Range: Europe, western Asia
Habitat: fresh water

Common frog
Rana temporaria

Size: up to 10 cm (4 in)
Range: Europe, east to Asia
Habitat: inhabited areas, farmland, deciduous forest, seasonal forest, fresh water

Much of this frog's life is spent on land, feeding on insects, spiders and other small creatures. It breeds in spring, when males attract females with their deep croaking calls. They mate in water and the females lay clusters of 3,000 to 4,000 eggs.

Size: up to 3.5 cm (1½ in)
Range: Africa, south of Chad
Habitat: temperate grassland, farmland

Mottled burrowing frog
Hemisus marmoratus

This frog has a small pointed head with a hard snout used for burrowing. It digs head first, pushing into the soil with its snout and clawing its way forward with its strong legs. The female lays her large eggs in a burrow. When the young hatch, she digs a tunnel for the tadpoles to swim to the nearest water.

Northern leopard frog
Rana pipiens

This frog adapts to any watery home and eats almost any small creatures it can find. If disturbed on land, it leaps away to water in a series of zig-zagging jumps. In the breeding season, males attract females with low, grunting calls. Each female lays up to 7,600 eggs, which lie at the bottom of the water until they hatch about four weeks later.

Size: 5–11 cm (2–4 in)
Range: most of northern North America
Habitat: temperate grassland, high ground, fresh water

Size: 9–20 cm (3½–8 in)
Range: Canada, USA, Mexico; introduced into South America, Europe, eastern Asia
Habitat: fresh water

Bullfrog
Rana catesbeiana

The largest North American frog, the bullfrog lives in water but also spends time on land at the water's edge. It hunts at night, catching insects, fish, smaller frogs and even birds and snakes. It is a good jumper and can leap nine times its own length. In the breeding season the female lays up to 20,000 eggs in water.

Children's Animal Encyclopedia

147

ARROW-POISON FROGS

Arrow-poison frogs live in the rainforests of Central and South America. Also known as poison-dart frogs, they are among the most colourful of all amphibians. For some, their jewel-like appearance is a warning to predators to keep their distance because the skin contains extremely strong poisons. The frogs cannot inject their poison into enemies. It is produced in special glands and simply released into the skin, making a dangerous meal for a predator. Some arrow-poison frogs are not poisonous at all, but mimic the bright colours to scare off predators.

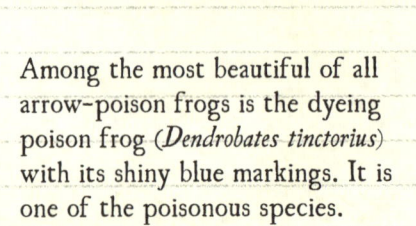

Among the most beautiful of all arrow-poison frogs is the dyeing poison frog (*Dendrobates tinctorius*) with its shiny blue markings. It is one of the poisonous species.

STRAWBERRY POISON-ARROW FROG

The poison in the skin of the strawberry poison-arrow frog (*Oophaga pumilio*) may come partly from its food, such as small beetles and millipedes. Although deadly to its enemies, the frog's poison may have a value. Doctors are investigating its use as a medicine for heart-attack patients.

CARING FOR YOUNG

The female flaming arrow-poison frog (*Oophaga pumilio*) looks after her tadpoles while they develop into frogs. She carries them up into a tree and places them in groups of about four in tiny pools of water contained in plants. She checks on them every few days and even gives them some unfertilized eggs to eat. The young are not poisonous at this stage, so they are very easy for other creatures to catch and eat.

1. The eggs are laid on a leaf.

2. Once hatched, the tadpoles wriggle on to the mother's back.

3. She carries them to a leaf-pool high in a tree.

SMALL BUT LETHAL

The golden arrow-poison frog is one of the most deadly of all arrow-poison frogs. It is only 5 cm (2 in) long, but its poison is at least 20 times as strong as that of any other frog and can be lethal for humans even to touch. It is one of only three species traditionally used by local tribesmen for tipping hunting arrows. The arrow is simply rubbed over the frog's body and it is ready to use. The poison remains strong for over a year.

Children's Animal Encyclopedia

Poisons and venoms

POISONS AND VENOMS

Many animals use poison for protection against enemies. By being unpleasant to eat, small creatures such as toads and caterpillars are able to defend themselves against larger creatures. Many have colourful markings that serve as a warning to others – predators learn to link these bright colours with the unpleasant taste and stay away. Venom is injected directly into the body, and makes a deadly weapon. Some snakes and spiders deliver a venomous bite to their prey with their fangs, while scorpions have venomous stings.

SNAKE

The rattlesnake uses venom to kill its prey. As it bites the animal, venom passes from glands in the head, through special canals in the fangs at the front of the jaw into its prey. The snake warns potential predators of its threat by making a rattling sound with its tail.

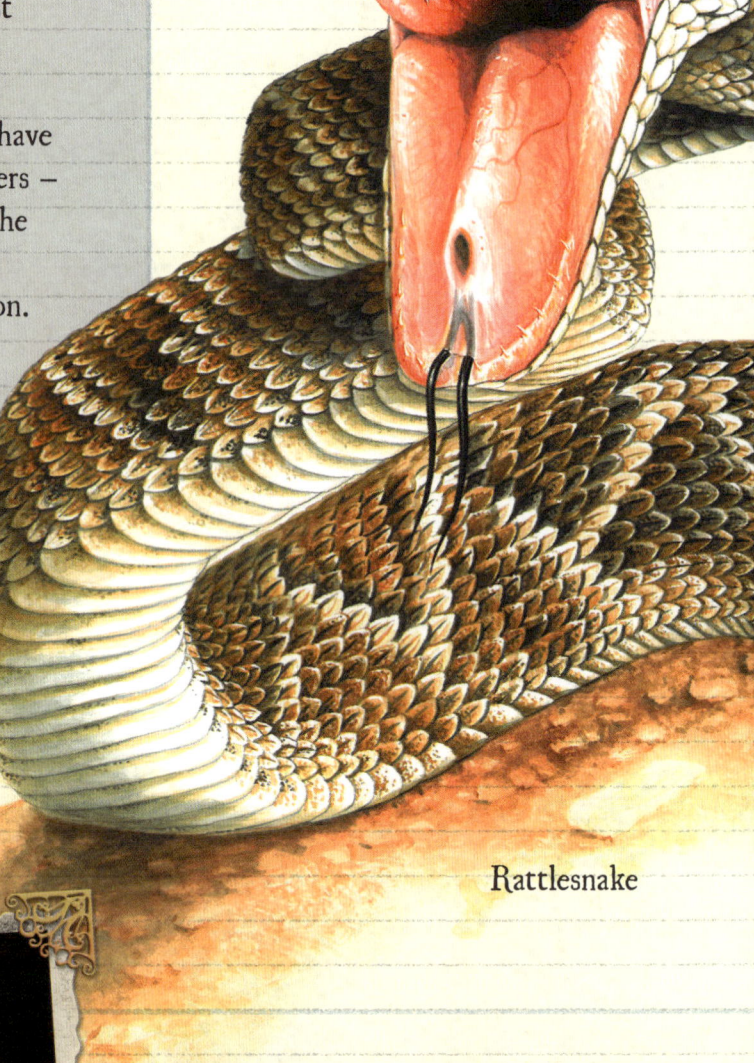

Rattlesnake

TOAD

The Oriental fire-bellied toad has small poison glands all over its body that produce an unpleasant-tasting substance. If threatened, the toad reveals the bright scarlet markings on the underside of its body to warn off its attacker.

Oriental fire-bellied toad

SPIDER

The funnel-web spider delivers a venom so strong that that it can kill humans. The spider digs a burrow and lines the entrance with trip-wires made of silk. It hides in the burrow and feels for vibrations in the silk with its legs. When it senses, an animal brushing the silk, the spider pounces, burying its fangs into its victim and injecting it with venom.

Funnel-web spider

CATERPILLAR

The monarch butterfly caterpillar feeds on the poisonous milkweed plant. The poison in the plant does not affect the caterpillar but is stored in its body and makes the caterpillar taste extremely unpleasant. Its bold stripes warn predators to leave it alone. Even as a butterly, this insect is poisonous.

Monarch butterfly caterpillar

FISH

There are about 32,500 species of fish, more than any other type of vertebrate. They range from tiny species such as the pygmy goby, which is only 1 cm (⅓ in) long, to giants such as the whale shark, which can measure as much as 12 m (40 ft). Most species of fish can live either in the sea or in fresh water, but not in both habitats. Some fish eat aquatic plants, others filter tiny animals from the water. Many are active, fast-moving hunters, while some lie hidden on the seabed and wait for prey to come close.

Children's Animal Encyclopedia

WHAT IS A FISH?

Fish were the first vertebrates – animals with backbones – to live on Earth. The earliest fish lived about 440–500 million years ago. All fish, except for the group that includes lampreys, have a spine made of bones called vertebrae, although in sharks and rays this is made of gristly, flexible cartilage.

Emperor angelfish

Mackerel

Coloration helps many fish to hide from their enemies. The angelfish's markings and the mackerel's light belly and darker back, break up their outlines and make them harder to see.

STRUCTURE OF A FISH

There are three main groups of fish and their relatives. The most primitive group includes the lampreys. These fish-like animals have no jaws, only sucker-like mouths. The second group includes all the sharks and rays. These are known as cartilaginous fish because their skeletons are made of a gristly substance called cartilage, not bone. The third, and largest, group contains the bony fish. As their name suggests, these fish have skeletons made of bone.

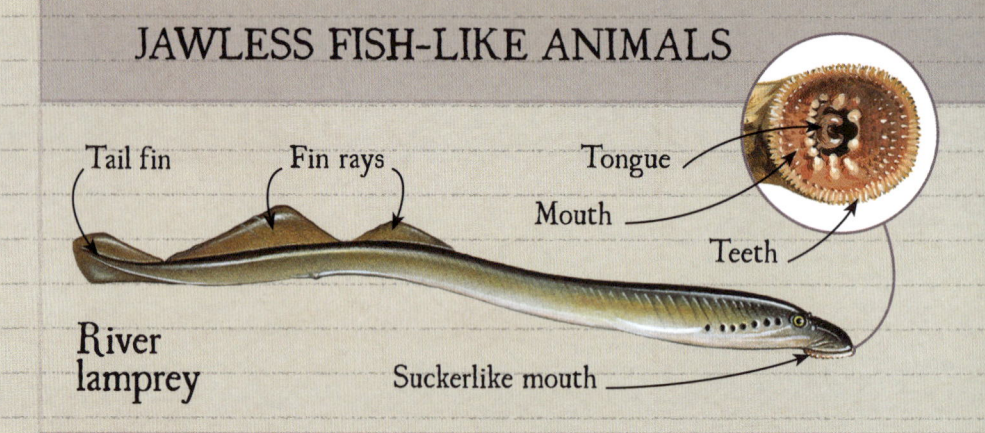

JAWLESS FISH-LIKE ANIMALS

River lamprey — Tail fin, Fin rays, Tongue, Mouth, Teeth, Suckerlike mouth

CARTILAGINOUS FISH

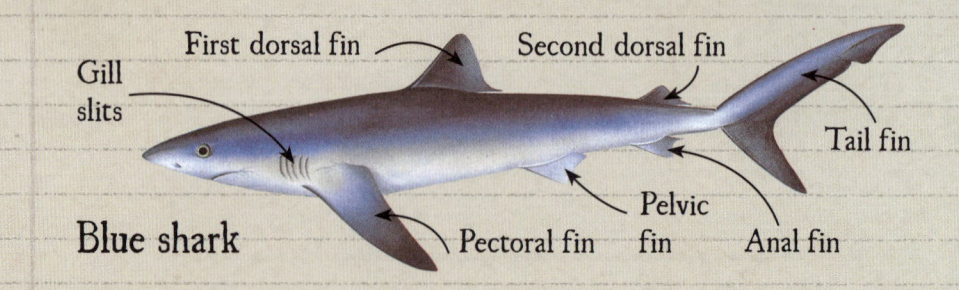

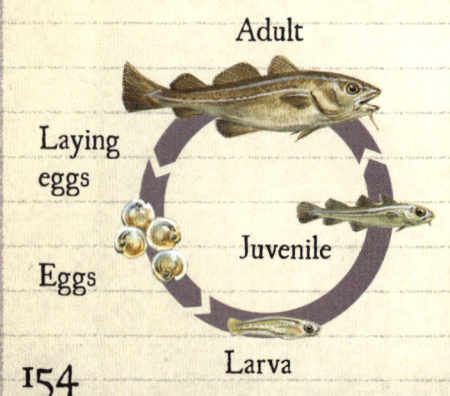

Blue shark — Gill slits, First dorsal fin, Second dorsal fin, Tail fin, Pectoral fin, Pelvic fin, Anal fin

EGGS AND YOUNG

Most female fish lay large numbers of eggs into the water. Males then release sperm to fertilize the eggs, which float in surface waters or sink to the bottom. The eggs hatch into larvae, many of which are eaten by predators. Some survive to become juveniles, with a more adult-like body. The juveniles feed and grow into adult fish.

Adult — Laying eggs — Eggs — Larva — Juvenile

Brood pouch

There are many exceptions to the normal way of breeding in fish. A male seahorse develops eggs in a small pouch on its body until they hatch.

Gills of bony fish

Mouth open
- Water
- Gills
- Gill flap
- Gills closed

Mouth closed
- Gills open

Gills of shark
- Water
- Gills
- Gill slit

HOW FISH BREATHE

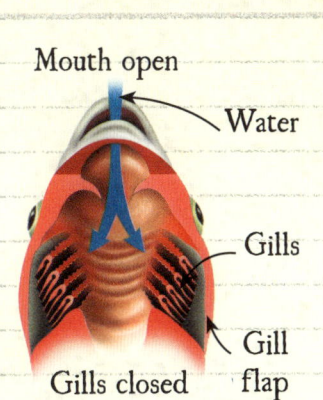

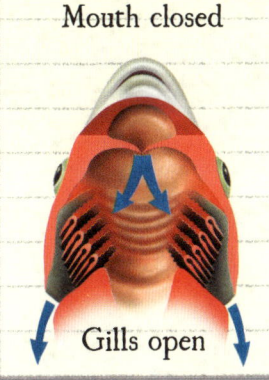

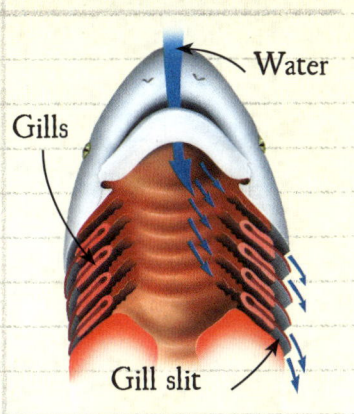

Fish breathe through special structures called gills at the sides of the head. These are made up of large numbers of delicate plates, packed with blood vessels. As water flows over the gills, molecules of oxygen pass into the blood, which is then carried around the body. The gills of a bony fish have one combined opening to the outside, which is covered by a protective flap. In sharks and rays, each gill has its own exit to the water.

BONY FISH

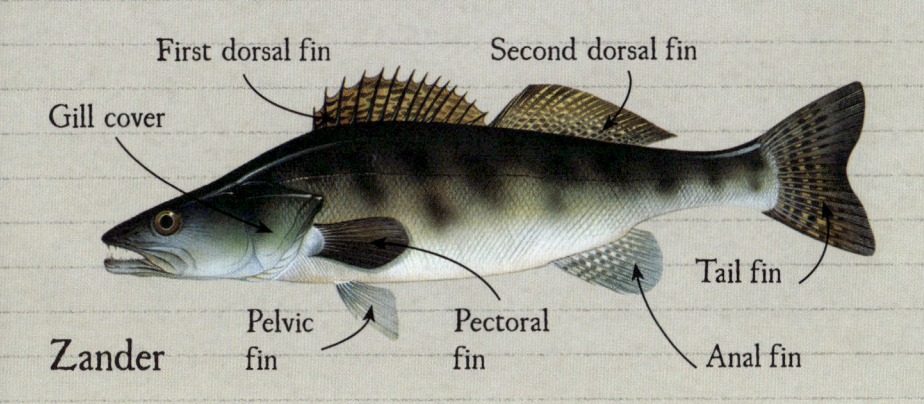

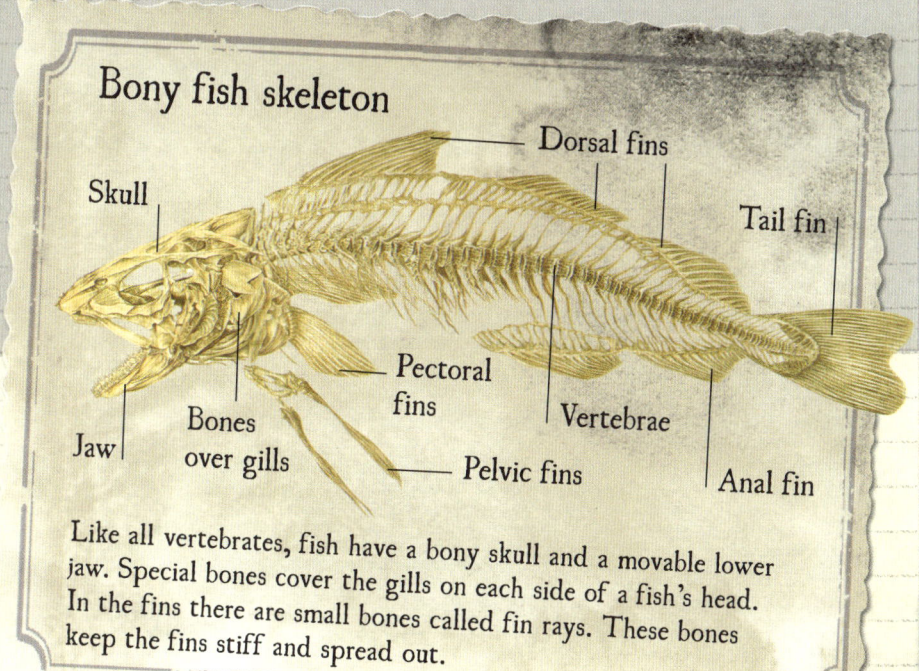

Zander
- Gill cover
- First dorsal fin
- Second dorsal fin
- Tail fin
- Anal fin
- Pectoral fin
- Pelvic fin

Bony fish skeleton
- Skull
- Dorsal fins
- Tail fin
- Jaw
- Bones over gills
- Pectoral fins
- Vertebrae
- Pelvic fins
- Anal fin

Like all vertebrates, fish have a bony skull and a movable lower jaw. Special bones cover the gills on each side of a fish's head. In the fins there are small bones called fin rays. These bones keep the fins stiff and spread out.

Pufferfish

Barracuda

FISH MOUTHS

The mouths of fish are adapted to suit the food that they eat. Fish that hunt, such as the barracuda, have long snouts and sharp teeth for seizing prey. The angler uses its wide mouth to engulf prey that it lures near with its fishing rod. Many, such as the parrotfish, have beak-like mouths for crushing hard-shelled creatures. The herring filters tiny plankton through special structures called gill rakers.

Herring

Angler fish

LAMPREYS, SHARKS AND RAYS

Lampreys are primitive fish-like animals that have no true jaws. They have sucking discs for feeding on the blood of other creatures. Sharks, sawfish, rays and their relatives have skeletons made of cartilage, not bone. There are about 1,200 known species of cartilaginous fish and all live in the sea. Most are active hunters with sharp-edged teeth. A few of the largest, such as the whale shark, are not hunters. They filter small creatures from the water.

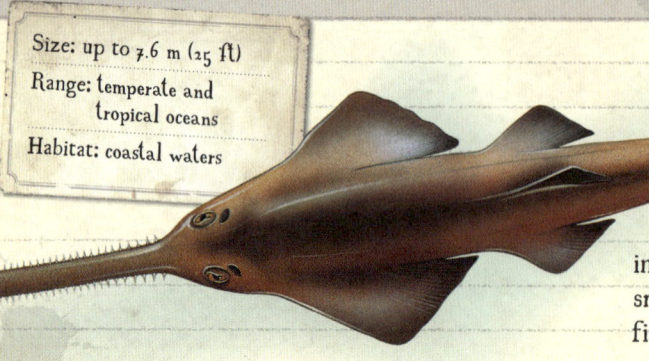

Size: up to 7.6 m (25 ft)
Range: temperate and tropical oceans
Habitat: coastal waters

Greater sawfish
Pristis pectinata

This fish's long, blade-like snout is studded with 24 or more large teeth on each side. It lives on the seabed in shallow water and uses its saw to dig in the sand and mud for small invertebrates to eat. It also swims into a school of smaller fish and lashes its toothed saw from side to side to stun prey.

Sandy dogfish
Scyliorhynus canicula

A small shark, the sandy dogfish lives on sandy and muddy seabeds, where it feeds on fish and bottom-living invertebrates. The female's eggs are laid in hard cases that lodge among weeds or other objects. The young dogfish hatch 5 to 11 months later and are about 10 cm (4 in) long.

Size: 15½–25½ in (40–65 cm)
Range: northeast Atlantic Ocean
Habitat: coastal waters

Size: 2.5–4 m (9–13 ft)
Range: Atlantic, Pacific, and Indian oceans
Habitat: all tropical and temperate seas

Mako shark
Isurus oxyrinchus

A powerful fish with a slender body and a pointed head, the mako is a fast, aggressive hunter and feeds on surface-living fish such as tuna and mackerel. The female gives birth to live young that develop inside her body.

Smooth hammerhead
Sphyrna zygaena

Size: 4.3 m (14 ft)
Range: all tropical and temperate seas
Habitat: oceanic

The hammerhead has a broad head that extends to each side. There is one eye and one nostril on either side of the elongated head. This spacing of eyes and nostrils may improve the shark's sight and sense of smell.

Children's Animal Encyclopedia

Great white shark
Carcharodon carcharias

A large aggressive hunter equipped with jagged triangular teeth, this shark kills seals, dolphins and even other sharks. It also scavenges dead animals and waste. White sharks have been involved in a number of attacks on humans.

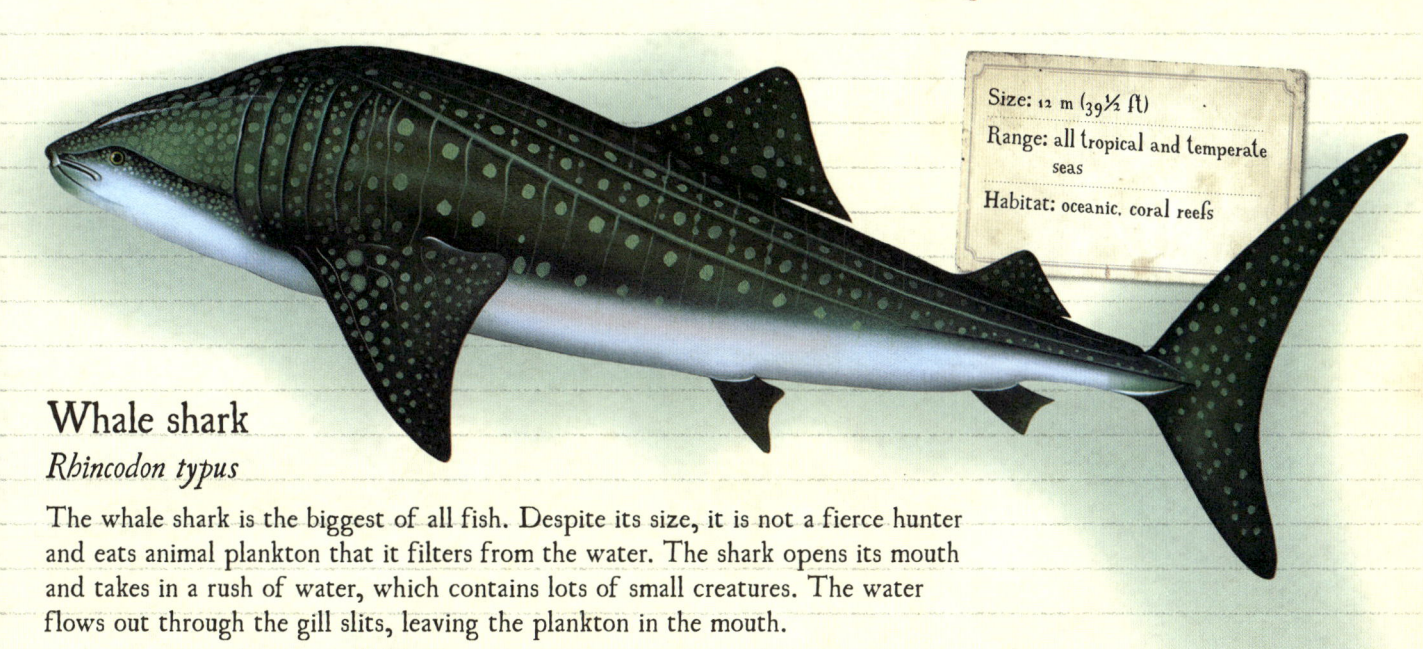

Size: 90 cm (35½ in)
Range: Atlantic coasts and Mediterranean Sea
Habitat: fresh water, coastal waters

Sea lamprey
Petromyzon marinus

The adult sea lamprey is a blood-feeding parasite. It has no true jaws and uses its sucking disclike mouth to attach itself to its victim so firmly that it is almost impossible to remove. A special substance in its mouth keeps the host's blood flowing so the lamprey can feed. Victims often die from blood loss.

Size: 6 m (19½ ft)
Range: Atlantic, Pacific and Indian oceans
Habitat: all tropical and temperate seas

Size: 12 m (39½ ft)
Range: all tropical and temperate seas
Habitat: oceanic, coral reefs

Whale shark
Rhincodon typus

The whale shark is the biggest of all fish. Despite its size, it is not a fierce hunter and eats animal plankton that it filters from the water. The shark opens its mouth and takes in a rush of water, which contains lots of small creatures. The water flows out through the gill slits, leaving the plankton in the mouth.

Giant manta
Manta birostris

With its huge, pointed pectoral fins, the manta is the biggest of the rays. Like the whale shark, this giant feeds mostly on tiny animal plankton, which it filters from the water. It also eats fish. The manta often basks near the surface with the tips of its pectoral fins out of the water.

Size: 5.2 m (17 ft) long; 6.7 m (22 ft) wide
Range: all tropical and temperate seas
Habitat: coastal waters

SKATES, RAYS AND SEABED SHARKS

There are more than 650 different species of skate and ray. Most have a very broad, flattened body and huge wing-like fins, giving them a diamond shape. As they swim, the fish flap their fins and appear almost to fly through the water. Skates and rays spend much of their lives on or near the seafloor. Their flat bodies make them hard to see. Openings called spiracles on the upper surface of the head allow them to breathe. Sharks are thought of as fast swimmers that live near the surface, but some, such as horn sharks and carpet sharks, lurk on the bottom.

Camouflaged by its colouring and the many flaps of skin at the sides of its body, the carpet shark lies on the seabed waiting for prey to come near.

SKATE

The skate's flattened body is covered with tiny spines and a line of larger spines runs down the middle of the tail. The spines help the skate defend itself against attackers. The female lays her eggs in a leathery case with long tips at each corner, which is left on the seabed. When the young hatch, they are about 20 cm (7¾ in) long.

Sting ray

Eagle ray

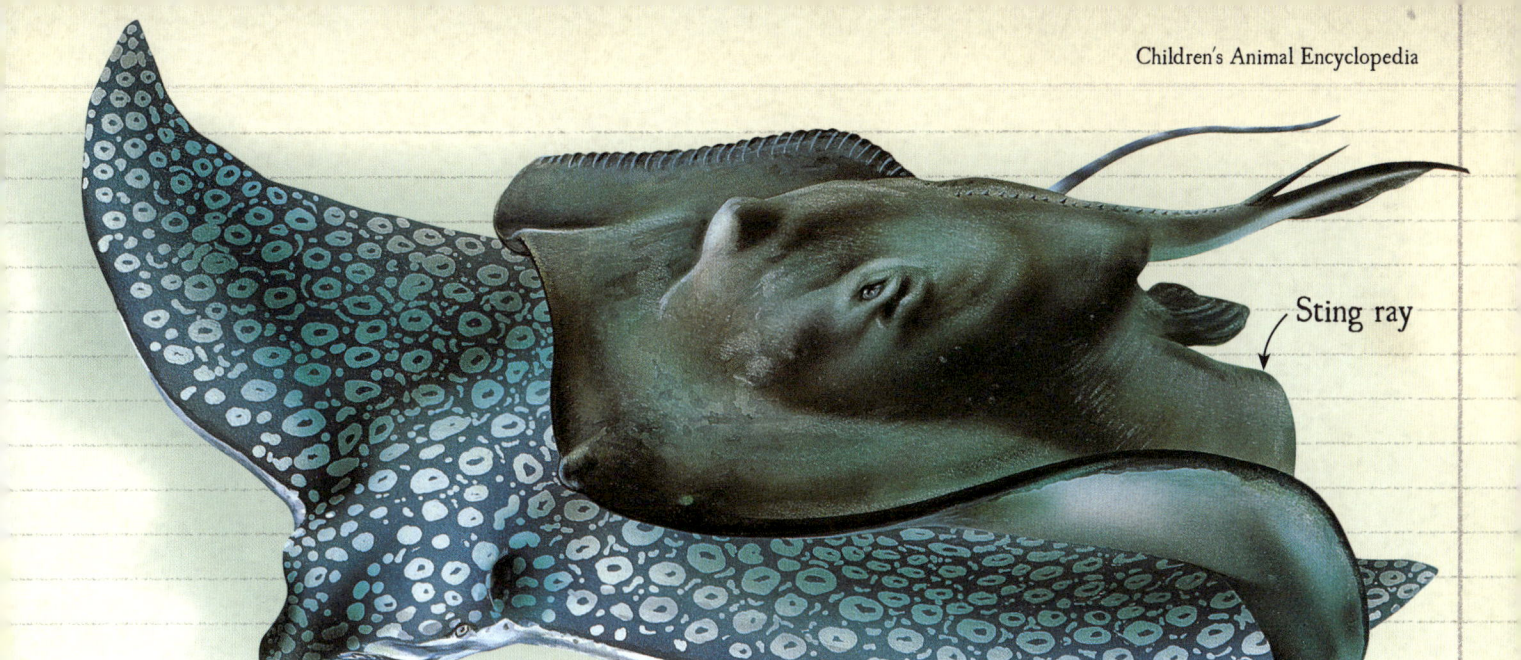

STING RAY AND EAGLE RAY

Both of these fish have long whip-like tails that they use to lash out at enemies to defend themselves. The spines are linked to venom glands and can cause serious injury to humans. Rays have flattened teeth with which they crush the hard shells of crabs and molluscs.

HORN SHARK

This shark has a long tapering body and a large blunt head. It gets its name from the sharp spines in front of the fins on its back. Active at night, it collects prey such as sea urchins, crabs and worms on the seabed. It crushes hard-shelled food with the large flat teeth at the back of its jaws.

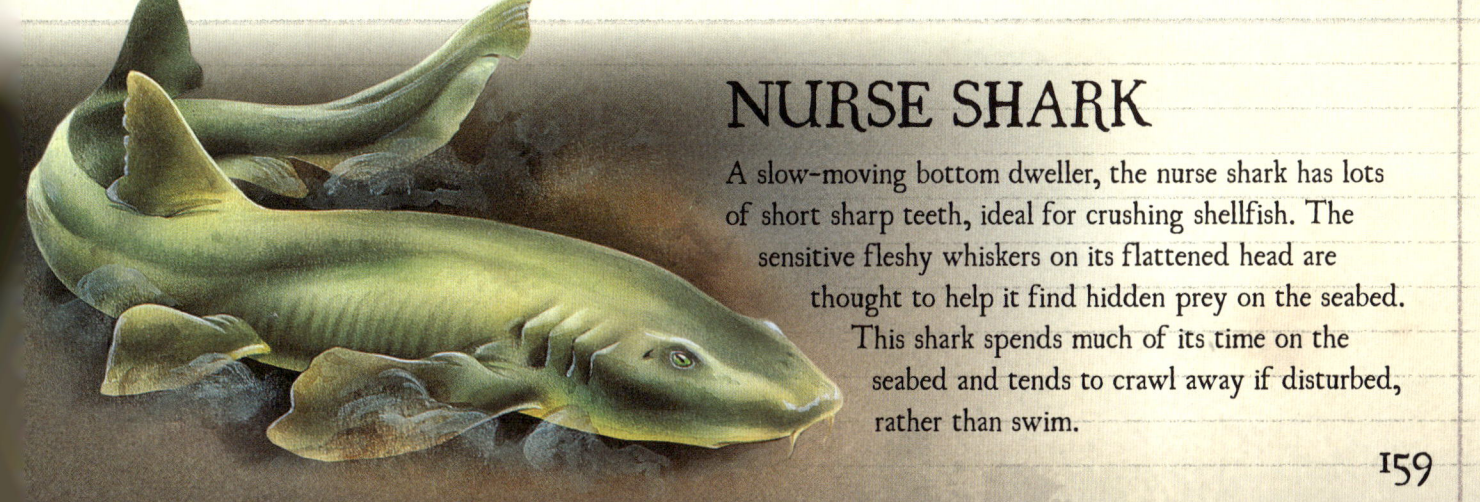

NURSE SHARK

A slow-moving bottom dweller, the nurse shark has lots of short sharp teeth, ideal for crushing shellfish. The sensitive fleshy whiskers on its flattened head are thought to help it find hidden prey on the seabed. This shark spends much of its time on the seabed and tends to crawl away if disturbed, rather than swim.

STURGEON, GARS AND RELATIVES

All of these fish live in fresh water, but most sturgeons spend part of their life in the sea. They travel into rivers to lay their eggs and the young remain there for several years, feeding and growing before making their first journey to the sea, where they spend their adult lives. Sturgeons are increasingly rare, partly because humans collect the female's unshed eggs to eat as a food called caviar. Gars, bichirs and bowfins are separate groups of fish. They generally occur in areas where there is a dense growth of water plants. Most goldeyes, pirarucus and elephant-snout fish live in the southern half of the world, but there are two species of goldeyes in North America. They all eat fish and insects.

Bowfin
Amia calva

This fish lives in slow-moving waters with dense plant life. In spring, the male clears a hollow in the riverbed, and makes a nest of plants roots and gravel. The female then lays her eggs and the male guards them for eight to ten days until they hatch out.

Size: up to 1 m (3¼ ft)
Range: northeastern USA, southeastern Canada
Habitat: fresh water

Mottled bichir
Polypterus weeksii

A long-bodied fish covered with hard, diamond-shaped scales, the bichir lives among water plants at the edges of rivers and lakes. It has an unusual dorsal fin made up of small flag-like sections, each supported by a bony ray. The bichir feeds mainly on fish, frogs and newts.

Size: 40 cm (15¾ in)
Range: Africa: central basin of the Congo River
Habitat: fresh water

Longnose gar
Lepisosteus osseus

As its name suggests, this gar has extremely long jaws, which are studded with sharp teeth. It hides among water plants, waiting for fish and shellfish to come near. It then dashes forwards and seizes its prey. It lays eggs in spring in shallow water. The eggs are sticky and attach themselves to water weed or stones so they are not carried away by the water current.

Size: up to 2 m (6½ ft)
Range: North and Central America
Habitat: fresh water

Children's Animal Encyclopedia

Size: 80 cm (31½ in)
Range: Africa: Nile River and East African lakes
Habitat: fresh water

Goldeye
Hiodon alosoides

The goldeye belongs to a small family of fish known as mooneyes. They have big golden eyes that provide good vision at night, when they are generally active. The goldeye has a large number of small fine teeth and it feeds mainly on insects and their larvae as well as on fish.

Elephant-snout fish
Mormyrus kannume

This fish gets its name from its long trunk-like snout. The muscles along its body are adapted to produce weak electric charges that set up an electric field in the water around the body. The fish can sense any disturbances in this field, which helps it find prey at night or in murky water.

Size: 30–40 cm (11¾–15¾ in)
Range: North America
Habitat: fresh water

Size: up to 4 m (13 ft)
Range: Amazon River basin
Habitat: fresh water

Pirarucu
Arapaima gigas

One of the largest freshwater fish in the world, South America's pirarucu may weigh up to 200 kg (440 lb). It has large scales on its body but none on its head. Other fish and insect larvae are its main food. Pirarucus breed in sandy-bottomed water. The eggs are laid in a hollow in the riverbed and the parents guard them until they hatch.

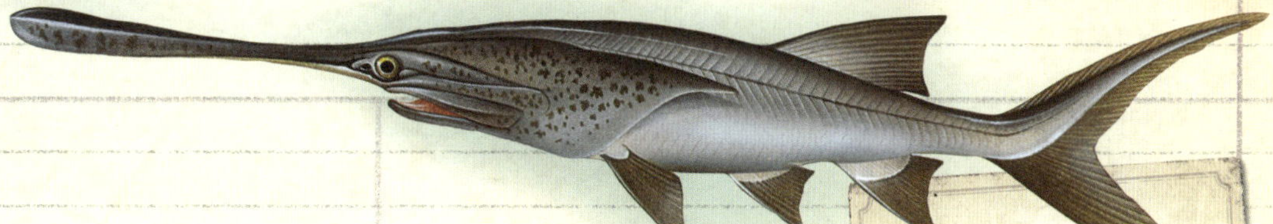

Common sturgeon
Acipenser sturio

Sturgeons spend most of their lives in the sea, feeding on worms and other invertebrates, but they lay their eggs in rivers. In spring, sturgeons migrate to rivers where each female lays thousands of sticky black eggs. The eggs hatch in about a week. The young fish remain in the river for about three years before travelling to the sea.

Paddlefish
Polyodon spathula

Size: up to 2 m (6½ ft)
Range: USA: Mississippi River
Habitat: fresh water

The paddlefish is a relative of the sturgeon. It swims with its large mouth open and uses the comb-like structures in its mouth to catch small creatures in the water. Eggs are laid in spring. Newly hatched fish do not have long snouts, but these develop in two or three weeks.

Size: 3 m (10 ft)
Range: European coastline
Habitat: fresh water, coastal waters

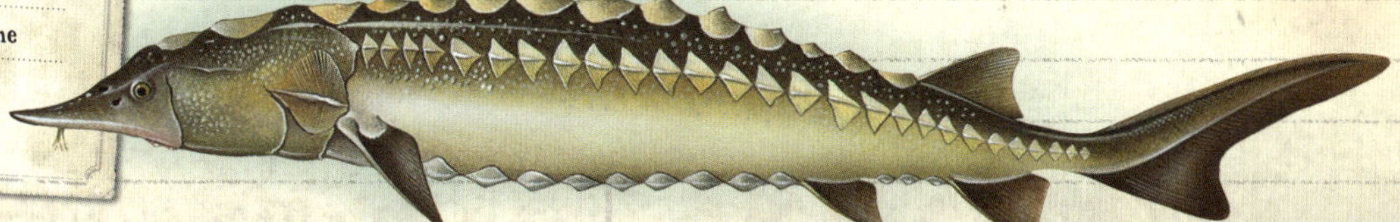

161

EELS, TARPONS AND HERRING

Most of these fish live in the sea, but some eels and tarpons spend at least part of their lives in fresh water. There are more than 800 species of eel. They live in all oceans, except in polar areas, and there are also a few freshwater species. All have slender bodies and long fins on the back and belly. The herring group includes about 392 species, some of which are important food fish, such as herrings themselves, sardines and anchovies. Most are marine and live in schools in surface waters in the open sea or near coasts. The tarpons belong to a small family of marine fish, which are related to eels and herrings. They are slender-bodied fish with deeply forked tails.

Sardine
Sardina pilchardus

The sardine is similar to the herring but has a more rounded body and larger scales. Shoals of sardines swim in surface waters, feeding on animal plankton. Sardines are a valued food fish and large numbers are caught every year.

Size: 25 cm (9¾ in)
Range: European and northwest African coasts
Habitat: coastal waters, oceanic

Alewife
Alosa pseudoharengus

A member of the herring group, the alewife feeds mostly on plankton and small fish. Although it lives in the sea, it swims into rivers to mate and lay its eggs, so is often found in fresh water. Some alewives spend all their lives in lakes and these are only about half the size of sea-living alewives.

Size: 38 cm (15 in)
Range: North American Atlantic coast
Habitat: fresh water, coastal waters

Size: 1.2–2.4 m (4–7¾ ft)
Range: Atlantic Ocean, Caribbean Sea, east Pacific Ocean via Panama Canal
Habitat: coastal waters, fresh water

Atlantic herring
Clupea harengus

Herring has long been an important food for humans, and large numbers of these fish are caught every year. In the sea, herring are also preyed on by birds, other fish, dolphins and seals. Herring themselves feed on plankton, small crustaceans and fish.

Tarpon
Megalops atlanticus

A strong, fast-swimming fish, the tarpon is related to eels and herrings. It feeds on many types of fish and on crabs. The female lays millions of eggs in coastal waters, but many of the larvae drift into rivers where they remain until they grow larger.

Size: 40 cm (15¾ in)
Range: North Atlantic Ocean
Habitat: coastal waters, oceanic

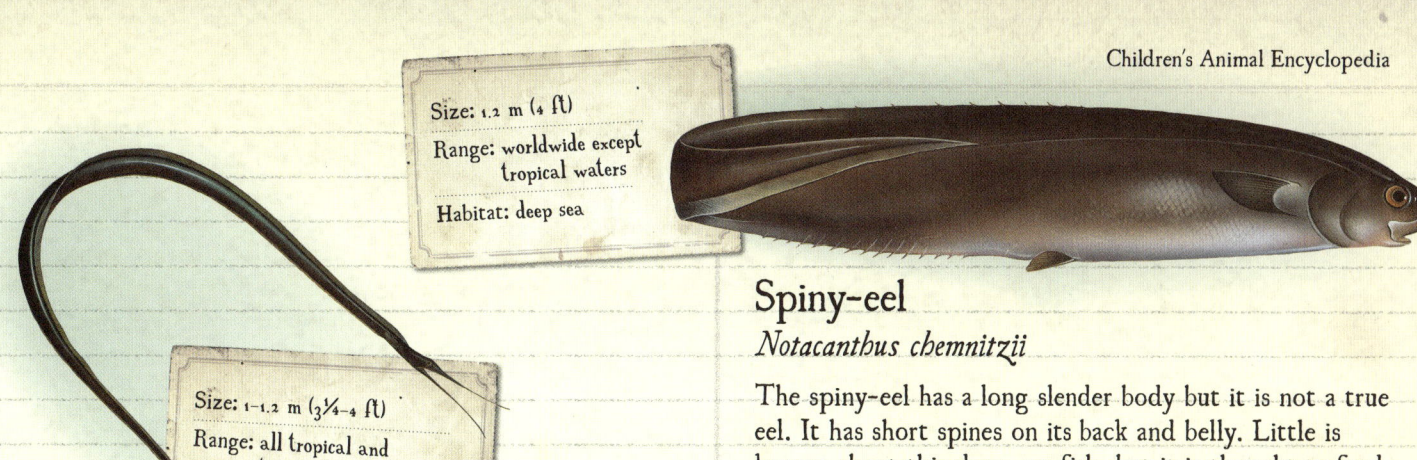

Children's Animal Encyclopedia

Size: 1.2 m (4 ft)
Range: worldwide except tropical waters
Habitat: deep sea

Spiny-eel
Notacanthus chemnitzii

The spiny-eel has a long slender body but it is not a true eel. It has short spines on its back and belly. Little is known about this deep-sea fish, but it is thought to feed head down on the seabed, eating bottom-living animals such as sea anemones.

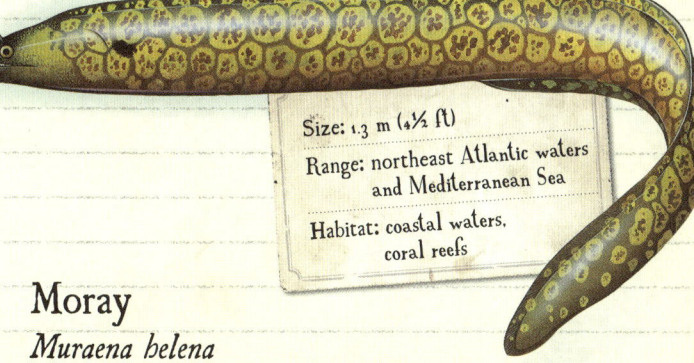

Size: 1–1.2 m (3¼–4 ft)
Range: all tropical and temperate seas
Habitat: oceanic

Slender snipe eel
Nemichthys scolopaceus

This deep-sea eel has an extremely long thin body with fins that run almost its whole length. It has narrow beak-like jaws and sharp backwards-facing teeth that it uses to trap prey such as fish and crustaceans.

Size: 1.3 m (4½ ft)
Range: northeast Atlantic waters and Mediterranean Sea
Habitat: coastal waters, coral reefs

Moray
Muraena helena

Like all of the 200 or so different species of moray eels found in warm seas, this moray has a scaleless, boldly patterned body, powerful jaws and strong, sharp teeth. A fierce hunter, the moray usually hides among underwater rocks with only its head showing, watching out for prey such as fish, squid and cuttlefish.

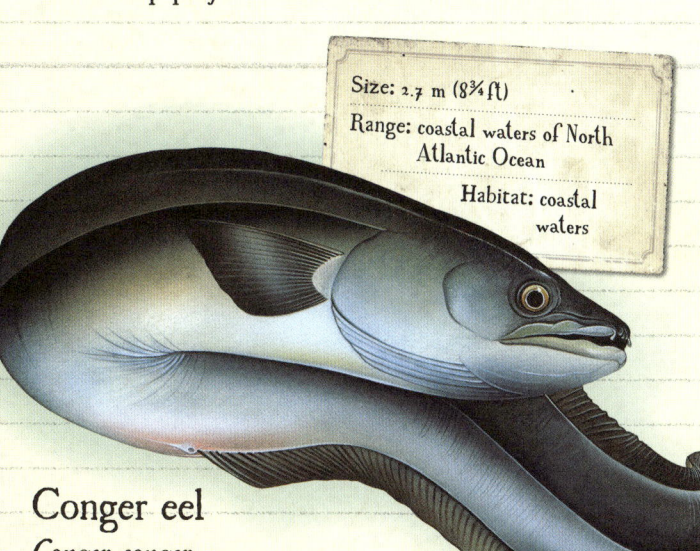

Size: 2.7 m (8¾ ft)
Range: coastal waters of North Atlantic Ocean
Habitat: coastal waters

Conger eel
Conger conger

This eel is common on rocky North Atlantic shores. It usually lives in shallow water, where it hides among rocks and comes out to find prey such as fish and octopus. It travels to deeper water to mate and lay its eggs. The eggs hatch out into small, transparent larvae which drift in the sea for a year or two before they develop into small eels.

Size: 50–100 cm (19¾–39½ in)
Range: North Atlantic Ocean, Mediterranean Sea
Habitat: fresh water, coastal waters, oceanic

European eel
Anguilla anguilla

Young eels live in fresh water where they feed in insects, crustaceans and fish. When they are ready to breed they swim to the sea where they mate, lay their eggs, then die. The eggs hatch and the larvae drift in surface waters for about three years. They then swim into rivers and the cycle starts again.

Carp, bream and piranhas

CARP, BREAM AND PIRANHAS

Carp, bream, roach and their relatives, such as the bigmouth buffalo and the white sucker, belong to a group of about 3,250 freshwater fish. They dominate the streams, rivers and lakes of Europe, northern Asia and North America and are also found in Africa. Most have scales on the body, but not on the head, and a single fin on the back. Pacus and piranhas belong to a separate group of freshwater fish, most of which live in lakes and rivers in Central and South America. Some relatives of the piranhas also live in Africa. Flesh-eating piranhas have sharp teeth for chopping flesh from their victims.

Common carp
Cyprinus carpio

The carp is a sturdy, deep-bodied fish. It usually lives in slow-moving water with plenty of plant life and feeds mostly on crustaceans, insect larvae and some plants. The eggs are laid in shallow water and stick to plants until they hatch.

Size: 50–100 cm (20–3¼ in)
Range: parts of Europe and Asia; introduced worldwide
Habitat: fresh water

Tench
Tinca tinca

A relative of the carp, the tench has a thickset body and rounded fins. The scales on the body are extremely small and covered with mucus. It usually feeds on the river or lake bed on insect larvae, crustaceans and molluscs. Tench breed in shallow water, shedding their eggs onto plants.

Size: up to 70 cm (27½ in)
Range: Europe and western to central Asia
Habitat: fresh water

Goldfish
Carassius auratus

The colourful goldfish belongs to the carp family. In the wild, it lives in ponds and lakes where there are plenty of water plants, but it is also bred for keeping in aquariums and ornamental pools.

Size: up to 30 cm (12 in)
Range: Europe and Asia; introduced worldwide
Habitat: fresh water

White sucker
Catostomus commersonii

This bottom-living fish has thick, suckerlike lips and feeds on insect larvae, crustaceans, molluscs and some plants. The eggs are laid at night in gravel-bottomed streams. They sink to the bottom and stay among the gravel until they hatch.

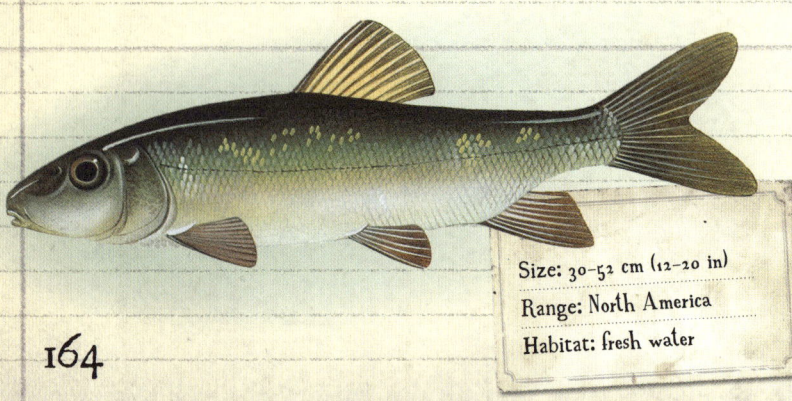

Size: 30–52 cm (12–20 in)
Range: North America
Habitat: fresh water

Children's Animal Encyclopedia

Size: 70 cm (27½ in)
Range: South America
Habitat: fresh water

Red piranha
Pygocentrus nattereri

Piranhas are not large fish but they swim in such large shoals that together they can catch and kill animals much larger than themselves. There are reports of shoals of piranhas stripping the flesh from animals such as cows in minutes.

Size: up to 30 cm (11 in)
Range: northern South America
Habitat: fresh water

Pacu
Colossoma macropomum

Not all piranhas are fierce hunters. Some are plant-eaters, such as the pacu. This fish feeds on the many fruits and seeds that fall from the forest trees bordering the rivers where it lives. It uses its strong teeth to crush them to a pulp. Plant-eating piranhas are slower swimmers than the hunting species and do not have such powerful jaws.

Size: up to 1 m (3¼ ft)
Range: North America
Habitat: fresh water

Bigmouth buffalo
Ictiobus cyprinellus

This powerful fish feeds on crustaceans and insect larvae and on some plant material. In spring, adults gather in shallow water where females lay as many as 500,000 eggs. The young fish stay in the shallow breeding area for some months, feeding on plankton.

Size: 25 cm (10 in)
Range: Europe and western Asia
Habitat: fresh water

Bream
Abramis brama

This fish uses its a tube-like mouth to gather insect larvae, snails and worms from the river bottom. It lives in shoals and usually feeds at night. Bream breed in late spring of summer in shallow water. The eggs stick to water plants and hatch in about 12 days.

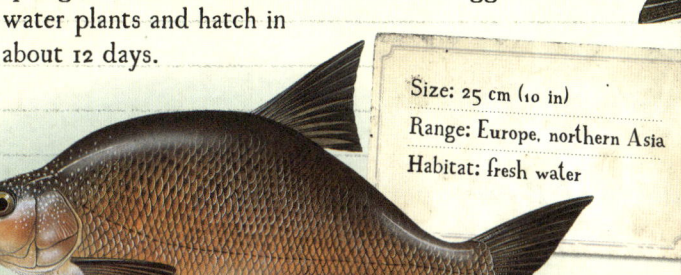

Size: 25 cm (10 in)
Range: Europe, northern Asia
Habitat: fresh water

Roach
Rutilus rutilus

This common river fish eats insects and their larvae as well as molluscs, crustaceans and plants. It, in turn, is food for many fish-eating birds and mammals. Roach breed in shallow water, where the eggs stick to plants. The young hatch in about two weeks.

165

CATFISH AND RELATIVES

There are more than 2,400 species in the catfish group, ranging from tiny fish just a few centimetres long to giant forms measuring 1.5 m (5 ft) or more and weighing as much as 45 kg (100 lb). Most live in rivers and freshwater lakes in the warmer parts of the world, but there are some sea-living species. Most catfish live in South America. These fish do not have ordinary scales, but some have bony plates which cover their bodies like armour. They are bottom-dwellers and find their food by touch and taste, digging in the mud of a river or lake bed until the sensitive whiskers, or barbels, around their mouth find prey.

Cascarudo
Callichthys callichthys

The body of this little catfish is covered with overlapping bony plates, which help protect it from enemies. The male fish makes a nest for the eggs among floating plants by blowing bubbles of air and mucus to form a foamy mass.

Size: up to 17 cm (6½ in)
Range: South America
Habitat: fresh water

Tandan catfish
Tandanus tandanus

The fins of this catfish run right around its body from its back to its belly. The spines on its back and on its pectoral fins can cause painful wounds if touched. Sensory whiskers, or barbels, around the mouth help it find food, mainly mussels, prawns and worms.

Size: 45 cm (18 in)
Range: southern and eastern Australia
Habitat: fresh water

Candirú
Vandellia cirrhosa

A tiny, delicate catfish, the candirú is a parasite – it lives on the blood of other fish. With small fish, it simply bites the skin and then feeds, but it may get inside the gill system of larger fish and stay there sucking blood. It is usually active at night and buries itself in the river bed when not feeding.

Size: 2.5 cm (1 in)
Range: South America: Amazon River basin
Habitat: fresh water

Barred sorubim
Pseudoplatystoma fasciatum

This South American catfish has a long snout and a slender body, marked with dark stripes and blotches. It spends most of its life on the river bed where it feeds on invertebrate animals. The sensitive whiskers, or barbels, around its mouth help it find food.

Size: up to 1 m (3¼ ft)
Range: South America
Habitat: fresh water

Blue catfish
Ictalurus furcatus

This catfish, one of the largest in North America, can grow to over 45 kg (100 lb) and is a valuable food fish. It often lives in fast-moving water, even waterfalls and rapids, and feeds on fish and crayfish. Its eggs are laid on the bottom and both parents guard the nest and then the young.

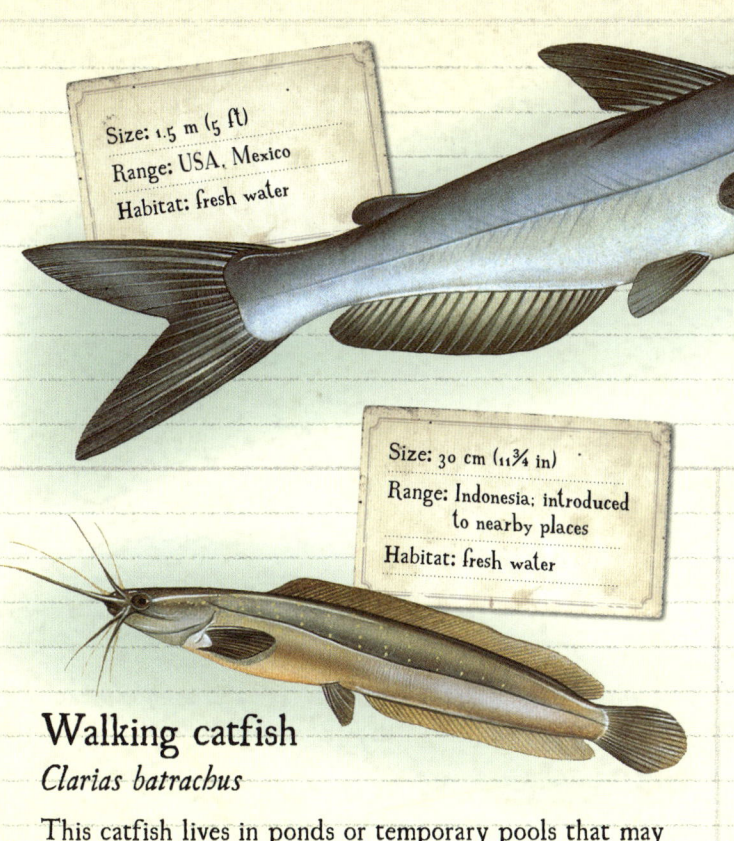

Size: 1.5 m (5 ft)
Range: USA, Mexico
Habitat: fresh water

Size: 30 cm (11¾ in)
Range: Indonesia; introduced to nearby places
Habitat: fresh water

Walking catfish
Clarias batrachus

This catfish lives in ponds or temporary pools that may disappear in long dry periods. When this happens, the fish can move over land to another pool, making snakelike movements of its body and using its pectoral fins as "legs". It feeds on fish and invertebrate animals.

Glass catfish
Kryptopterus bicirrhis

As its name suggests, this fish is transparent and many of the internal organs can be seen through the body. Unlike most catfish, it moves in small schools in surface waters during the day.

Size: 10 cm (4 in)
Range: Cambodia, Indonesia, Laos, Malaysia, Thailand, Vietnam
Habitat: fresh water

Wels
Silurus glanis

A large catfish, the wels has a broad head and long anal fin. It lives in slow-moving or still waters and is usually active at night, hiding in plants near the bottom during the day. Fish are its main food, but it also eats frogs, birds and even small mammals such as water voles.

Size: 30 cm (11¾ in)
Range: west Atlantic Ocean
Habitat: coastal waters

Sea catfish
Ariopsis felis

This sea-living catfish is most active at night when it feeds on crabs, shrimp and fish. It breeds in summer and as the eggs are laid, the male takes them in his mouth, where they incubate. He cannot eat during this time. The young fish may also swim into the male's mouth for safety after hatching.

Size: up to 3 m (10 ft)
Range: Europe and western Asia
Habitat: fresh water

Children's Animal Encyclopedia

ELECTRIC EEL, SALMON, HATCHETFISH AND PIKE

The electric eel is one of about 39 species in its family. It is not a true eel but has a similar long body and is able to produce electric charges. In a separate group of about 73 species is the hatchetfish, a deep-sea fish which has light-producing organs on its body. These help the hatchetfish recognise its own kind in the darkness of the deep sea. The salmon family contains about 222 species which live in fresh water and the sea. Some migrate from the sea into rivers to lay eggs. The smelts belong to a different group of sea fish but they, too, travel up rivers to breed. Pike are a small group of freshwater fish.

Size: 1.5 m (5 ft)
Range: central Asia, Europe, Russia, Alaska, Canada, northern USA
Habitat: fresh water

Northern pike
Esox lucius

A fierce predator, the pike lurks among plants, keeping watch for any prey. Young pike feed mainly on invertebrates, but adults catch other fish and even birds and mammals. Female pike are larger than males and may weigh 23 kg (50 lb) or more.

Size: 7 cm (2¾ in)
Range: warm and tropical areas of all oceans
Habitat: oceanic, deep sea

Lovely hatchetfish
Argyropelecus aculeatus

This fish lives in water 100–600 m (330–2,000 ft) deep, but at night it comes up near the surface to feed on plankton. On its belly, rows of light-producing organs give out a pale blue light. This confuses predators about its size and shape, making it harder to catch.

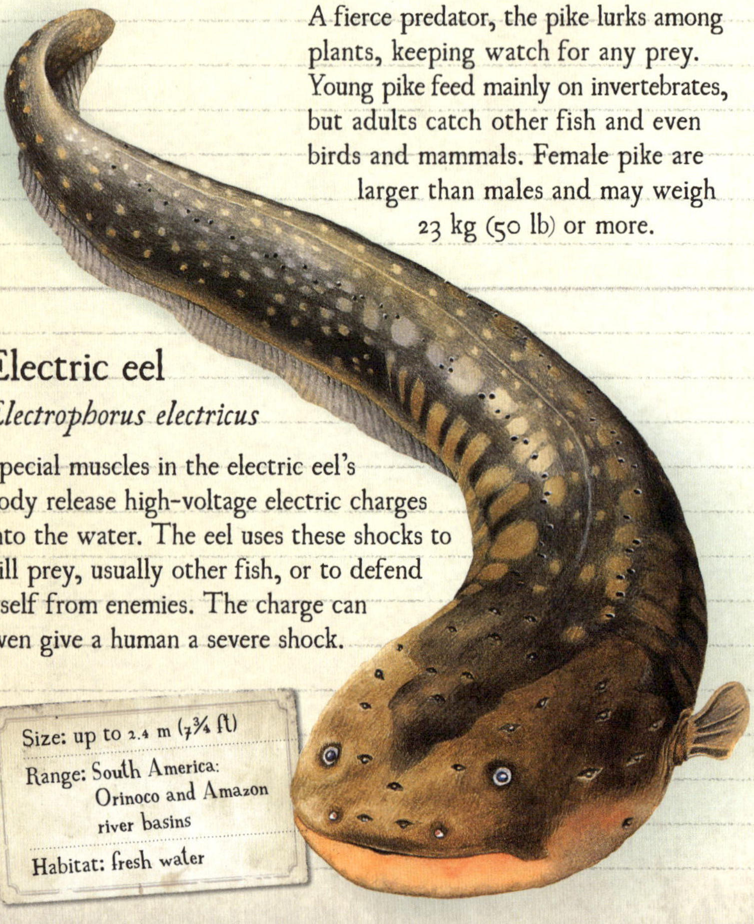

Electric eel
Electrophorus electricus

Special muscles in the electric eel's body release high-voltage electric charges into the water. The eel uses these shocks to kill prey, usually other fish, or to defend itself from enemies. The charge can even give a human a severe shock.

Size: up to 2.4 m (7¾ ft)
Range: South America: Orinoco and Amazon river basins
Habitat: fresh water

Size: 17 cm (7 in)
Range: North Atlantic Ocean
Habitat: fresh water, coastal waters

Smelt
Osmerus eperlanus

Smelts are sea-living fish but in winter, adult fish leave the sea to travel up rivers to breed. In spring, the females shed their eggs onto gravel on the riverbed or onto plants. When the young fish are large enough, they swim to the sea where they grow and mature.

Children's Animal Encyclopedia

Size: 46 cm (18 in)
Range: northern Europe
Habitat: fresh water

Size: up to 84 cm (33 in)
Range: North Pacific Ocean
Habitat: fresh water, coastal waters, oceanic

Sockeye salmon
Oncorhynchus nerka

Sockeye salmon live in the ocean until they are two to four years old. They then enter rivers and swim to the breeding grounds where they were hatched, sometimes as far as 1,600 km (1,000 miles) inland. After laying their eggs, the adult salmon die. The young spend up to three years in fresh water before migrating to the sea.

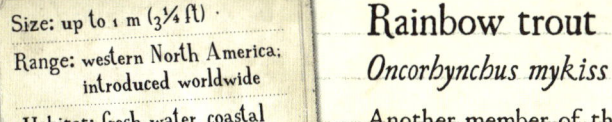

Grayling
Thymallus thymallus

A member of the salmon family, the grayling has a high, sail-like fin on its back and a forked tail. It eats insects and their larvae as well as crustaceans and molluscs. In spring, the female grayling makes a hollow in shallow water for her eggs. The eggs hatch three to four weeks after laying.

Size: up to 1 m (3¼ ft)
Range: western North America; introduced worldwide
Habitat: fresh water, coastal waters

Rainbow trout
Oncorhynchus mykiss

Another member of the salmon family and now farmed in large quantities, this trout is an important food fish. In the wild, rainbow trout live in rivers and feed on insect larvae, molluscs and crustaceans. In spring, the female makes a shallow nest and lays her eggs, which are then fertilised and covered over by the male.

Arctic char
Salvelinus alpinus alpinus

This member of the salmon family spends most of its life in polar seas, feeding on fish and molluscs. When ready to breed, it swims into rivers, and lays its eggs among gravel on the riverbed. The young eventually make their way back to the sea. Some Arctic char live in lakes.

Size: 40 cm (16 in)
Range: Arctic and North Atlantic oceans
Habitat: fresh water, coastal waters, oceanic

Size: up to 1.5 m (5 ft)
Range: North Atlantic Ocean
Habitat: fresh water, coastal waters, oceanic

Atlantic salmon
Salmo salar

Like the sockeye salmon, most Atlantic salmon swim into rivers to breed. The female makes a shallow nest on the riverbed in winter and lays her eggs, which are fertilised by the male. The eggs hatch the following spring and the young spend two to six years in the river before going to sea.

COD, ANGLERS AND CUSK-EELS

There are about 611 species of fish in the cod group. All but five live in the sea, mostly in the northern hemisphere. They include popular food fish such as cod, haddock, hake and ling. Many have a sensory whisker, or barbel, on the chin, which helps them find prey on the seabed. The anglers include about 323 species, all with a large head, a wide mouth and rows of sharp teeth. Most have a spine on the head, which they use as a lure to attract prey. Cusk-eels are a group of small, eel-like fish.

New Providence cusk-eel
Lucifuga spelaeotes

This little eel-like fish is mostly known from a few fresh water pools in the Bahamas. It has a broad, flattened head and a tapering body with a continuous back, tail and anal fin. Most of its head is bare, but small scales cover its body.

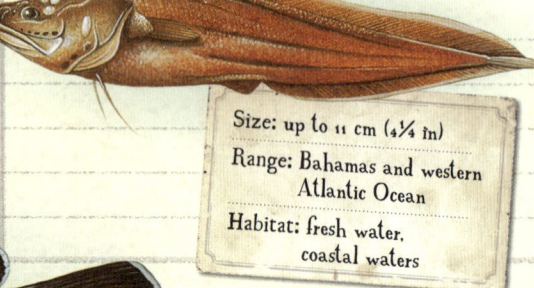

Size: up to 11 cm (4¼ in)
Range: Bahamas and western Atlantic Ocean
Habitat: fresh water, coastal waters

Size: 1.5–2 m (5–6½ ft)
Range: northeastern Atlantic Ocean, Arctic Ocean
Habitat: oceanic, deep sea

Ling
Molva molva

The ling is most common in rocky-bottomed waters where it eats fish and large crustaceans. Although usually a deep-water fish, it may live in shallower areas where there are rocks. It breeds in spring and summer and one female may lay as many as 60 million eggs.

Roughhead grenadier
Macrourus berglax

A relative of the cod, this deep-sea fish has a large head and a tapering tail. Its body scales are rough and toothed. Males make loud sounds by vibrating the swim bladder (a gas-filled sac inside the body) with special muscles.

Size: 90–100 cm (35½–39½ in)
Range: North Atlantic Ocean
Habitat: deep sea

Size: 40 cm (16 in)
Range: Canada, northern USA, northern Europe, Asia
Habitat: fresh water

Burbot
Lota lota

One of the few freshwater fish in the cod group, the burbot hides among water plants by day and comes out at dawn and dusk to feed. Adults eat fish, crustaceans and insects; young feed on insect larvae and small shrimps. Eggs are laid at night in winter – up to three million eggs per female.

Children's Animal Encyclopedia

Size: 35 cm (14 in)
Range: North Atlantic Ocean
Habitat: coastal waters

Haddock
Melanogrammus aeglefinus

The haddock is a member of the cod family and feeds on bottom-living worms, molluscs and brittlestars as well as fish. It gathers in shoals to spawn and the eggs are left to float in the surface waters until they hatch. Young haddock often shelter among the tentacles of large jellyfish.

Atlantic footballfish
Himantolophus groenlandicus

This deep-sea angler has a round body studded with bony plates, each with a central spine. On its head is a lure, which carries a light-producing organ. It uses this lure to attract prey in the darkness of the deep sea.

Size: up to 60 cm (23½ in)
Range: all temperate and tropical oceans
Habitat: deep sea

Size: 1.2 m (4 ft)
Range: North Atlantic Ocean
Habitat: coastal waters

Atlantic cod
Gadus morhua

The cod has three fins on its back, a long whisker, or barbel, on its chin and a mouth lined with sharp teeth. It usually swims in schools in surface waters but will search for food such as fish and worms on the seabed. It is an extremely valuable food fish.

Size: 1–2 m (3¼–6½ ft)
Range: European and north African coasts
Habitat: coastal waters, deep sea

Angler
Lophius piscatorius

The angler, or monkfish, has a special spine on its head, tipped with a flap of skin which it uses as a fishing lure. The fish lies on the seabed and moves its lure to attract other fish. When prey comes within reach, the angler opens its huge mouth and water flows in, with the prey.

Size: up to 90 cm (35½ in)
Range: North Pacific and Arctic oceans
Habitat: coastal waters, oceanic, deep sea

Alaska pollock
Theragra chalcogramma

The pollock has a long, tapering body, with three fins on its back and two on its underside. Its head and mouth are large and it has bigger eyes than most other cod. Unlike most cod, it feeds in mid-waters, catching crustaceans and small fish.

171

PERCH-LIKE FISH

This is the largest and most varied of all groups of fish and species live in almost every watery habitat. It includes more than 10,000 types of fish such as the sea bass, cichlids, gobies and wrasses. They have a wide range of body forms and include fish as different as the barracuda, angelfish, swordfish and Siamese fightingfish. Despite their differences, all perch-like fish have one or two fins on the back and most have pelvic fins close to the head. The pelvic fins usually have a spine and five rays.

Perch
Perca fluviatilis

Barred markings camouflage this fish among water plants. Perch live in slow-moving water, feed on fish and breed in shallow water in spring. Long strings of eggs hatch in about eight days and the young fish feed on plankton.

Size: 25 cm (10 in)
Range: Europe and parts of Asia
Habitat: fresh water

Size: up to 8 cm (3¼ in)
Range: central USA
Habitat: fresh water

Orangethroat darter
Etheostoma spectabile

This little member of the perch family feeds on insects and animal plankton. A breeding male has an orange throat and breast, while females have pale throats. The male chooses a nest site and guards the eggs once they are laid.

Greater amberjack
Seriola dumerili

A relative of the pompano, the greater amberjack is a large fish with a sleek body and a deeply forked tail. It feeds on many species of fish and is itself caught as a food fish.

Size: up to 1.8 m (6 ft)
Range: all temperate and tropical seas
Habitat: coastal waters, coral reefs

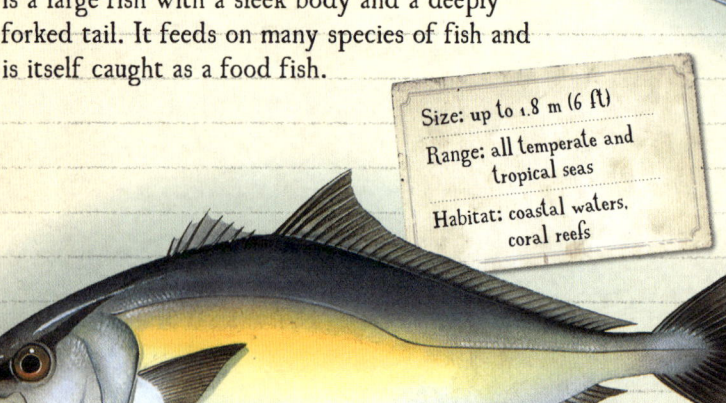

Size: 45–65 cm (17¾–25½ in)
Range: western Atlantic Ocean
Habitat: coastal waters

Florida pompano
Trachinotus carolinus

The pompano has a rounded snout and a fairly deep body, which tapers sharply to a forked tail. It feeds mainly on molluscs and crustaceans, which it finds in the mud and sand of the seabed. It is an excellent and valuable food fish.

Children's Animal Encyclopedia

Size: 2 m (6½ ft)
Range: eastern and northwestern Pacific Ocean
Habitat: coastal waters

Red mullet
Mullus surmuletus

This fish uses the sensory whiskers, or barbels, on its chin to help it find bottom-living invertebrates, which it then digs it out of the sand or mud. Red mullet are able to change colour to blend in to their surroundings, varying between day and night.

Giant sea bass
Stereolepis gigas

Some of these fish weigh more than 250 kg (550 lb) and live for more than 70 years. They eat fish and crustaceans and are popular food fish. The young are reddish in colour but slowly develop the adult appearance by about 12 or 13 years of age.

Size: 40 cm (15¾ in)
Range: eastern Atlantic Ocean and Mediterranean Sea
Habitat: coastal waters

Size: up to 2 m (6½ ft)
Range: warm and tropical waters of all oceans
Habitat: coastal

Dolphinfish
Coryphaena hippurus

The brightly coloured dolphinfish is easily identified by the large fin along its back. The forehead of the male becomes steeper with age; otherwise male and female look alike. Dolphinfish move in small shoals and eat fish, squid and crustaceans. They are often seen around patches of floating seaweed where their prey may hide.

Size: 35-50 cm (13¾-19¾ in)
Range: Atlantic Ocean and Mediterranean Sea
Habitat: coastal waters, oceanic

Size: 40 cm (15¾ in)
Range: western Atlantic Ocean
Habitat: coastal waters, coral reefs

Blackspot seabream
Pagellus bogaraveo

This fish has a reddish flush and a dark spot above its pectoral fin. The young are paler in colour and may not have a dark spot. They swim in large shoals in shallow waters, feeding on crustaceans. Adults live in smaller groups in deeper waters and eat fish as well as crustaceans.

Yellowtail snapper
Ocyurus chrysurus

Snappers are common around coral reefs and are a popular fish for humans to eat. This species is easily recognised by its bright yellow tail and the yellow stripe along each side. It feeds mostly on other fish and small crustaceans.

Perch-like fish

Queen angelfish
Holacanthus ciliaris

Size: up to 45 cm (17¾ in)
Range: western Atlantic Ocean and Caribbean Sea
Habitat: coral reefs

This colourful angelfish has long fins on its back and belly that extend past the tail fin. It feeds on sponges and other invertebrate animals. Young queen angelfish may act as cleaners – they pick and eat parasites off other fish.

Rock goby
Gobius paganellus

There are more than 1,800 kinds of goby, mostly in the sea. The rock goby is one of the larger gobies but typical of the group with its big blunt head and rounded tail. It uses its pelvic fins to cling to rocks. It feeds on small invertebrates and fish.

Size: up to 12 cm (4¾ in)
Range: North Atlantic Ocean and Mediterranean Sea
Habitat: coastal waters

Size: up to 90 cm (35½ in)
Range: northern and western Australia and islands
Habitat: coastal waters, coral reefs

Sweetlip emperor
Lethrinus miniatus

This heavy-bodied fish is one of the many that hunt for their food around coral reefs. It has a rather large head for its body, a long snout and no scales on its cheeks. It has deep red fins, dark barring on its sides and red patches around the eyes. It can grow to more than 9 kg (20 lb) and is an extremely popular food fish.

Dragonet
Callionymus lyra

The male dragonet has long, blue and yellow fins. Females are smaller and do not have extended fins. Dragonets lie half-buried in the sand on the seabed, watching for bottom-dwelling crustaceans and worms – their main food. They breed in spring or summer and males perform displays with their decorative fins to win females.

Size: up to 20 cm (7¾ in)
Range: Indian and Pacific oceans
Habitat: coral reefs, coastal waters

Size: up to 30 cm (11¾ in)
Range: east Atlantic Ocean and Mediterranean Sea
Habitat: coastal waters, oceanic

Copperband butterflyfish
Chelmon rostratus

This fish uses its long beak-like snout to reach into crevices in the coral and find small creatures to eat. The large "eyespot" near its tail fin may confuse predators into thinking the copperband is larger than it really is.

Black drum
Pogonias cromis

This large fish can weigh as much as 51 kg (112 lb). A bottom-feeder, it eats molluscs and crustaceans, which it crushes with the special flat teeth in its throat. Oysters are a favourite food and black drums can cause a great deal of damage to commercial oyster beds.

Size: 1.2–1.8 m (4–6 ft)
Range: western Atlantic Ocean
Habitat: coastal waters

Atlantic spadefish
Chaetodipterus faber

This fish has a deep, flattened body and long dorsal and anal fins. The young are black, becoming silvery grey as they grow, with dark vertical bars that become less clear in large adults. Spadefish feed mostly on small invertebrates.

Size: 46–90 cm (18–35½ in)
Range: western Atlantic Ocean
Habitat: coastal waters

Size: 25 cm (10 in)
Range: western Atlantic Ocean and Caribbean Sea
Habitat: coastal waters, coral reefs

Blue tang
Acanthurus coeruleus

This fish has extremely sharp, movable spines on each side of its tail, which it can raise to wound an enemy. The young are bright yellow with blue markings, as shown above. This colour changes as the fish matures, becoming blue all over by the time it is an adult.

Northern clingfish
Gobiesox maeandricus

This common fish has a smooth body and a broad head. Its dorsal and anal fins are set back near its tail. Like all clingfish, its pelvic fins form part of a sucking disc on its belly. It uses this to cling to rocks to avoid being washed away by strong tides in the coastal waters where it lives. Molluscs and crustaceans are its main foods.

Size: 21 cm (8 in)
Range: Indian and Pacific oceans
Habitat: coastal waters, coral reefs

Moorish idol
Zanclus cornutus

This relative of the blue tang has bold stripes, a protruding snout and long swept-back fins. It lacks tail spines, but the young have a sharp spine at each corner of the mouth, which drop off as the fish grow bigger.

Size: up to 16 cm (6½ in)
Range: eastern Pacific Ocean
Habitat: coastal waters

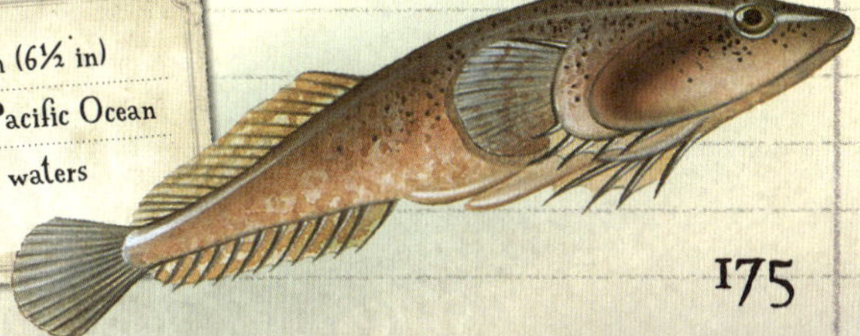

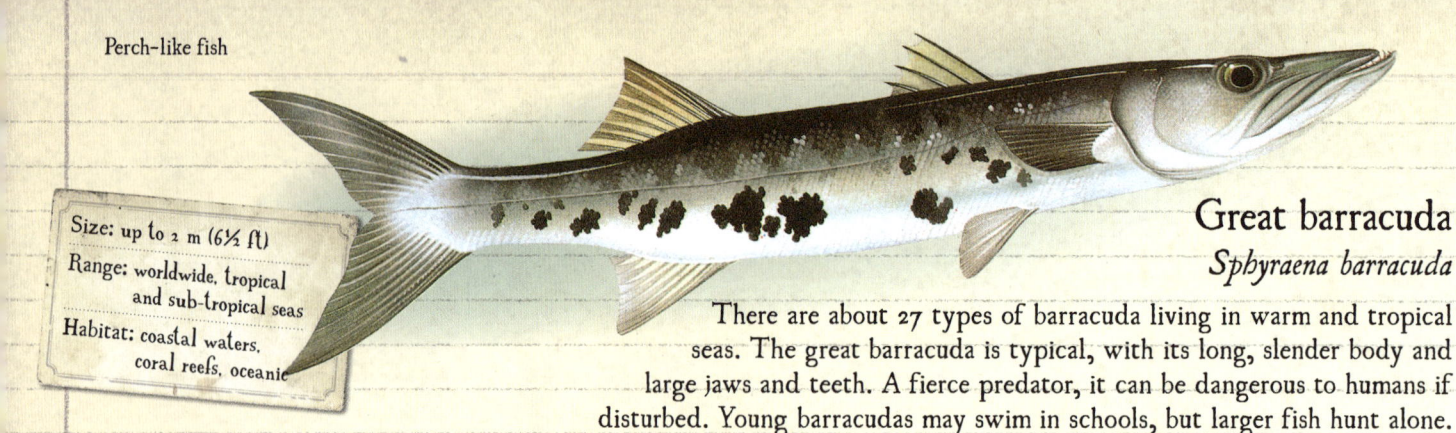

Perch-like fish

Great barracuda
Sphyraena barracuda

Size: up to 2 m (6½ ft)
Range: worldwide, tropical and sub-tropical seas
Habitat: coastal waters, coral reefs, oceanic

There are about 27 types of barracuda living in warm and tropical seas. The great barracuda is typical, with its long, slender body and large jaws and teeth. A fierce predator, it can be dangerous to humans if disturbed. Young barracudas may swim in schools, but larger fish hunt alone.

Northern stargazer
Astroscopus guttatus

Size: up to 59 cm (23½ in)
Range: Atlantic coast of North America
Habitat: coastal waters

The northern stargazer has a large head with its mouth pointing upwards and eyes on top of its head, also facing upwards. This allows the stargazer to lie partly buried on the seabed, with only its eyes and mouth uncovered, watching for prey such as fish and crustaceans.

Siamese fightingfish
Betta splendens

Size: up to 6 cm (2¼ in)
Range: Cambodia, Laos, Thailand, Vietnam
Habitat: fresh water

Male Siamese fightingfish are bred in captivity to take part in staged fights, but wild males battle with rivals over territory. In the breeding season, the male blows a bubble nest from air and mucus. When the female lays her eggs, the male fertilises them and spits them into the nest to keep them safe.

Striped snakehead
Channa striata

Size: up to 1 m (3¼ ft)
Range: India, China, and Southeast Asia
Habitat: fresh water

This long-bodied fish belongs to a small group of freshwater fish that live in tropical Africa and Asia. Usually found in oxygen-poor waters, it has special structures in its gills that help it take oxygen from the air. It can even survive out of water if it burrows into mud to keep its skin moist.

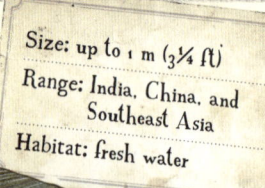

Man-of-war fish
Nomeus gronovii

Size: up to 39 cm (15½ in)
Range: tropical and temperate waters
Habitat: oceanic, coastal waters

Named for its habit of living among the trailing tentacles of the Portuguese man-of-war, this little fish does not seem to be affected by the jellyfish's stinging cells. It may even prevent them working and remove parasites and other debris from its host's body.

Redlip blenny
Ophioblennius macclurei

This fish is identified by the bristles on its rounded snout as well as its red lips and red-tipped fin. It lives on rocky- or coral-bottomed seabeds, where it searches for small invertebrates to eat. The female lays her eggs among coral or under rocks and the male guards them until they hatch.

Size: up to 12 cm (4¾ in).
Range: western Atlantic Ocean, Gulf of Mexico and Caribbean Sea
Habitat: coastal waters, coral reefs

Atlantic mackerel
Scomber scombrus

In spring and summer, large schools of mackerel go north to breed; in winter they return south. A female may produce as many as 450,000 eggs, which float until they hatch about four days later. Adult mackerel eat small fish and crustaceans, while young fish feed mainly on plankton and fish larvae.

Size: 41–66 cm (16–26 in)
Range: Atlantic Ocean and Mediterranean Sea
Habitat: coastal waters, oceanic

Children's Animal Encyclopedia

Size: up to 5 m (16½ ft)
Range: Atlantic Ocean tropical and temperate waters
Habitat: oceanic

Blue marlin
Makaira nigricans

One of the fastest of all fish, the blue marlin has the streamlined body and crescent-shaped tail typical of high-speed swimmers. It weighs at least 180 kg (400 lb) and has a long beak-like nose, which it may use to stun its prey such as smaller schooling fish and squid.

Size: up to 4.6 m (15 ft)
Range: worldwide, warm and tropical seas
Habitat: oceanic, coastal waters

Indo-pacific sailfish
Istiophorus platypterus

This fast-swimming fish has a tall, sail-like fin on its back and long pointed jaws. It is a fierce predator and eats almost any fish it can find, as well as squid. Sailfish breed in open sea. The female sheds several million eggs, which float in surface waters until they hatch.

Swordfish
Xiphias gladius

The huge, spectacular swordfish is a fast, active hunter with a streamlined body and a sickle-shaped fin on its back. It feeds on small fish as well as squid, and it may use its extremely long snout to strike at schooling fish. Young swordfish do not have a long snout; it develops as they grow.

Size: up to 3.6 m (12 ft)
Range: worldwide, warm and tropical waters
Habitat: oceanic, coastal waters

Tuna

TUNA

Among the fastest of all fish, tuna are shaped for speed and can swim at 70 km/h (44 mph). They are among the most streamlined fish, with a pointed head and a torpedo-shaped body tapering to a narrow tail stalk and a crescent tail. The 14 species of tuna usually live near the surface waters of warm and tropical oceans. All are hunters, feeding mainly on fish and squid. Many swim in large schools, but the biggest fish swim in smaller groups or alone. Fish obtain oxygen from water, not air; the oxygen is taken out of the water flowing past the gills. Most fish pump water over the gills by muscle action – but not tuna. Instead, tuna must keep swimming at all times, with their mouths open, to create a constant flow of water over the gills. The faster they swim, the more water passes over the gills and the more oxygen can be absorbed.

Albacore
Thunnus alalunga

Skipjack
Katsuwonus pelamis

Bluefin
Thunnus thynnus

Bigeye
Thunnus obesus

TYPES OF TUNA

The bluefin is the biggest tuna. It can grow up to 4.5 m (14¾ ft) long and weigh more than 685 kg (1,500 lb) – as much as nine people. A fast swimmer, it has been known to cross the Atlantic in 60 days. The bigeye grows to nearly 2.4 m (7¾ ft) long and can weigh more than 180 kg (400 lb). The albacore and skipjack are smaller – up to 1.5 m (5 ft) and 1.1 m (3½ ft) respectively. The skipjack gets its name from its habit of "skipping" over the surface of the water as it chases its prey.

178

Children's Animal Encyclopedia

YELLOWFIN

This tuna swims in schools that often attack mackerel. It has long pectoral fins and yellow finlets as well as yellow markings on its sides. The yellowfin lives in the Atlantic, Indian and Pacific oceans. It grows to about 1.5 m (5 ft) long and weighs up to 200 kg (440 lb).

Yellowfin tuna (*Thunnus albacares*) are the most valuable of all the tuna as food fish. Fishermen pursue schools of these tuna all over the world and catch large numbers.

179

FLYINGFISH, LANTERNFISH AND LIZARDFISH

The flyingfish belongs to a large group of mostly sea-living fish, which also includes halfbeaks, needlefish, sauries and garfish. Most are active near or at the surface of the water, and flyingfish can actually lift themselves into the air with their pectoral fins and use their rapidly beating tails to help them glide short distances. Lanternfish are deep-sea fish and are found in all oceans. They have light-producing organs on the body. The lizardfish and its relative, the bummalow, both live in shallow coastal waters, where they prey on small fish.

Wrestling halfbeak
Dermogenys pusilla

Size: up to 7 cm (2¾ in)
Range: Southeast Asia: from India to Malaysia and the Philippines
Habitat: fresh water

This small, slender fish feeds on mosquito larvae and so helps to control these pests. Male fish are aggressive and fight one another by wrestling with their long jaws.

Tropical two-wing flyingfish
Exocoetus volitans

Size: up to 30 cm (11¾ in)
Range: worldwide, tropical and sub-tropical seas
Habitat: coastal waters, oceanic

The flyingfish escapes its enemies by leaping up and gliding over the surface of the water with the aid of its wing-like fins. It can glide 90 m (300 ft), up to 1.5 m (5 ft) above the surface.

Garfish
Belone belone

The slender garfish has long jaws, studded with many needle-like teeth. An active hunter, the garfish eats small fish and crustaceans. It breeds in coastal waters and its small, round eggs attach themselves to floating debris or seaweed.

Size: up to 94 cm (37 in)
Range: North Atlantic Ocean; Mediterranean and Black seas
Habitat: coastal waters, oceanic

Atlantic saury
Scomberesox saurus saurus

Size: 32 cm (13 in)
Range: Arctic and Atlantic oceans, Mediterranean Sea
Habitat: oceanic

The saury swims in shoals in surface waters, feeding on small fish and crustaceans. It has beaklike jaws, the lower longer than the upper. Young fish hatch with short jaws of equal length; the long lower jaw develops as they grow.

Children's Animal Encyclopedia

Spotted lanternfish
Myctophum punctatum

This fish has groups of light-producing organs on its body. The light organs may help the fish to light up the dark depths of the sea to find prey or they may be used to confuse its own enemies. Lanternfish feed on animal plankton.

Size: up to 32 cm (12½ in)
Range: warm waters of the Atlantic Ocean
Habitat: coastal waters, coral reefs

Diamond lizardfish
Synodus synodus

The lizardfish has unusually long pelvic fins and often lies on the seabed, supporting its body on these fins. A fierce hunter, it lies in wait for prey, then suddenly darts up from the seabed and catches the victim in its long sharp teeth.

Size: up to 10 cm (4 in)
Range: North Atlantic Ocean, Mediterranean Sea
Habitat: deep sea, oceanic

Bummalow
Harpadon nehereus

The bummalow has a long body and huge jaws, armed with sharp curving teeth. It is often found near the mouths of large rivers, where it eats small fish and crustaceans. This fish is split and dried in the sun for eating. In this form it is known as Bombay duck.

Size: up to 41 cm (16¼ in)
Range: Indian and western Pacific oceans
Habitat: coastal waters, deep sea

Needlefish
Belonian apodion

This tiny freshwater fish has an extremely slender body, with small fins near its tail. It has a long lower jaw that it uses to scoop up animal plankton.

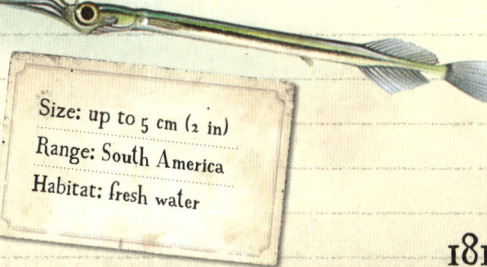

Size: 35 cm (14 in)
Range: warm waters of the Atlantic Ocean
Habitat: coastal waters

Ballyhoo
Hemiramphus brasiliensis

This fish cannot leap above the water like its relative the flyingfish, but it can skim over the surface. It moves in schools, feeding on sea grass and small fish, and it may use its long lower jaw to scoop up food from the water surface.

Size: up to 5 cm (2 in)
Range: South America
Habitat: fresh water

GUPPIES, GRUNIONS AND RELATIVES

Guppies belong to a group of freshwater fish that contains more than 1,250 species, including lyretails, mummichogs, sheepshead minnows and the four-eyed fish. Most are surface swimmers, feeding on insects and plant matter that has fallen on to the water, and are able to survive in slow-moving or even stagnant water. Grunions belong to a group of about 341 species that includes silversides, sand smelts and rainbow fish. Most feed on animal plankton and live in large shoals in lakes, estuaries and shallow coastal waters.

Size: 18 cm (7 in)
Range: eastern Pacific Ocean
Habitat: coastal waters

California grunion
Leuresthes tenuis

Grunions time their breeding with the tides. On a night of an extreme high, or spring, tide, they swim ashore, lay their eggs in the sand and swim back out to sea on next wave. Two weeks later, at the next spring tide, the eggs hatch and the young are carried out to sea.

Size: 9 cm (3½ in)
Range: Australia
Habitat: fresh water

Size: 7.5 cm (3 in)
Range: western Atlantic Ocean
Habitat: coastal waters

Hardhead silverside
Atherinomorus stipes

During the day the slender body of this little fish looks almost transparent, with a narrow silvery stripe running down each side. When night falls, the colour darkens. Silversides are common fish and they swim in large schools. Their eggs have tiny threads which attach them to water plants while they develop.

Murray River rainbowfish
Melanotaenia fluviatilis

This colourful fish is one of about 59 types of rainbow fish found in Australia and New Guinea. In early summer it lays eggs, which become anchored to water plants by fine threads.

Size: 15–20 cm (6–7¾ in)
Range: eastern Atlantic Ocean, Mediteranean
Habitat: coastal waters

Sand smelt
Atherina presbyter

This small fish has a long slender body and two widely spaced fins on its back. It swims in schools and eats mainly animal plankton, but also tiny fish. Sand smelts are themselves eaten by larger fish and by seabirds such as terns.

Guppy
Poecilia reticulata

The guppy is an extremely common fish. It is popular with humans because it feeds on mosquito larvae and so helps to control this pest. It also eats other insect larvae, small crustaceans, and the eggs and young of other fish. Many colourful forms of the guppy are bred as aquarium fish.

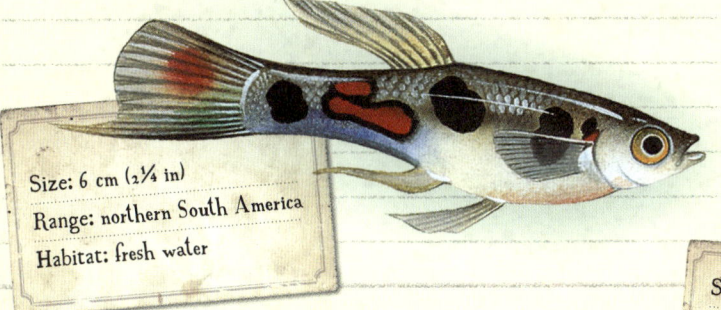

Size: 6 cm (2¼ in)
Range: northern South America
Habitat: fresh water

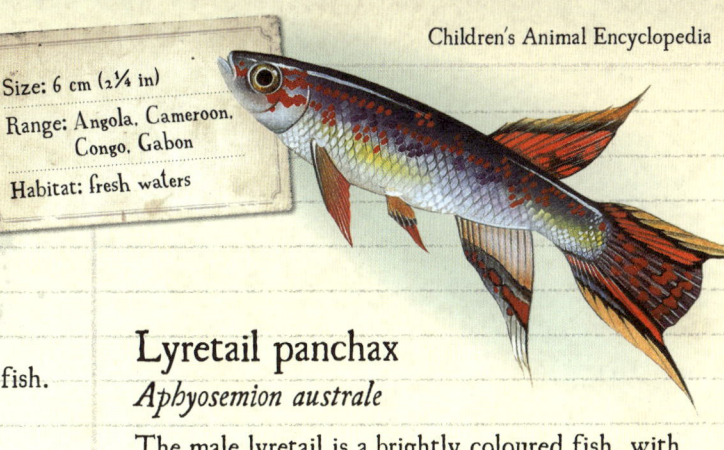

Lyretail panchax
Aphyosemion australe

Size: 6 cm (2¼ in)
Range: Angola, Cameroon, Congo, Gabon
Habitat: fresh waters

The male lyretail is a brightly coloured fish, with large pointed fins. The female is plainer, with smaller fins. The lyretail lays its eggs among mud. If there is then a long dry season, the eggs stop developing until the rains return. The embryos then start to grow again and hatch shortly afterwards.

Sheepshead minnow
Cyprinodon variegatus variegatus

Outside the breeding season, male and female sheepshead minnows look similar, but breeding males develop brighter coloration. The female lays her eggs a few at a time and the male fertilises them as they are shed. The eggs have sticky threads on the surface, which attach them to each other and to plants.

Size: up to 9 cm (3½ in)
Range: east coast of North and South America
Habitat: coastal waters

Mummichog
Fundulus heteroclitus heteroclitus

The mummichog is a hardy little stout-bodied fish that can survive in salt or fresh water and eats almost any plants and animals it can find. It breeds in spring, in shallow water. The male clasps the female with his fins so he can fertilise the eggs as they are laid. The eggs stick together and sink to the bottom in a cluster.

Size: 10–15 cm (4–6 in)
Range: east coast of North America
Habitat: fresh water, coastal waters

Four-eyed fish
Anableps anableps

This unusual fish has, in fact, only two eyes that are divided into two parts. The top part of each eye is for seeing in the air and the lower part is for seeing in water. The two parts are separated by a dark band. The fish swims at the surface, the water reaching the dividing bands on the eyes. It is able to watch for insect prey in the air or other prey in the water at the same time.

Size: 30 cm (11¾ in)
Range: northern South America
Habitat: fresh water, coastal waters

Oarfish, squirrelfish and relatives

OARFISH, SQUIRRELFISH AND RELATIVES

All of these fish live in the sea. The pinecone fish, squirrelfish, roughie and beardfish all belong to a group of about 163 species of deep-bodied fish with spiny fins. The John Dory belongs to a separate group of deep-bodied fish, many of which live in deep sea. The whalefish is also a deep-sea species. Although their body shapes appear to be very different, the oarfish and the opah both belong to a rare group of fish, about which little is known.

Size: 12.5 cm (5 in)
Range: Indian and Pacific oceans
Habitat: oceanic, coastal waters

Pinecone fish
Monocentris japonica

The body of the pinecone fish is protected by an armour of heavy, plate-like scutes, or scales. It has a dorsal fin made up of thick spines, more spines on in its belly and two light-producing organs under the lower jaw. Pinecone fish swim in schools near the bottom of the sea.

Size: up to 11 m (36 ft)
Range: worldwide, especially in cool waters
Habitat: oceanic

Oarfish
Regalecus glesne

This unusual fish has a long, ribbonlike body, with a dorsal fin running along most of its length. It swims with rippling, snake-like movements and is thought to have been the cause of many tales about giant sea serpents. The oarfish has no teeth in its small mouth and feeds mainly on small shrimp-like crustaceans.

Size: 30 cm (11¾ in)
Range: Atlantic Ocean
Habitat: deep sea

Stout beardfish
Polymixia nobilis

This fish gets its name from the pair of whiskers, or barbels, that hang from its lower jaw. These may help it find food on the seabed. It usually lives at depths of about 100 to 770 m (330 to 2,500 ft).

Size: 1.2 m (5 ft)
Range: worldwide, except the Southern Ocean
Habitat: oceanic

Opah
Lampris guttatus

Despite its almost comical appearance, this fish is a successful hunter, feeding on squid and fish such as hake and whiting. It has a large, rounded body, dotted with white spots, and bright red fins. It may weigh as much as 73 kg (161 lb).

John Dory
Zeus faber

The John Dory has 9 or 11 thick spines in the front part of its dorsal fin and four on the belly in front of its anal fin. Not a fast swimmer, it slowly approaches its prey – mostly crustaceans and small fish – until near enough to snap them up in its huge mouth.

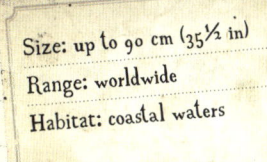

Size: 30 cm (11¾ in)
Range: Atlantic, Indian and Pacific oceans
Habitat: deep sea

Orange roughy
Hoplostethus atlanticus

The brightly coloured roughy has a large head and a deep body. It has sharp spines on its back in front of its dorsal fin and on its belly. Its mouth is large and upturned, its jaws are lined with lots of tiny teeth and it feeds on small crustaceans.

Size: up to 90 cm (35½ in)
Range: worldwide
Habitat: coastal waters

Whalefish
Cetichthys indagator

The whalefish belongs to a small group of deep-sea fish. It has a big head for its size and no scales on its body. The area at the base of the dorsal and anal fins is thought to glow in the dark. It hunts for its food and seizes prey in its large jaws lined with many tiny teeth.

Size: 61 cm (24 in)
Range: Atlantic Ocean
Habitat: coastal waters, coral reefs

Squirrelfish
Holocentrus adscensionis

This brightly coloured fish is common on coral reefs. Hiding in crevices by day, it comes out at night to hunt for small crustaceans and other prey. Its large eyes help it to see well in the dark, and it can make a range of sounds by vibrating its swim bladder (a gas-filled sac inside the body) with special muscles.

Size: up to 12 cm (4¾ in)
Range: Atlantic, Pacific and Indian oceans
Habitat: deep sea

SEAHORSES, STONEFISH AND RELATIVES

Seahorses and sticklebacks belong to a group of about 323 fish, which also includes tubesnouts and pipefish. Sticklebacks have between 3 and 16 spines on their backs and are found in the sea and in fresh water. Seahorses, with their horse-like heads, all live in the sea. The stonefish, lionfish, northern searobin and sculpin all belong to the scorpionfish group. This includes more than 1,300 species, most of which live in the sea. Many of these fish are chunky and spiny. The flying gurnard belongs to a small group of only seven species of marine fish. Despite their name, these fish have never been seen flying above the surface of the water.

Size: 38 cm (15 in)
Range: Indian and Pacific oceans
Habitat: coastal waters, coral reefs

Lionfish
Pterois volitans

With its brightly striped body and large fan-like fins, this fish is one of the most extraordinary in the sea. The spines on its back are poisonous and can be dangerous even for humans. The fish uses its spines to defend itself against its enemies, not to attack prey.

Size: 27 cm (10½ in)
Range: Indian and Pacific oceans
Habitat: coastal waters, coral reefs

Stonefish
Synanceia verrucosa

The stonefish's mottled coloration and irregular shape keep it well hidden as it lies half-buried among stones on the seabed. The sharp spines on its back are linked to glands containing a deadly poison. It can even kill any human unlucky enough to tread on a stonefish's spines.

Size: 25–60 cm (9¾–23½ in)
Range: Arctic and North Atlantic oceans
Habitat: coastal waters

Shorthorn sculpin
Myoxocephalus scorpius

This fish has spines on its head, near its gills and along each side. Females are usually larger than males. A bottom-dweller, the shorthorn sculpin has mottled colouring that blends well with the seabed. It eats seabed crustaceans, worms and small fish.

Children's Animal Encyclopedia

Size: 46 cm (18 in)
Range: coasts of southern Australia
Habitat: coastal waters, coral reefs

Size: up to 50 cm (19¾ in)
Range: Atlantic Ocean and Mediterranean Sea
Habitat: coastal waters, coral reefs

Weedy seadragon
Phyllopteryx taeniolatus

The many leaf-like flaps of skin on the body of this strange little seahorse are thought to help it hide from its enemies among fronds of seaweed. The male incubates his mate's eggs on a flap of skin beneath his tail.

Flying gurnard
Dactylopterus volitans

A bottom-dwelling fish, the flying gurnard uses its long, wing-like pelvic fins to "walk" over the seabed as it searches for crustaceans to eat. If alarmed, the gurnard spreads its fins wide, showing their blue spots.

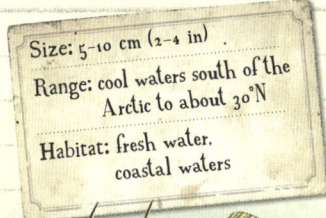

Size: 5–10 cm (2–4 in)
Range: cool waters south of the Arctic to about 30°N
Habitat: fresh water, coastal waters

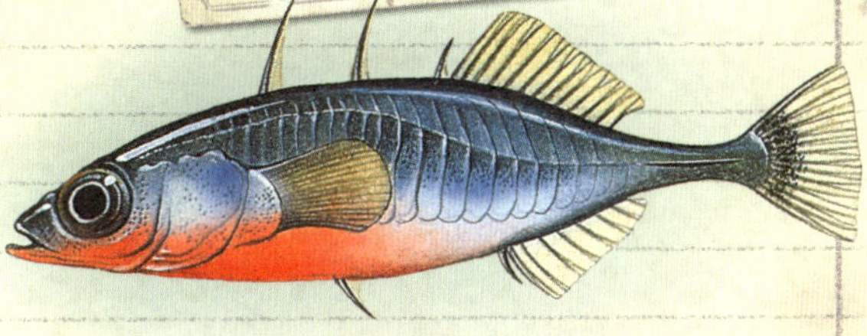

Size: 4 cm (1½ in)
Range: western Atlantic Ocean and Caribbean Sea
Habitat: coastal waters

Dwarf seahorse
Hippocampus zosterae

This unusual fish moves slowly, gently pushing itself along with movements of its tiny dorsal fin. It can also attach itself to seaweed with its curling tail. In the breeding season, the female lays 50 or more eggs, which she places in a pouch on the male's body where they incubate.

Three-spined stickleback
Gasterosteus aculeatus

In the breeding season, the male stickleback develops a bright red belly. He make a nest from tiny bits of plants, glued together with mucus. He then displays to attract females to his nest, where they lay their eggs. He fertilises the eggs and guards them carefully until they hatch about three weeks later.

Size: 30 cm (11¾ in)
Range: western Atlantic Ocean
Habitat: coastal waters

Northern searobin
Prionotus carolinus

A relative of the lionfish, the northern sea robin spends much of its life on the seabed, often supporting itself on its pectoral fins. It uses the first three rays of its pectoral fins to feel for prey on the seabed. If in danger, the sea robin buries itself in sand, leaving only the top of its head and eyes showing.

Flatfish

FLATFISH

The flatfish belong to a group of about 777 species. All but three of these live in the sea. Young flatfish have normal bodies at first, but as they grow, their bodies flatten and the eye on one side moves so that both eyes are on the upper surface. A typical flatfish spends much of its life on the seabed, lying with the eyed side facing up. Some flatfish have both eyes on the right side and lie on the left; others have both eyes on the left side and lie on the right.

Size: up to 64 cm (25 in)
Range: Red Sea, Indian Ocean, western Pacific Ocean
Habitat: coastal waters

Adalah
Psettodes erumei

The adalah is less dramatically flattened than most other flatfish. Some have both eyes on the left side, others on the right, but one eye is on the edge of the head. Like other flatfish, the adalah spends much of its life on the seabed, but it also swims in midwaters looking for fish and other creatures to eat.

Size: 1 m (3¼ ft)
Range: eastern Atlantic Ocean and Mediterranean and Baltic seas
Habitat: coastal waters

Turbot
Scophthalmus maximus

This extremely broad-bodied flatfish varies in colour, but usually has speckled markings that help to camouflage it on the seabed. A food fish, the adult turbot preys mostly on fish, but young turbots eat small crustaceans. Turbot breed in spring or summer and females produce as many as 10 million eggs.

Summer flounder
Paralichthys dentatus

A slender active fish, the summer flounder feeds on crustaceans, molluscs and fish and will chase prey up into surface waters if necessary. But although a fast swimmer, it spends much of its time lying half-buried on the seabed. Its colour varies according to the type of seabed it is on, but is usually greyish brown with dark spots.

Size: up to 1 m (3¼ ft)
Range: western Atlantic Ocean
Habitat: coastal waters

Children's Animal Encyclopedia

Size: 1.5 m (5 ft)
Range: eastern Pacific Ocean
Habitat: coastal waters

European plaice
Pleuronectes platessa

The topside of this important food fish is brown, dotted with orange spots. Both eyes are usually on the top, right side of the body. Plaice breed in early spring and the larvae live in surface waters for up to six weeks before settling on the seabed.

Size: 40 cm (15¾ in)
Range: North Atlantic Ocean
Habitat: coastal waters

California flounder
Paralichthys californicus

This flounder has a large mouth and strong sharp teeth. It feeds on fish, particularly anchovies, and is itself eaten by creatures such as rays, sea lions and porpoises. It is also an important food fish for humans. A large individual can weigh up to 32 kg (70 lb).

Size: 30–70 cm (11¾–27½ in)
Range: eastern Atlantic Ocean and Mediterranean Sea
Habitat: coastal waters

Sole
Solea solea

A food fish, the common or Dover sole usually feeds at night and spends the day buried in sand or mud. It breeds in shallow water and its eggs float at the surface. The larvae move to the seabed when they are about 1.25 cm (½ in) long.

North American naked sole
Gymnachirus melas

With no scales on its skin, the naked sole has dark stripes on its uppermost side and a whitish underside. Mostly both eyes are on the right side and the small mouth is also twisted to the right. This flatfish spends most of its life on the seabed, but it is an active hunter and can swim well when necessary.

Size: 20 cm (7¾ in)
Range: western Atlantic Ocean
Habitat: coastal waters

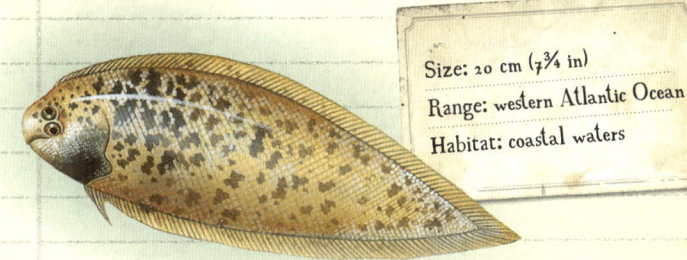

Blackcheek tonguefish
Symphurus plagusia

This flatfish's body tapers to a pointed tail, and its dorsal and anal fins join with the tail fin. Both its eyes are on the left side and its small mouth is twisted to the left. Like other flatfish, it lives on the seabed and feeds on small invertebrate animals such as worms and crustaceans.

Size: up to 23 cm (9 in)
Range: western Atlantic Ocean
Habitat: coastal waters

COELACANTH, LUNGFISH, TRIGGERFISH AND RELATIVES

The coelacanth is thought to resemble some of the earliest fish and is more closely related to amphibians than any other living fish. Common millions of years ago, only two species now survive. Lungfish are related to early air-breathing fish. They have lung-like breathing organs which they use to take breaths of air at the surface of the water. Triggerfish, pufferfish, boxfish and relatives belong to a group of about 340 species. Many of these have round or boxlike bodies, and most live in the sea.

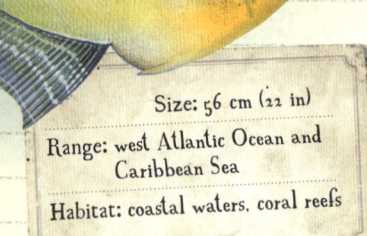

Size: 56 cm (22 in)
Range: west Atlantic Ocean and Caribbean Sea
Habitat: coastal waters, coral reefs

Queen triggerfish
Balistes vetula

On the triggerfish's back are three spines. When the first spine is upright, it is locked into place by the second. If in danger, the triggerfish can wedge itself into a crevice with this "locking" spine and is extremely hard to move. It feeds on small invertebrate creatures, particularly sea urchins.

Size: 2 m (6½ ft)
Range: African coast of Indian Ocean
Habitat: coastal waters

Coelacanth
Latimeria chalumnae

Coelacanths were thought to have been extinct for millions of years until one was caught off South Africa in 1938. This living species is very like its fossil relatives. It has a heavy body and fleshy sections at the base of all its fins except the first dorsal fin. It may hunt other fish to eat.

South American lungfish
Lepidosiren paradoxa

This lungfish lives in swamps that dry out for part of the year. During this time, it lives in a burrow that it digs in the mud and breathes air with the help of lung-like organs in its body. When the rains return, the fish comes out of its burrow.

Size: 1.25 m (4½ ft)
Range: central South America
Habitat: fresh water

Ocean sunfish
Mola mola

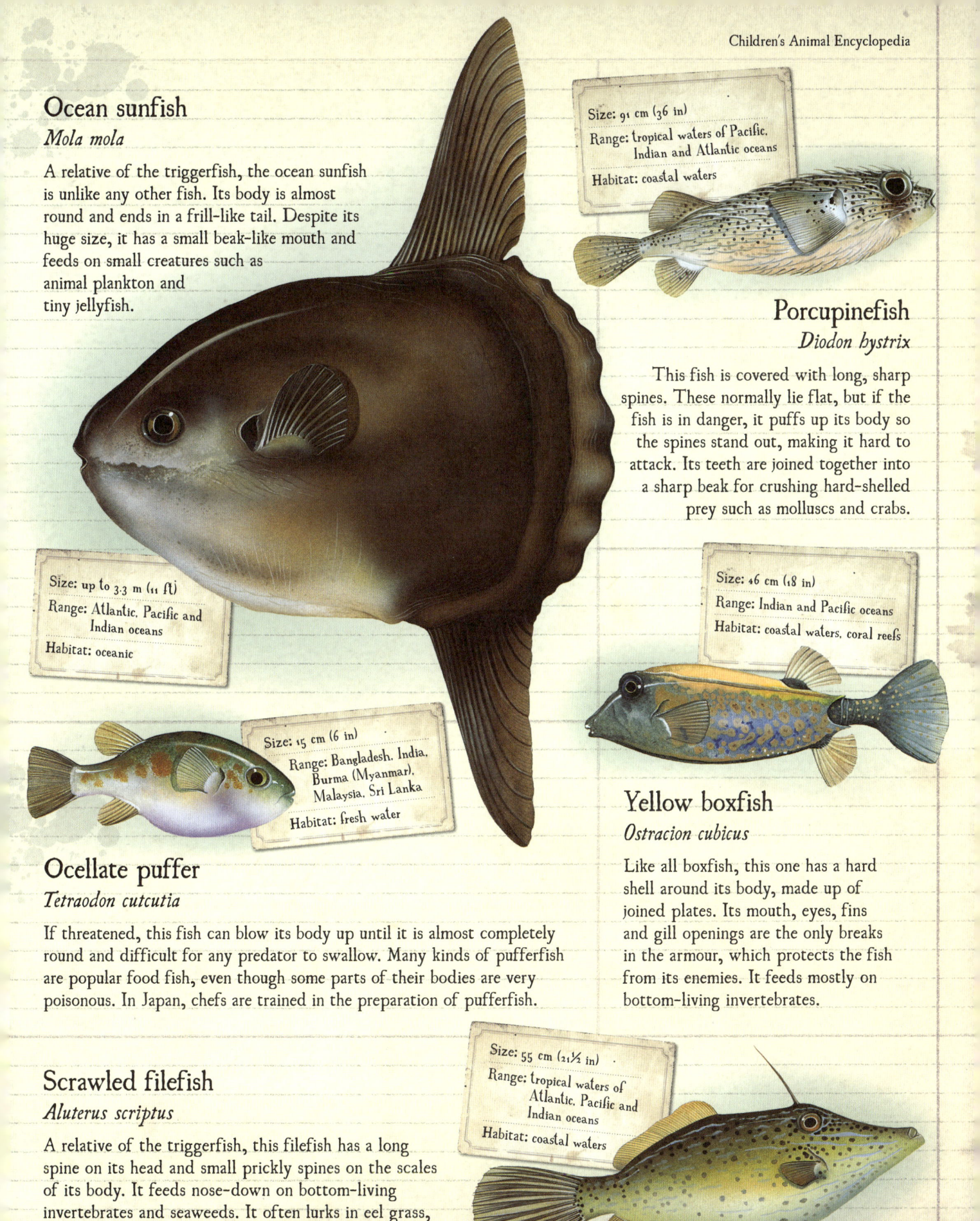

A relative of the triggerfish, the ocean sunfish is unlike any other fish. Its body is almost round and ends in a frill-like tail. Despite its huge size, it has a small beak-like mouth and feeds on small creatures such as animal plankton and tiny jellyfish.

Size: up to 3.3 m (11 ft)
Range: Atlantic, Pacific and Indian oceans
Habitat: oceanic

Size: 91 cm (36 in)
Range: tropical waters of Pacific, Indian and Atlantic oceans
Habitat: coastal waters

Porcupinefish
Diodon hystrix

This fish is covered with long, sharp spines. These normally lie flat, but if the fish is in danger, it puffs up its body so the spines stand out, making it hard to attack. Its teeth are joined together into a sharp beak for crushing hard-shelled prey such as molluscs and crabs.

Size: 46 cm (18 in)
Range: Indian and Pacific oceans
Habitat: coastal waters, coral reefs

Size: 15 cm (6 in)
Range: Bangladesh, India, Burma (Myanmar), Malaysia, Sri Lanka
Habitat: fresh water

Ocellate puffer
Tetraodon cutcutia

If threatened, this fish can blow its body up until it is almost completely round and difficult for any predator to swallow. Many kinds of pufferfish are popular food fish, even though some parts of their bodies are very poisonous. In Japan, chefs are trained in the preparation of pufferfish.

Yellow boxfish
Ostracion cubicus

Like all boxfish, this one has a hard shell around its body, made up of joined plates. Its mouth, eyes, fins and gill openings are the only breaks in the armour, which protects the fish from its enemies. It feeds mostly on bottom-living invertebrates.

Size: 55 cm (21½ in)
Range: tropical waters of Atlantic, Pacific and Indian oceans
Habitat: coastal waters

Scrawled filefish
Aluterus scriptus

A relative of the triggerfish, this filefish has a long spine on its head and small prickly spines on the scales of its body. It feeds nose-down on bottom-living invertebrates and seaweeds. It often lurks in eel grass, where its greenish coloration keeps it well hidden.

Children's Animal Encyclopedia

191

WHY DO SOME ANIMALS WORK TOGETHER?

When animals develop close links with creatures of another species both partners can benefit. The cleaner fish, for example, feeds on parasites and tiny scraps of food it finds on the bodies of larger fish. The cleaner fish gains a good meal and the host has its body cleared of debris and harmful parasites. Sometimes only one partner benefits. Cattle egrets follow large mammals such as elephants to feed on the insects disturbed as they pass. The egrets get plenty of food but there is no clear advantage to the elephant.

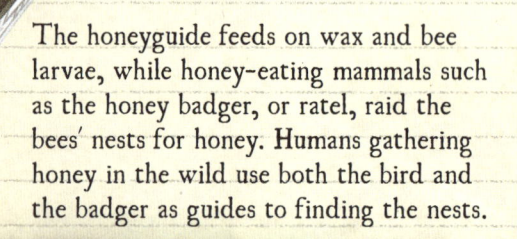

The honeyguide feeds on wax and bee larvae, while honey-eating mammals such as the honey badger, or ratel, raid the bees' nests for honey. Humans gathering honey in the wild use both the bird and the badger as guides to finding the nests.

Ant

Aphids

PROTECTION

Black ants protect groups of the tiny bugs called aphids from other insects. When an ant strokes an aphid's body with its antennae, the aphid produces a drop of a sugary substance called honeydew – delicious food for the ant.

The oxpecker provides a very useful service for this buffalo while getting a good meal for itself. The bird eats the ticks and other parasites that live on the buffalo's skin.

SAFETY

The clownfish finds safety from enemies among a sea anemone's stinging tentacles. Its own skin is immune to the sting. The clownfish may attract other fish near enough for the anemone to catch.

Children's Animal Encyclopedia

Insects, spiders and other invertebrates

INSECTS, SPIDERS AND OTHER INVERTEBRATES

Insects outnumber every other creature on Earth. There are almost two million known animal species in the world, and about half of those species are insects. Arachnids, like insects, are found all over the world in every kind of habitat. There are at least 103,000 species of arachnid, of which spiders are the biggest group. Other invertebrates include worms, snails, centipedes and millipedes on land and an amazing range of species at sea, including sponges, clams, mussels, jellyfish and crabs.

WHAT IS AN INVERTEBRATE?

An invertebrate is an animal without a backbone – creatures such as crabs, worms, insects and spiders are all invertebrates. There are invertebrates on land, in the sea and in fresh water, and many insects fly in the air. These animals have an extraordinary range of lifestyles and feeding habits.

ARTHROPODS

Arthropods are the largest group of invertebrates and some of the most successful creatures of all time. They include such creatures as insects, spiders and crabs. One of the reasons for their success is that they have a hard external skeleton, called an exoskeleton, which protects the soft body within.

A spider's body

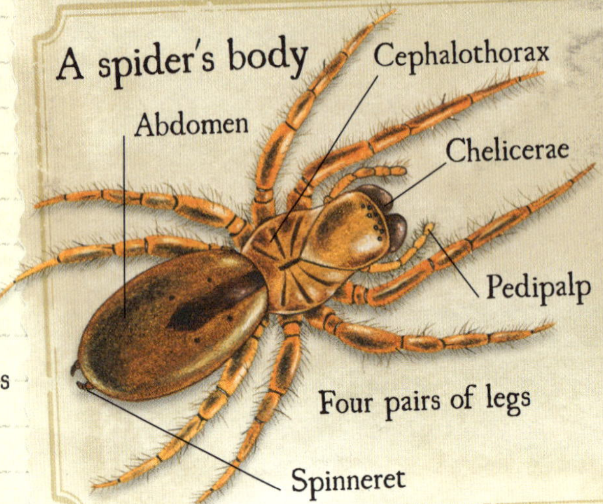

- Cephalothorax
- Abdomen
- Chelicerae
- Pedipalp
- Four pairs of legs
- Spinneret

The typical spider's body is divided into two parts. The head and thorax are joined to make one structure called the cephalothorax. This is linked to the abdomen by a narrow waist. At the front of the head are the spider's jaws, called chelicerae, and behind these is the mouth. Spiders have four pairs of segmented legs, and each leg is tipped with claws.

Spider

Centipede

Crustacean

Millipede

Insect

An insect's body

An insect is divided into three parts – head, thorax and abdomen. The head carries the eyes, a pair of sensory antennae, which the insect uses to find out about its surroundings, and the mouthparts. These vary in shape according to the insect's diet. On the thorax are three pairs of legs and usually two pairs of wings.

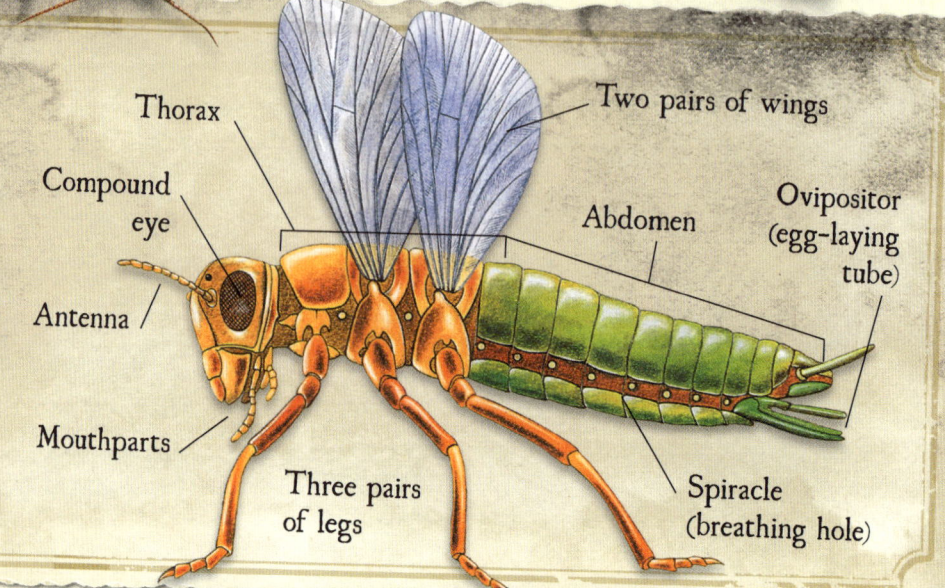

- Thorax
- Compound eye
- Antenna
- Mouthparts
- Three pairs of legs
- Two pairs of wings
- Abdomen
- Ovipositor (egg-laying tube)
- Spiracle (breathing hole)

196

OTHER INVERTEBRATE GROUPS

COMB JELLIES

Comb jellies have a simple bag-like body, with eight lines of tiny hairs that beat to move the comb jelly through the water.

Beroe comb jelly

ANNELID WORMS

There are about 21,000 species of these worms, in water and on land. Their bodies are divided into segments.

Medical leech

LAMP SHELLS

There are about 400 species in this group, also known as brachiopods. All lamp shells have an upper and a lower shell.

Lamp shell

MOLLUSCS

The three main groups of molluscs are the gastropods (creatures such as limpets); bivalves (clams, scallops and mussels); and cephalopods (squid, octopus and the nautilus).

Nautilus

ECHINODERMS

There are four main groups of echinoderms – brittle stars, starfish, sea cucumbers, and sea urchins and sand dollars. Most move around using tiny stilts called tube feet.

Flower urchin

CNIDARIANS

This group includes creatures such as sea anemones and corals. Most have tube-like bodies with a central mouth surrounded by tentacles.

Purple jellyfish

SPONGES

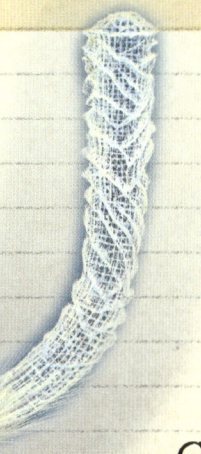

Sponges are the simplest many-celled animals. Their shapes vary from tiny cups, tube-like pipes and tall vases to rounded masses. Special filtering cells in their bodies trap food particles in the water.

Glass sponge

COCKROACHES, EARWIGS, CRICKETS, GRASSHOPPERS AND RELATIVES

While these insects are not closely related, they share certain features. They all have strong jaws for chewing, mobile heads, and most have large back wings. They also include some of the most ancient of all insect groups – cockroaches have been around for about 350 million years. Most of these creatures are familiar to humans, and some are even unwelcome guests in our homes.

COCKROACHES, EARWIGS AND BRISTLETAILS

Although most cockroaches live outdoors, in every kind of habitat from mountains to rainforest, they are best known as indoor pests. Earwigs, found in every garden, are also considered pests, since many feed on plants and flowers. Also common in houses, but less often seen, are the wingless insects known as silverfish or bristletails.

Family: Blattidae
Size: 1.9–5 cm (¾–2 in) long
Number of species: about 650
Habitat: worldwide

American cockroach

Common in buildings, these cockroaches hide by day and feed on anything they can find by night. The female lays her eggs in a case attached to her body, which she leaves in a dark safe place before the eggs hatch.

Family: Forficulidae
Size: 0.9–2.5 cm (⅜–1 in) long
Number of species: about 450
Habitat: worldwide

Common earwig

The female earwig lays her eggs in a burrow and stays close to look after them. Unusually for an insect, she tends her young until they are able to manage by themselves. The abdomen ends in a pair of pincers that is used to capture prey and defend against attack.

Children's Animal Encyclopedia

Family: Lepismatidae
Size: 0.8–1.9 cm (⅓–¾ in) long
Number of species: about 295
Habitat: worldwide

Family: Labiduridae
Size: 0.9–2.5 cm (⅜–1 in) long
Number of species: 75
Habitat: worldwide

Firebrat
The firebrat is a bristletail. It usually lives indoors near warm places such as ovens or boilers. A fast runner, it scurries around finding crumbs and scraps of food to eat.

Long-horned earwig
These insects are also known as striped earwigs because of the dark markings on the thorax and short front wings. Like all earwigs, the long-horned hides by day and comes out at night to hunt other insects. If attacked, it can squirt a bad-smelling liquid from special glands on the abdomen.

Silverfish
Fast-moving, silverfish usually shy away from the light and live in dark corners indoors, where they eat paper, glue and spilled foods. The long, tapering body is covered with tiny scales.

Family: Lepismatidae
Size: 0.8–1.9 cm (⅓–¾ in) long
Number of species: about 295
Habitat: worldwide

Madagascan hissing cockroach
Large and wingless, these cockroaches make a hissing sound through breathing holes in their abdomen to warn off any enemies. Males also make a softer hissing noise when courting females.

Family: Blattellidae
Size: 0.6–2.5 cm (¼–1 in) long
Number of species: about 2,240
Habitat: worldwide

Family: Blaberidae
Size: 5–7.5 cm (2–3 in) long
Number of species: about 1,200
Habitat: tropical

German cockroach
These cockroaches are found all over the world, usually indoors. They are fast runners and their flattened bodies are ideally shaped for squeezing into cracks and under floorboards.

199

CRICKETS, GRASSHOPPERS AND RELATIVES

More often heard than seen, grasshoppers are best known for their calls, usually made by the male rubbing together its wings or legs when courting females. There are two main families of grasshoppers: short-horned, such as locusts, and long-horned, such as katydids. Crickets are relatives of grasshoppers and also make chirping sounds. Stick and leaf insects are famous for their ability to hide themselves by looking like twigs or leaves.

Locust
Locusts are a type of grasshopper and are among the most damaging of all insects. Swarms of locusts swoop down on to crops and feed until there are scarcely any leaves left. A swarm may contain as many as 50 billion insects.

Family: Acrididae
Size: 1.2–7.5 cm (½–3 in) long
Number of species: about 10,500
Habitat: worldwide

Family: Acrididae
Size: 1.2–7.5 cm (½–3 in) long
Number of species: about 10,500
Habitat: worldwide

Long-horned grasshopper
As their name suggests, long-horned grasshoppers have long antennae. They feed on plants but also catch and eat small insects. Many are green or brown in colour and can be hard to spot in the trees and bushes where they live.

Family: Tettigoniidae
Size: 1.2–7.5 cm (½–3 in) long
Number of species: about 6,750
Habitat: worldwide

Short-horned grasshopper
Short-horned grasshoppers have short antennae. Like all grasshoppers, they have powerful back legs and can leap more than 200 times their own length.

Children's Animal Encyclopedia

Leaf insect

These extraordinary insects are shaped just like the leaves they live on, complete with veins. Even their eggs look like the plant's seeds. Leaf insects live in tropical parts of Asia and Australia.

Family: Phylliidae
Size: 5–10 cm (2–4 in) long
Number of species: about 30
Habitat: tropical

Family: Gryllidae
Size: up to 5 cm (2 in) long
Number of species: about 4,700
Habitat: tropical

True cricket

True crickets "sing" by rubbing together specially ridged and thickened areas of their front wings to make a high-pitched sound. They are usually coloured green, black or brown and have broad bodies and well-developed feelers at the end of the abdomen.

Mole cricket

Like tiny moles, these crickets live under the ground, where they burrow with their large, spadelike front legs. Fine hairs protects the body from soil. Plant roots are their main food and they often damage crops and trees. They also catch and eat worms and larvae.

Family: Gryllotalpidae
Size: 2–5 cm (¾–2 in) long
Number of species: about 105
Habitat: worldwide

Family: Phasmatidae
Size: up to 30 cm (11¾ in) long
Number of species: about 2,450
Habitat: worldwide

Stick insect

With its slender green or brown body, the stick insect looks so like a leafless twig that it is hard for hungry birds to see. During the day it clings to a plant, with only its long, thin legs swaying gently, as though blown by a breeze. At night the stick insect moves around, feeding on leaves.

Katydid

This insect has wings that look like leaves to help it hide among plants. The female katydid has a knife-like ovipositor, which is an egg-laying tube. She uses this to insert her eggs into slots that she cuts in the stems of plants.

Family: Tettigoniidae
Size: 1.2–7.5 cm (½–3 in) long
Number of species: about 6,750
Habitat: worldwide

Ovipositor

201

MANTIDS, DRAGONFLIES AND RELATIVES

These insects are some of the fiercest hunters in the insect world. Mantids are equipped with long front legs, which they extend at lightning speeds to grasp their prey. More energetic hunters are the dragonflies, some of the fastest-flying of all insects. They seize their prey in the air or pluck tiny creatures from leaves. Lacewings, antlions, snakeflies and mantidflies are known as nerve-winged insects. They have two pairs of delicate, veined wings that can be folded like an arch over the body. Their larvae feed on other small creatures, which they catch in their powerful jaws.

Flower mantis

Some mantids are coloured to match the flowers that they perch on. This helps them to stay hidden from both their victims and their enemies. Mantids usually prey on other insects but they can also catch frogs and small lizards.

Family: Hymenopodidae
Size: up to 13 cm (5 in) long
Number of species: 290
Habitat: tropical

Family: Mantidae
Size: 1.2–15 cm (½–6 in) long
Number of species: about 1,100
Habitat: worldwide

Angola mantis

This mantis is hard to see when it lies on a lichen-covered branch. It remains very still as it watches for food but can reach out to grab its prey in a fraction of a second. Mantid larvae hatch as tiny versions of their parents and start hunting for themselves right away.

Family: Mantidae
Size: 1.2–15 cm (½–6 in) long
Number of species: about 1,100
Habitat:

Praying mantis

When a mantid holds its front legs up together, it may look like it is at prayer, but these two powerful limbs are its hunting tools. They are lined with sharp spines, which help the insect hold on to its struggling prey as it feeds. Females are usually larger than males and sometimes attack or even eat males after mating.

Children's Animal Encyclopedia

Mantisfly

This relative of the lacewing looks like a small praying mantis and catches prey in the same way. Some mantisfly larvae burrow into the nests of wasps or bees and eat their larvae. Others feed on spider eggs.

Family: Mantispidae
Size: 0.3–2.5 cm (⅛–1 in) long
Number of species: about 415
Habitat: worldwide, in warm places

Family: Perlidae
Size: 0.9–4 cm (⅜–1½ in) long
Number of species: about 450
Habitat: worldwide

Common stonefly

Stonefly nymphs (young) live in streams, where they feed mostly on plants, although some hunt insects. They take in oxygen through their body surface, but gills also help them to breathe in water. The adults are poor fliers and spend much of the day resting on stones, with wings folded. They live only two or three weeks and most do not feed.

Family: Myrmeleontidae
Size: 0.9–5 cm (⅜–2 in) long
Number of species: about 3,350
Habitat: tropical and sub tropical

Family: Raphidiidae
Size: 0.6–2.5 cm (¼–1 in) long
Number of species: about 185
Habitat: temperate

Antlion

The adult antlion looks like a dragonfly but has longer antennae, with club-like tips. The name antlion comes from the larvae, which are fierce hunters with spiny jaws. The larva digs a pit in sandy soil. When an insect comes near, the antlion tosses soil at it until it falls into the pit.

Snakefly

The snakefly gets its name from the way it lifts its long neck as it searches for prey and then lunges forwards to grab its victim. Adults and larvae hunt insects such as aphids and caterpillars.

Green lacewing

Both adult lacewings and their larvae feed on small insects such as aphids. The larvae suck out the body juices of their prey with special mouthparts.

Family: Chrysopidae
Size: 0.9–1.9 cm (⅜–¾ in) long
Number of species: about 2,060
Habitat: worldwide

203

Mantids, dragonflies and relatives

Darner dragonfly

Darners are some of the largest and fastest of all dragonflies. When hunting, they zoom back and forth with legs held ready to seize prey. The male is very territorial – he has a particular area that he patrols and defends. Females are allowed to enter the territory, but other male darners are chased away.

Family: Aeshnidae
Size: 6–12 cm (2¼–4¾ in) long
Number of species: about 450
Habitat: worldwide

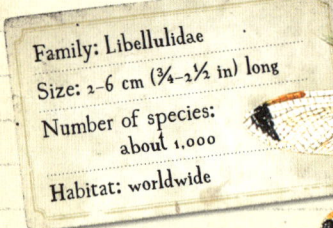

Family: Libellulidae
Size: 2–6 cm (¾–2½ in) long
Number of species: about 1,000
Habitat: worldwide

Darter

This type of dragonfly gets its name from its fast, darting flight. Like all dragonflies, darters lay their eggs in or close to water. The young are called nymphs or naiads. They look quite different from adults and live in water, catching prey such as tadpoles.

Skimmer

A skimmer is a kind of dragonfly with a wide, flattened body that is shorter than its wings. Some have a wingspan of up to 10 cm (4 in). Skimmers are usually seen flying near still or slow-moving water, such as ponds and swamps.

Family: Libellulidae
Size: 2–6 cm (¾–2½ in) long
Number of species: about 1,000
Habitat: worldwide

Family: Lestidae
Size: 3–5 cm (1¼–2 in) long
Number of species: about 150
Habitat: worldwide

Damselfly

These insects are sometimes known as spread-winged damselflies because they hold their wings partly spread out when at rest. They live around ponds and marshes, where they catch insects such as small flies.

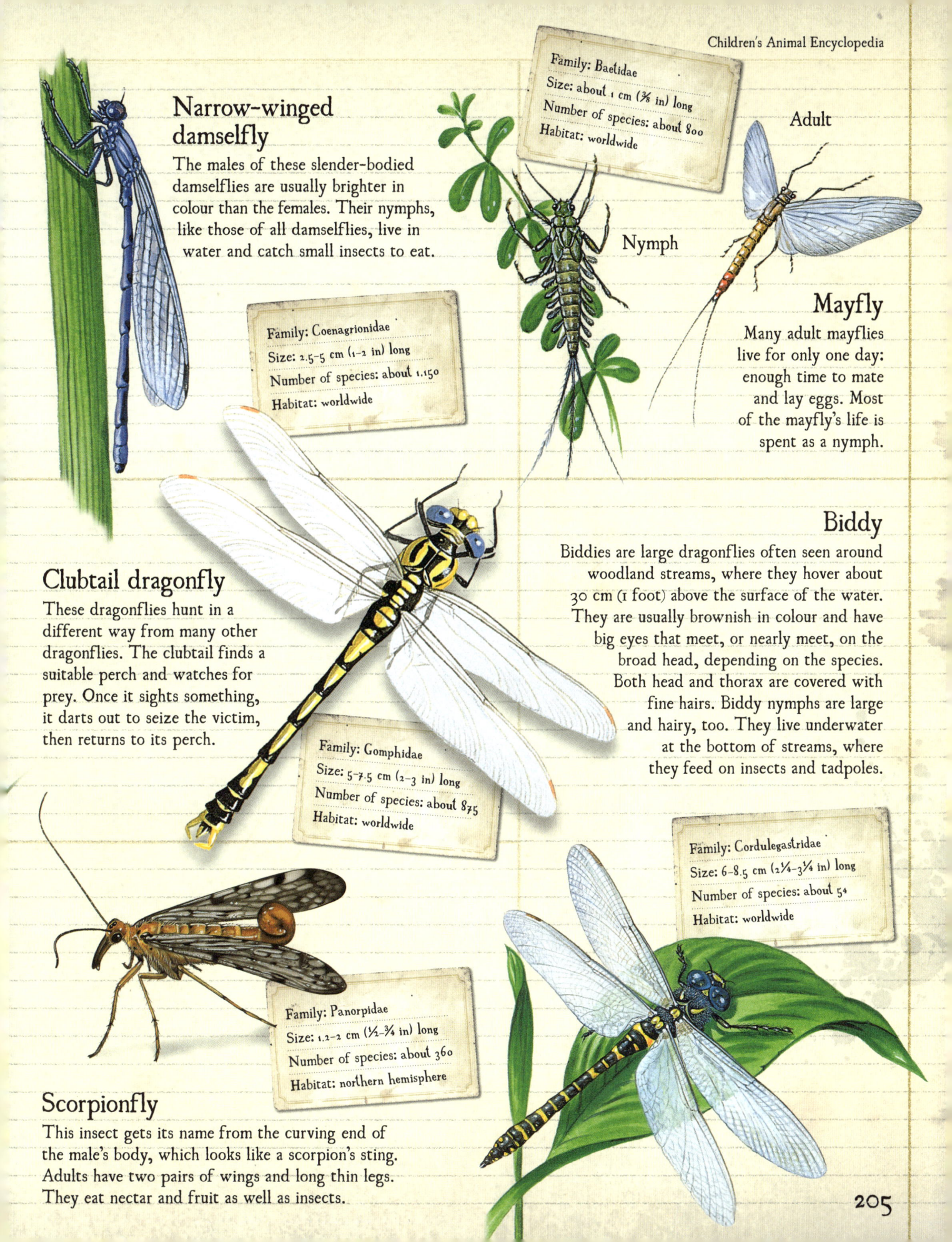

Narrow-winged damselfly

The males of these slender-bodied damselflies are usually brighter in colour than the females. Their nymphs, like those of all damselflies, live in water and catch small insects to eat.

Family: Coenagrionidae
Size: 2.5-5 cm (1-2 in) long
Number of species: about 1,150
Habitat: worldwide

Family: Baetidae
Size: about 1 cm (⅜ in) long
Number of species: about 800
Habitat: worldwide

Nymph

Adult

Mayfly

Many adult mayflies live for only one day: enough time to mate and lay eggs. Most of the mayfly's life is spent as a nymph.

Clubtail dragonfly

These dragonflies hunt in a different way from many other dragonflies. The clubtail finds a suitable perch and watches for prey. Once it sights something, it darts out to seize the victim, then returns to its perch.

Family: Gomphidae
Size: 5-7.5 cm (2-3 in) long
Number of species: about 875
Habitat: worldwide

Biddy

Biddies are large dragonflies often seen around woodland streams, where they hover about 30 cm (1 foot) above the surface of the water. They are usually brownish in colour and have big eyes that meet, or nearly meet, on the broad head, depending on the species. Both head and thorax are covered with fine hairs. Biddy nymphs are large and hairy, too. They live underwater at the bottom of streams, where they feed on insects and tadpoles.

Family: Cordulegastridae
Size: 6-8.5 cm (2¼-3¼ in) long
Number of species: about 54
Habitat: worldwide

Family: Panorpidae
Size: 1.2-2 cm (½-¾ in) long
Number of species: about 360
Habitat: northern hemisphere

Scorpionfly

This insect gets its name from the curving end of the male's body, which looks like a scorpion's sting. Adults have two pairs of wings and long thin legs. They eat nectar and fruit as well as insects.

BUGS, LICE, FLEAS AND BEETLES

These are some of the most numerous of all insects. Beetles form the largest group of insects and account for 40 per cent of known insect species. One of the reasons for their success is that they can adapt to almost any type of food. Bugs, too, eat a wide range of foods from plant juices to human blood. Lice and fleas live as parasites, feeding on the blood, skin, feathers or hair of other animals.

BUGS, LICE AND FLEAS

The name bug is used for insects generally, but it also describes a particular group of insects. These include a wide variety of aphids, cicadas and stinkbugs. All have special needlelike mouthparts for piercing food and sucking out the juices. Lice are small wingless insects which live on birds and mammals. There are two types: sucking lice and chewing lice. Fleas, too, are wingless. They have powerful legs to help them leap on to other animals to feed.

Family: Cicadidae
Size: up to 5 cm (2 in) long
Number of species: about 2,500
Habitat: worldwide

Adult

Cicada
This insect is best known for the shrill, almost constant call from the males. The sound is made by tymbals, a pair of structures located on the abdomen, which are vibrated by special muscles. Female cicadas usually lay their eggs in slits they make in tree branches. The nymphs live under the ground and feed on plant roots. As they grow, they moult – shedding the exoskeleton – until they finally make their way to the surface and emerge as adults.

Family: Membracidae
Size: 0.6–1.2 cm (¼–½ in) long
Number of species: about 2,500
Habitat: worldwide

Family: Pentatomidae
Size: 0.6–2 cm (¼–¾ in) long
Number of species: about 5,500
Habitat: worldwide

Stinkbug
Stinkbugs squirt a foul-smelling liquid at any creature that tries to attack them. The liquid comes from glands on the underside of the stinkbug's body. The bug uses its beak-like snout for piercing the surface of a plant or animal to get at the sap or body juices.

Treehopper
Many of these little bugs have strangely shaped extensions on the thorax, which makes them look like the sharp thorns of plants. They feed mostly on sap from trees and other plants.

Children's Animal Encyclopedia

Plant bug
The biggest group of true bugs, plant bugs live in every kind of habitat. Most feed on leaves, seeds and fruit and some are serious pests of food crops such as alfalfa. Other plant bugs are more welcome to farmers since they feed on insects such as aphids, which are also pests. Plant bugs have delicate, often brightly coloured bodies.

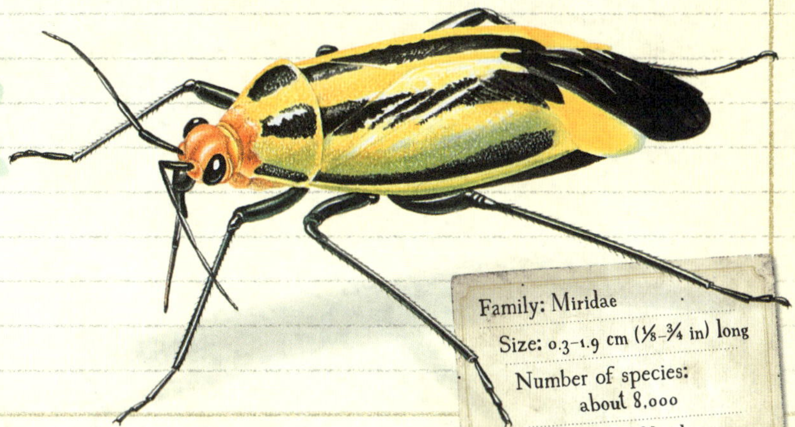

Family: Aphididae
Size: up to 0.9 cm (⅜ in) long
Number of species: about 2,250
Habitat: worldwide

Aphid
These small, soft-bodied insects are familiar to gardeners because they feed on sap from the leaves and stems of plants and can damage them. They reproduce extremely quickly, but many are destroyed by insects such as ladybirds and parasitic wasps.

Family: Miridae
Size: 0.3–1.9 cm (⅛–¾ in) long
Number of species: about 8,000
Habitat: worldwide

Family: Cercopidae
Size: up to 2 cm (¾ in) long
Number of species: about 2,400
Habitat: worldwide

Bedbug
Bedbugs usually stay hidden during the day, then come out at night to feed on the blood of birds and mammals. They do not live on their host but in its home or nest, and their flattened bodies make it easy for them to hide in crevices. Adults can survive for weeks without food.

Family: Cimicidae
Size: up to 1.2 cm (½ in) long
Number of species: 90
Habitat: worldwide

Family: Pediculidae
Size: 0.15–0.6 cm (1⁄16–¼ in) long
Number of species: 7
Habitat: worldwide

Froghopper
Like tiny frogs, froghoppers hop about on plants as they feed. They lay their eggs on plant stems and when the nymphs hatch they cover themselves with a substance much like spit, or saliva. This comes from glands on the abdomen and mixes with air to form a frothy mass. The froth helps to protect the nymphs and hides them from enemies.

Head louse
The head louse is a sucking louse that lives on human heads, feeding on blood. It stays on the head by holding on to hairs with its strong legs and claws, and also glues its small eggs to the hairs of its host.

Bugs, lice and fleas

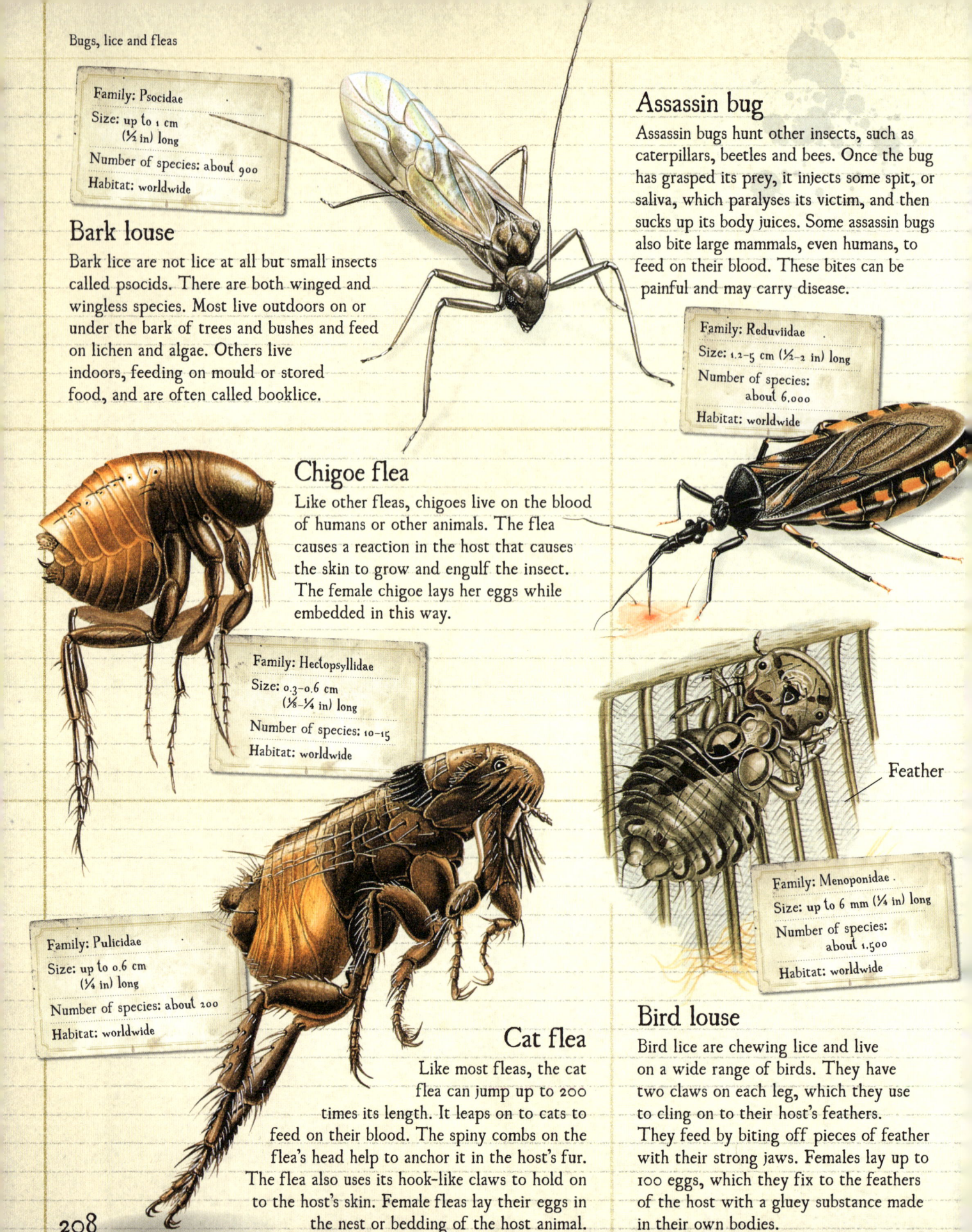

Family: Psocidae
Size: up to 1 cm (½ in) long
Number of species: about 900
Habitat: worldwide

Bark louse
Bark lice are not lice at all but small insects called psocids. There are both winged and wingless species. Most live outdoors on or under the bark of trees and bushes and feed on lichen and algae. Others live indoors, feeding on mould or stored food, and are often called booklice.

Assassin bug
Assassin bugs hunt other insects, such as caterpillars, beetles and bees. Once the bug has grasped its prey, it injects some spit, or saliva, which paralyses its victim, and then sucks up its body juices. Some assassin bugs also bite large mammals, even humans, to feed on their blood. These bites can be painful and may carry disease.

Family: Reduviidae
Size: 1.2–5 cm (½–2 in) long
Number of species: about 6,000
Habitat: worldwide

Chigoe flea
Like other fleas, chigoes live on the blood of humans or other animals. The flea causes a reaction in the host that causes the skin to grow and engulf the insect. The female chigoe lays her eggs while embedded in this way.

Family: Hectopsyllidae
Size: 0.3–0.6 cm (⅛–¼ in) long
Number of species: 10–15
Habitat: worldwide

Feather

Family: Menoponidae
Size: up to 6 mm (¼ in) long
Number of species: about 1,500
Habitat: worldwide

Family: Pulicidae
Size: up to 0.6 cm (¼ in) long
Number of species: about 200
Habitat: worldwide

Cat flea
Like most fleas, the cat flea can jump up to 200 times its length. It leaps on to cats to feed on their blood. The spiny combs on the flea's head help to anchor it in the host's fur. The flea also uses its hook-like claws to hold on to the host's skin. Female fleas lay their eggs in the nest or bedding of the host animal.

Bird louse
Bird lice are chewing lice and live on a wide range of birds. They have two claws on each leg, which they use to cling on to their host's feathers. They feed by biting off pieces of feather with their strong jaws. Females lay up to 100 eggs, which they fix to the feathers of the host with a gluey substance made in their own bodies.

BEETLES

About 370,000 species of beetle are known and there are certainly many more yet to be discovered. They live in almost every type of habitat, from polar lands to rainforests, and feed on almost every type of food with their strong, chewing mouthparts. Typically, beetles have two pairs of wings – the front pair, called elytra, are thick and hard and act as covers for the more delicate back wings. When the beetle is at rest, its back wings are folded safely away under the front wings.

Family: Staphylinidae
Size: up to 4 cm (1½ in) long
Number of species: about 29,000
Habitat: worldwide

Children's Animal Encyclopedia

Rove beetle
This beetle has a long body and short wing cases that cover only a little of the abdomen. When it is disturbed, it holds the back end of its body up, like a scorpion does. Both adult rove beetles and their larvae prey on insects and other small creatures such as worms.

Family: Scarabaeidae
Size: 0.2–17 cm (1/16–6¾ in) long
Number of species: about 16,500
Habitat: worldwide

Tiger beetle
The colourful tiger beetle has long legs and is a fast runner. A fierce, active hunter, it catches smaller insects in its strong jaws. The female beetle lays its eggs in the sand. When the larvae hatch, they dig burrows where they hide, waiting to grab passing prey.

Family: Carabidae
Size: 0.2–8 cm (1/16–3 in) long
Number of species: about 29,000
Habitat: worldwide

Whirligig beetle
Glossy whirligig beetles swim on the surface of ponds and streams, feeding on insects that fall into the water. Their eyes are divided into two parts so that they can see above and below the water surface at the same time. Larval whirligigs eat water insects, but they also hunt other small creatures such as snails.

Goliath beetle
One of the largest and heaviest of all insects is the goliath beetle, found in Africa. Males are the giants; females are smaller and less brightly patterned. These beetles have strong front legs and are excellent climbers. They clamber up into trees in search of sap and soft fruit to eat.

Family: Gyrinidae
Size: 0.3–1.5 cm (⅛–⅝ in) long
Number of species: 750
Habitat: worldwide

209

Beetles

Diving beetle

Diving beetles live in ponds and lakes. They swim by moving their paddle-like back legs together as oars. When they dive, these beetles can stay under for some time, using air trapped under the wing cases. Both adults and larvae hunt prey.

Family: Dytiscidae
Size: 0.15–4 cm (1/16–1 5/8 in) long
Number of species: about 3,500
Habitat: worldwide

Jewel beetle

With their gleaming metallic colours, jewel beetles deserve their name. They live in woodland, usually in tropical areas, where the adults feed on flower nectar and leaves. The larvae bore into dead or living wood as they eat, and can cause a great deal of damage.

Family: Buprestidae
Size: 2–6 cm (3/4–2 1/2 in) long
Number of species: about 15,000
Habitat: worldwide

Boll weevil

This insect belongs to the weevil family, all of which eat plants and can cause serious damage. The boll weevil uses its long snout to bore into the seedpods – called bolls – and buds of cotton plants. Females also lay their eggs in holes made in seedpods.

Family: Curculionidae
Size: 0.15–9 cm (1/16–3 1/2 in) long
Number of species: about 48,000
Habitat: worldwide

Carrion beetle

These brightly coloured beetles and their larvae feed on dead animals, such as mice and birds. Some carrion beetles dig under the corpse so that it sinks into the ground. They then lay their eggs on the buried, decaying creature so that their young have a ready supply of food to eat when they hatch.

Family: Silphidae
Size: up to 4 cm (1 1/2 in) long
Number of species: about 250
Habitat: worldwide

Family: Elateridae
Size: up to 6 cm (2 1/4 in) long
Number of species: about 9,000
Habitat: worldwide

Click beetle

The clicking sound made as they leap in the air to escape predators and to right themselves gives these beetles their name. They can jump as high as 30 cm (12 in). Adult beetles feed on plants and live on the ground or in rotting wood.

Longhorn beetle

This beetle has extremely long antennae – up to three times the length of its body. Adults feed on mainly on leaves, roots and pollen and do not usually catch prey. While her mate stands guard, the female lays her eggs in crevices in living trees or logs. When the larvae hatch, they tunnel into the wood as they feed and may cause considerable damage to timber and trees.

Family: Cerambycidae
Size: up to 18 cm (7 in) long, including antennae
Number of species: about 30,000
Habitat: worldwide

Family: Tenebrionidae
Size: 2–4.5 cm (¾–1¾ in) long
Number of species: about 17,000
Habitat: worldwide

Darkling beetle

Common in dry areas, where they lurk under stones, darkling beetles scurry out at night to feed. They are scavengers and eat many kinds of foods, including rotting wood, insect larvae and stored grain. Some desert-living darklings have long legs and can move quickly as they run from one patch of shade to another.

Ladybird

The ladybird's round spotted body makes it one of the most easily recognisable of all insects. The ladybird's bright colours warn its enemies that it tastes unpleasant and may be poisonous. Adults and larvae feed mainly on aphids, which suck the juices of plants and can be serious pests. Without ladybirds, these insects would be a far greater problem for farmers and gardeners.

Family: Coccinellidae
Size: up to 1.5 cm (½ in) long
Number of species: 5,000
Habitat: worldwide

Firefly

Fireflies can produce a yellowish-green light in a special area at the end of the abdomen. Each species of firefly flashes its light in a particular pattern to attract mates of its own kind. Male fireflies have wings, but females are often wingless and look like larvae.

Family: Lampyridae
Size: up to 2.5 cm (1 in) long
Number of species: about 2,000
Habitat: worldwide

STAG BEETLES

With their large heads and massive jaws, male stag beetles look fierce, but these insects are harmless and feed mostly on tree sap and other liquids. There are about 1,300 species of stag beetle, some as long as 10 cm (4 in). Mostly black or brownish in colour, they usually live in woodland and are particularly common in tropical areas. The jaws of the males are branched like the antlers of a stag and, like stags, these beetles take part in fierce battles with one another to win females. They rarely bite, but they do sometimes damage each other's wing cases. The beetle with the biggest jaws usually wins the contest. Female stag beetles lay their eggs in cracks in logs or dead tree stumps. When the larvae hatch, they feed on the juices of the rotting wood.

Its wing cases raised, this magnificent stag beetle is about to take to the air. When the beetle is not in flight, the tough wing cases, formed from the front wings, protect the more delicate back wings, which are folded underneath.

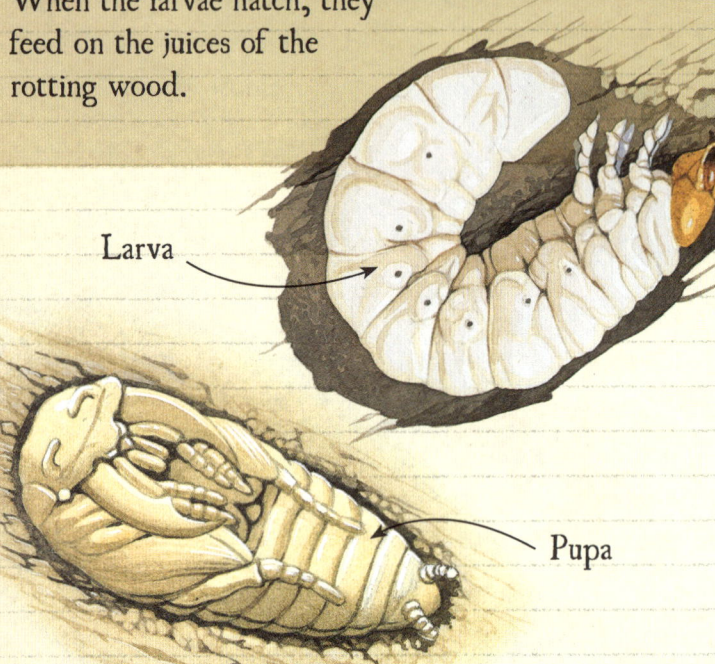

Larva

Pupa

FEMALE STAG BEETLE

The female stag beetle is smaller than the battling male and does not have such large jaws. However, she can give a much more powerful nip if under threat. The male's mighty jaws are so specialised for fighting that they are almost useless for feeding or biting.

LARVA AND PUPA

Stag beetle eggs hatch into wormlike, C-shaped larvae called grubs. They spend most of their time feeding and grow quickly. As a larva grows, it moults several times – it sheds its skin to allow for the increase in body size. When the larva is full grown, it becomes a pupa – the stage during which the larva changes into an adult beetle. Finally, a winged, adult beetle comes out of the pupa.

THE HELPLESS LOSER

If a stag beetle lands on its back after a battle, it is very hard for it to right itself again. In this position, it is extremely easy for other enemies, such as birds, to snap the beetle up.

BATTLING RIVALS

The beetles usually meet on the branch of a tree. As they struggle, each male tries to lock the other in its jaws — the jaws are just the right shape to fit around the top part of the stag beetle's body. Once one competitor succeeds in grabbing the other, he lifts the loser up and tries to throw him off the branch.

Flies, moths and butterflies

FLIES, MOTHS AND BUTTERFLIES

Flies are sometimes thought of as dirty and disease-carrying but, like bees, they pollinate plants as they feed and they are an important source of food for many other creatures, such as birds. Also, their scavenging habits help to get rid of decaying waste, such as dung and dead bodies. With large, often beautifully patterned wings, butterflies and moths pollinate plants too, as they flit from flower to flower sipping nectar.

Family: Chironomidae
Size: 0.15–0.9 cm (1/16 – 3/8 in) long
Number of species: about 5,000
Habitat: worldwide

Midge
Tiny, delicate insects, these midges do not bite. They fly in huge swarms, usually in the evening, and are often seen near ponds and streams. Their larvae live in damp places or in water. Most feed on rotting plants and algae but some are predators.

FLIES

Among the larger groups of insects, with more than 150,000 known species, flies are common almost everywhere – one of the few land-based creatures in Antarctica is a midge, a type of fly. Flies have only one pair of wings. The hind wings are reduced to small, knobbed structures called halteres, which help the fly to balance in flight. Flies usually take liquid food. Many sip nectar and sap from plants or lap up juices from rotting plants. Some, such as mosquitoes, suck blood from humans and other animals.

Family: Asilidae
Size: 0.6–4.5 cm (1/4–1 3/4 in) long
Number of species: about 5,000
Habitat: worldwide

Family: Tabanidae
Size: 0.6–2.5 cm (1/4–1 in) long
Number of species: about 4,100
Habitat: worldwide

Horse fly
These flies have particularly large, iridescent (shimmering) eyes. Males feed on pollen and nectar, but female horse flies take blood from mammals, including humans. Their bites can be painful and the flies may carry diseases such as anthrax.

Robber fly
A fast-moving hunter, the robber fly chases and catches other insects in the air or pounces on them on the ground. It has strong, bristly legs for seizing its prey. Once it has caught its victim, the robber fly sucks out its body fluids with its sharp mouthparts. Larvae live in soil or rotting wood, where they feed on the larvae of other insects.

Hover fly

Also known as flower flies, adult hover flies feed on pollen and nectar and are often seen around flowers. They are expert fliers and can hover with ease and even fly backwards. Many species are brightly coloured and look much like bees or wasps but do not sting. Some hover fly larvae hunt insects such as aphids. Others feed on plants or live in the nests of bees or wasps, where they feed on their larvae.

Family: Syrphidae
Size: 0.6–3 cm (¼–1¼ in) long
Number of species: about 6,000
Habitat: worldwide

Family: Tipulidae
Size: 0.6–6 cm (¼–2½ in) long
Number of species: about 15,000
Habitat: worldwide

Crane fly

With their long, thin legs, crane flies look like large mosquitoes, but they do not bite or suck blood. The largest have a wingspan of as much as 7 cm (2¾ in). Most adults live only a few days and probably do not eat at all. The larvae feed mainly on plant roots and rotting plants, although some do hunt for their food.

Blow fly

Many blow flies are coloured metallic blue or green. Adults feed on pollen and nectar as well as fluids from rotting matter. Many lay their eggs in carrion – the bodies of dead animals – or in dung, so that the larvae, called maggots, have plenty of food to eat when they hatch.

Family: Calliphoridae
Size: 0.6–1.5 cm (¾–⅝ in) long
Number of species: about 1,200
Habitat: worldwide

Family: Muscidae
Size: 0.3–1.2 cm (⅛–½ in) long
Number of species: about 4,000
Habitat: worldwide

House fly

Found almost everywhere in the world, house flies suck liquids from manure and other decaying matter and from fresh fruit and plants. These insects can be dangerous as they may carry diseases.

Fruit fly

These little flies are common around flowers and overripe fruit. Their larvae feed on plant matter and some are serious pests, causing great damage to fruit trees and other crops.

Family: Tephritidae
Size: 0.3–0.9 cm (⅛–⅜ in) long
Number of species: about 4,500
Habitat: worldwide

BUTTERFLIES AND MOTHS

Wherever plants grow, there are butterflies and moths. Known as the Lepidoptera, this is the second largest group of insects, containing about 165,000 species. Caddisflies look similar to butterflies and moths but are in fact a separate group called the Trichoptera. The young butterfly or moth is called a caterpillar. It spends most of its life feeding on plants and growing fast. When it has reached its full size, a caterpillar becomes a pupa. During this stage, it makes its transformation from wingless larva to winged adult.

Family: Tineidae
Size: wingspan 0.6–2 cm (¼–¾ in) long
Number of species: about 2,500
Habitat: worldwide

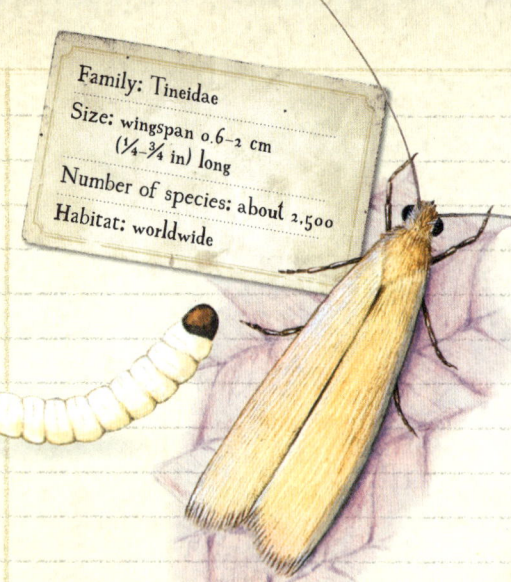

Clothes moth

The caterpillars of the clothes moth feed on hair and feathers in animal nests and on the dried corpses of small mammals and birds. Few creatures, other than some beetle larvae, can digest these tough foods. Because our clothes are often made of animal wool, the caterpillars often come into our homes to feed on cloth. The adult moths are small and brownish in colour, with narrow front wings that are folded neatly over the body when at rest. They do not usually eat anything.

Family: Geometridae
Size: wingspan 1.7–7.4 cm (¾–3 in) long
Number of species: about 20,000
Habitat: worldwide

Geometrid moth

Geometrids have slender bodies and fragile wings. When they are at rest, they spread their wings out flat. Their caterpillars are known as inchworms because they seem to be measuring inch by inch as they move. They eat leaves and may cause serious damage to trees.

Family: Sphingidae
Size: wingspan 3–15 cm (1¼–6 in) long
Number of species: about 1,100
Habitat: worldwide

Hummingbird hawkmoth

Many of the scales on the wings of this hawk moth drop off after its first flight, leaving large, clear areas. It feeds on flower nectar, using its long proboscis, or feeding tube, to reach deep into the flowers. It hovers as it feeds, making a noise like the sound of a hummingbird's wings.

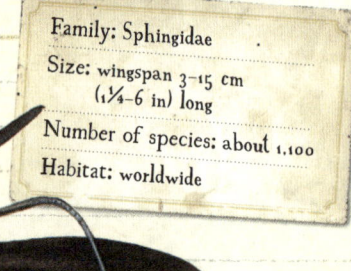

Children's Animal Encyclopedia

Large caddis fly

Caddis flies look like moths but have hairs not scales on the body and wings, and short mouthparts for lapping up food instead of a proboscis. The caterpillar-like larvae are usually aquatic and live and pupate in water, in cases made of leaves, stones or twigs.

Family: Phryganeidae
Size: wingspan 1.2–2.5 cm (½–1 in) long
Number of species: about 450
Habitat: worldwide

Larva

Large Caddis fly

Cotton boll moth

This moth belongs to one of the biggest families of moths. Most moths in this family are night-flying and dull in colour. The cotton boll caterpillar feeds on cotton seedpods and can damage the plants.

Family: Noctuidae
Size: wingspan 1.2–7.5 cm (½–3 in) long
Number of species: about 22,000
Habitat: worldwide

Atlas moth

These brightly patterned moths are some of the largest in the world. Most have transparent, scaleless patches on their broad wings and feathery antennae. The antennae help male moths pick up the scent signals given off by females when looking for mates. Adults have very small mouthparts and do not generally feed during their short lives.

Family: Saturniidae
Size: wingspan 2.5–25 cm (1–10 in) long
Number of species: about 1,200
Habitat: worldwide

Luna moth

This beautiful moth has wings that can measure up to 11 cm (4½ in) across with long tails trailing from them. It lives in forests and its caterpillars feed on the leaves of trees such as hickory, walnut and birch. The caterpillars pupate in a cocoon on the ground.

Family: Saturniidae
Size: wingspan 2.5–25 cm (1–10 in) long
Number of species: about 1,200
Habitat: worldwide

Tiger moth

Tiger moths have broad, hairy bodies and boldly patterned wings. The bright markings of these moths, and of their hairy caterpillars, warn birds and mammals that they are unpleasant to eat. The caterpillars feed on plants that are poisonous to vertebrate animals, and then store the poison for their own protection.

Family: Arctiidae
Size: wingspan 2–7 cm (¾–2¾ in) long
Number of species: 2,500
Habitat: worldwide

217

Butterflies and moths

Family: Papilionidae
Size: wingspan 5–28 cm (2–11 in) long
Number of species: about 600
Habitat: worldwide

Cairns birdwing

Birdwings are the biggest butterflies in the world. They are only found in Southeast Asia and northern Australia, and many are now rare. Females are bigger than males, but males are more colourful. Adults feed on flower nectar, but caterpillars eat the leaves of plants that are poisonous to most creatures.

Family: Lycaenidae
Size: wingspan 2.5–5 cm (1–2 in) long
Number of species: about 6,000
Habitat: worldwide

Copper

These little butterflies have brightly coloured, often iridescent wings. When at rest or feeding on flowers, they hold their wings together above the back. The plump, slug-shaped caterpillars feed on the leaves of plants such as dock and sorrel.

Swallowtail

Boldly patterned swallowtail butterflies get their name from the tail-like extensions on the back wings. These may help to distract enemies away from the vulnerable head area. Adult swallowtails feed on flower nectar, and their caterpillars usually eat the leaves of trees such as ash and bay.

Family: Papilionidae
Size: wingspan 5–28 cm (2–11 in) long
Number of species: about 600
Habitat: worldwide

Fluminense swallowtail

This beautiful butterfly is one of Brazil's most endangered insects. Drainage of its habitat to build houses and factories and to lay out banana plantations has caused it to die out in many sites. Conservationists hope to be able to catch some butterflies and establish new colonies in safer places.

Family: Papilionidae
Size: wingspan 5–28 cm (2–11 in) long
Number of species: about 600
Habitat: worldwide

218

Children's Animal Encyclopedia

Cabbage white

The cabbage white, like others in its family, is a very common butterfly. Unlike many butterflies, it has well-developed front legs, which are used for walking. Adults feed on nectar. Their caterpillars eat cabbage and other leafy crops, and can do great damage.

Family: Pieridae
Size: wingspan 0.9-7 cm (¾-2¾ in) long
Number of species: about 1,200
Habitat: worldwide

Family: Nymphalidae
Size: wingspan 3-15 cm (1¼-6 in) long
Number of species: about 5,000
Habitat: tropical

Morpho

Morpho butterflies live in the rainforests of Central and South America. The males are brilliantly coloured – the beautiful iridescence of their wings is caused by the arrangement of the rows of scales, which reflect the light. Females are much plainer.

Monarch

Every autumn, millions of monarch butterflies fly south from Canada to Mexico – a distance of about 3,200 km (2,000 miles). The following spring, the females lay their eggs as they return north. The new monarch butterflies then fly north to Canada before autumn comes again.

Family: Papilionidae
Size: wingspan 5-28 cm (2-11 in) long
Number of species: about 600
Habitat: worldwide

Family: Nymphalidae
Size: wingspan 3-15 cm (1¼-6 in) long
Number of species: about 5,000
Habitat: worldwide

Queen Alexandra's birdwing

The female of this giant butterfly is the biggest in the world, with a wingspan of up to 28 cm (11 in). It is highly prized by collectors, so local people catch it to sell to traders. It is hoped that if some of the forest in which the butterflies live can be saved in reserves, local people might be able to earn a living from tourism instead.

219

HAWK MOTHS

Of all butterflies and moths, hawk moths – also called sphinx moths (Sphingidae) – are some of the most powerful fliers. Their wings beat so fast that they make a whirring noise. Some hawk moths can even hover like hummingbirds in front of flowers as they feed. Like all moths, the adults eat liquid food such as nectar. They suck up the food with a straw-like tongue called a proboscis, which is coiled under the head when not in use. They have the longest tongues of any moths and can feed on nectar at the bottom of long tube-like flowers. There are about 1,100 species of hawk moth, some with wingspans of up to 15 cm (6 in). Most have large, heavy bodies and long, narrow front wings.

A privet hawkmoth lands on a flower to feed on nectar with the help of its long proboscis. The moth's caterpillar feeds on the leaves of privet, lilac and ash.

BEE SPHINX MOTH

A bee sphinx moth plunges its long tongue deep into a flower. With its broad striped body and the large clear areas without scales on its wings, this moth looks amazingly like a bee as it hovers over plants – the resemblance to a stinging insect may help to scare away potential predators. Many moths are nocturnal, but the bee sphinx flies by day, not at night.

OLEANDER HAWK MOTH

This is one of the most beautifully patterned of all moths. Its caterpillar feeds on the leaves of plants such as oleander and grows up to 15 cm (6 in) long. It has bold eyespots on its body, which can fool a predator into thinking it a much larger creature than it really is.

Children's Animal Encyclopedia

WHITE-LINED SPHINX MOTH

The white-lined sphinx moth visits flowers at night to feed. Like most moths, it has antennae that are extremely sensitive to smell as well as touch. It can pick up the faintest scents, which helps it to find flowers in the darkness.

POPLAR SPHINX MOTH

The colour and irregular shape of the poplar sphinx moth's wings help it to hide on bark as it rests during the day. Its caterpillars feed on the leaves of trees such as poplar and willow.

EGG TO PUPA

As soon as a caterpillar hatches from its egg it starts to feed, devouring plants with its strong, chewing mouthparts. It grows fast and sheds its skin several times as it gets bigger. When fully grown, the caterpillar becomes a pupa. The bee sphinx moth pupates on the ground in a cocoon made of silk.

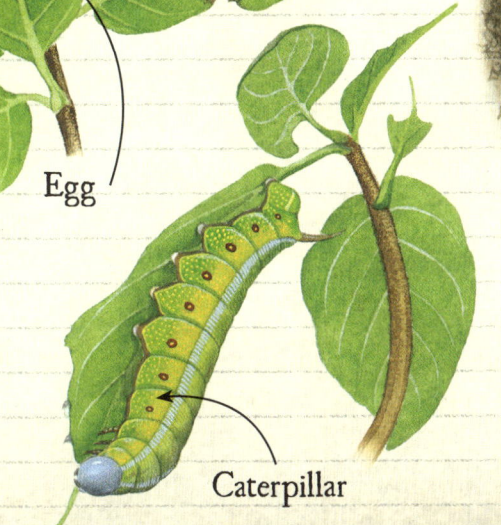

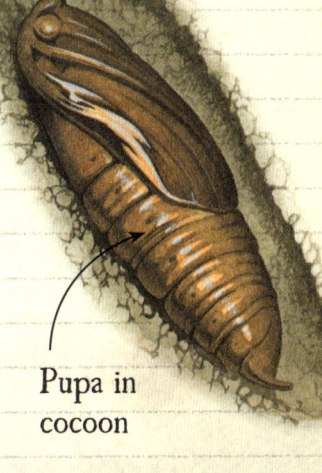

Egg

Caterpillar

Pupa in cocoon

221

Bees, wasps, ants and termites

BEES, WASPS, ANTS AND TERMITES

Bees, wasps and ants belong to a large group of about 198,000 insects. Although they vary greatly, most have a definite "waist" at the front of the abdomen. They have mouthparts for chewing and tongue-like structures for sipping liquids such as flower nectar. Species that have wings have two pairs, but many worker ants are wingless. Ants and some bees and wasps live in social colonies in elaborate nests. Termites are not related to ants, bees and wasps, but they too live in huge colonies. They make nests in soil or trees, or in specially built mounds.

BEES

These flying insects have two pairs of wings and their bodies are covered with tiny hairs. Some, such as leafcutter bees, live alone and make their own nests for their young. Others, such as honeybees and bumblebees, live in huge colonies, which may contain thousands of bees. Only bee colonies produce honey.

Family: Megachilidae
Size: 0.9–2 cm (⅜–¾ in) long
Number of species: about 3,000
Habitat: worldwide

Leafcutter bee
This bee gets its name from its habit of cutting circular pieces of leaves and flowers with its jaws. It uses these pieces to line larval cells in its tunnel nest, made in soil or rotting wood. Stores of nectar and pollen are put into the cells and an egg is then laid in each one.

Family: Colletidae
Size: 0.3–2 cm (⅛–¾ in) long
Number of species: over 2,000
Habitat: worldwide

Plasterer bee
Plasterer bees nest in the ground in burrows with branching tunnels. They line the tunnels with a secretion from glands in the abdomen, which dries to a clear, waterproof substance. Cells for larvae are made in the tunnels.

Family: Apidae
Size: 0.3–2.5 cm (⅛–1 in) long
Number of species: about 1,000
Habitat: worldwide

Bumblebee
Bumblebees are large, hairy insects, usually black in colour with some yellow markings. In spring, queens look for underground nest sites. Each queen collects pollen and nectar and makes food called beebread. Later, she lays eggs, and when the larvae hatch they feed on the beebread. These larvae become adult worker bees and they take over the work of the colony, while the queen continues to lay eggs.

Children's Animal Encyclopedia

Orchid bee
Most orchid bees live in tropical areas and are brightly coloured. Males are attracted to orchid flowers for their nectar. They pollinate the flowers and collect scent, which may play a part in their mating rituals.

Family: Apidae
Size: 0.3–2.5 cm (⅛–1 in) long
Number of species: about 1,000
Habitat: worldwide

Family: Apidae
Size: 0.3–2.5 cm (⅛–1 in) long
Number of species: about 1,000
Habitat: worldwide

Carpenter bee
The female carpenter bee chews a tunnel-like nest in wood. She makes a line of separate cells inside the tunnel, fills them with pollen and nectar food stores and lays one egg in each cell. She stays nearby and guards the nest against any enemies.

Cuckoo bee
Like its namesake the cuckoo bird, this wasp-like bee lays its eggs in the nests of other bees, which have prepared food stores for their eggs. The cuckoo bee's eggs hatch first and the larvae eat up all the food intended for the host's larvae.

Family: Anthophoridae
Size: 0.9–1.2 cm (⅜–½ in) long
Number of species: about 4,200
Habitat: worldwide

Family: Apidae
Size: 0.3–2.5 cm (⅛–1 in) long
Number of species: about 1,000
Habitat: worldwide

Family: Andrenidae
Size: 0.3–2 cm (⅛–¾ in) long
Number of species: about 4,000
Habitat: worldwide

Stingless bee
As their name suggests, these bees cannot sting, but they have strong jaws that they use to bite any intruders. They live in colonies and make nests under the ground in a tree trunk or even in part of a nest of a termite colony.

Mining bee
Mining bees nest in long branching tunnels that they dig in the ground. Cells in the tunnels are stocked with nectar and pollen, and an egg is laid in each one. Each bee digs its own nest but large numbers may live close together.

223

Wasps

WASPS

Wasps feed their young on other insects, such as caterpillars and aphids that harm garden and food plants. Without wasps there would be many more of these pests. Adult wasps feed mainly on nectar and the juice of ripe fruit. Many wasps, including mud daubers and spider wasps, live alone and make their own nests for their eggs. Others, such as common wasps and hornets, live in large colonies and make group nests. Wasp colonies do not store food like honeybees. Only the new queens survive the winter, in other shelters.

Family: Vespidae
Size: 1–3 cm (⅜–1¼ in) long
Number of species: about 4,000
Habitat: worldwide

Family: Pompilidae
Size: 0.5–8 cm (¼–3 in) long
Number of species: about 4,000
Habitat: worldwide

Blue-black spider wasp
Adult spider wasps feed on nectar but the female catches spiders to feed her young. She paralyses the spider with her sting and then places it in a nest cell with an egg and seals the top with mud. When the wasp larva hatches, it eats the spider.

Giant hornet
Adult hornets feed on insects and nectar and grow to up to 3 cm (1¼ in) long. They live in colonies, in nests built of a papery material they make by mixing their saliva with chewed-up plant material. The nest is usually in a tree or an old building. Larvae feed on insects caught by the adults.

Family: Vespidae
Size: 1–3 cm (⅜–1¼ in) long
Number of species: about 4,000
Habitat: worldwide

Paper wasp
The paper wasp builds her nest with a papery material that she makes from chewed wood mixed with her spit. She lays her eggs in the cells, and more females join her to help feed the young with other insects. About 20 wasps usually live in a nest.

Velvet ant
Velvet ants are not ants but hairy wasps. Only the males have wings. The females search for the nests of bees and other kinds of wasp and lay their eggs on their larvae. When each velvet ant hatches, it eats its host.

Family: Mutillidae
Size: 0.6–2.5 cm (¼–1 in) long
Number of species: about 5,000
Habitat: worldwide

Children's Animal Encyclopedia

Family: Cynipidae
Size: 0.15–0.9 cm (1/16–3/8 in) long
Number of species: about 1,250
Habitat: worldwide

Gall wasp

These tiny wasps lay their eggs on particular species of plants. For reasons that are not fully understood, the host plant forms a growth, called a gall, around the egg. When the larva hatches it feeds on the gall tissue.

Common wasp

Common wasps, or yellow jackets, feed on nectar and other sweet things such as ripe fruit. They also catch other insects to feed their young. Like other vespid wasps, the females are well known for their sting. The pointed sting is at the end of the body and is linked to a bag of poison. The wasp uses its sting to kill prey and to defend itself against enemies – including humans.

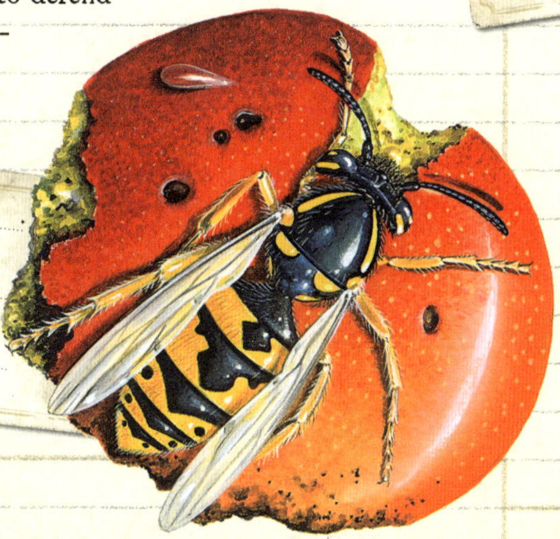

Family: Vespidae
Size: 1–3 cm (3/8–1 1/4 in) long
Number of species: about 4,000
Habitat: worldwide

Family: Ichneumonidae
Size: 0.3–5 cm (1/8–2 in) long
Number of species: about 60,000
Habitat: worldwide

Ichneumon wasp

The female ichneumon wasp can bore through wood to lay her eggs near the larvae of other insects such as wood wasps. She has a special long egg-laying tube, called an ovipositor. When the egg hatches, the ichneumon larva feeds on the host larva.

Mud dauber

Mud daubers are solitary wasps, which feed on other insects and nectar. The female mud dauber wasp makes a nest of damp mud. Into each cell she puts an egg and some paralysed insects for her young to eat when it hatches.

Family: Sphecidae
Size: 0.9–5 cm (3/8–2 in) long
Number of species: 8,000
Habitat: worldwide

Family: Tenthredinidae
Size: up to 3.2 cm (1 1/4 in) long
Number of species: about 6,000
Habitat: worldwide

Sawfly

The sawfly is related to wasps but lacks the "waist" between the abdomen and thorax. The female sawfly uses her ovipositor (egg-laying tube) to cut slits in the stems and leaves of plants where she then lays her eggs. The caterpillar-like larvae feed on leaves when they hatch.

HONEYBEES

Honeybees are probably the best known bees of all. They pollinate countless food crops and produce billions of pounds' worth of honey and wax every year. They live in huge colonies of thousands of bees, with a complex social organisation. Each colony has a queen. The queen bee is larger than the other bees and lays all the eggs of the colony. Most of the members of the colony are female workers. They care for the young, build and repair the nest and gather food, but they do not lay eggs. At certain times of year the colony includes male bees, called drones, whose only role is to mate with new queens. The nest is made in a hollow tree or in a beekeeper's hive and consists of sheets of hexagonal (six-sided) cells that make up the honeycomb. These cells contain eggs and young as well as food stores of pollen and honey.

BUSY BEES

When a worker bee returns from a foraging trip laden with pollen and nectar, the other bees gather around to collect the food stores. Workers also make the nest cells, building them from wax produced in glands on the underside of the bee's abdomen. The bee pulls out thin flakes of wax and kneads it with her mouthparts until it is soft enough to use for building the honeycomb.

WORKERS

A worker honeybee lives only about six weeks. For the first week of her adult life she cares for the eggs and larvae of the colony. Then she helps to build cells and maintain the nest. Finally she becomes a food gatherer, bringing nectar and pollen back to the nest.

A worker honeybee has just returned to the nest, with her pollen baskets full of golden-yellow pollen. Other workers gather round to help her unload the pollen and pack it into cells.

ROYAL CELLS

Special cells for future queens hang from the edge of the comb. The larvae in queen cells are fed on royal jelly – a protein-rich substance from glands on the heads of workers. Worker larvae are fed royal jelly for a few days and then given pollen and nectar.

Children's Animal Encyclopedia

EQUIPPED FOR WORK

All the tools needed by a worker bee are on her own body. On each front leg there are long hairs used for removing pollen from the body and a special notch for cleaning the antennae. On the middle legs there are fringes of hair for removing pollen from the forelegs and a spike for taking wax from glands in the abdomen. On each hind leg there is a pollen basket – a special area lined with hairs where pollen is carried.

ANTS AND TERMITES

Ants live in huge well-organised groups of thousands of individuals, called colonies. Most colonies make a nest of interconnecting tunnels in rotting wood or under the ground. Each colony includes at least one queen that lays all the eggs. The workers are also female but cannot lay eggs. They do all the work, gathering food and looking after eggs and young. Termites are more closely related to cockroaches than to ants, but they too build large nests.

Family: Formicidae
Size: 0.15–2.5 cm (1/16–1 in) long
Number of species: about 9,000
Habitat: worldwide

Fire ant
This ant gets its name from its powerful bite and sting, which is extremely painful even to humans. It hunts other insects, which it stings to death, but also eats seeds, fruit and flowers. Fire ants make nests in the ground or under logs or stones.

Family: Formicidae
Size: 0.15–2.5 cm (1/16–1 in) long
Number of species: about 9,000
Habitat: worldwide

Harvester ant
These ants get their name from their habit of feeding on seeds and grain crops. When the ants find a plentiful supply of seeds near their nest, they leave scent trails to lead others in their colony to the food. In times of plenty, the ants collect more seeds than they can eat and store them in special granary areas in the nest.

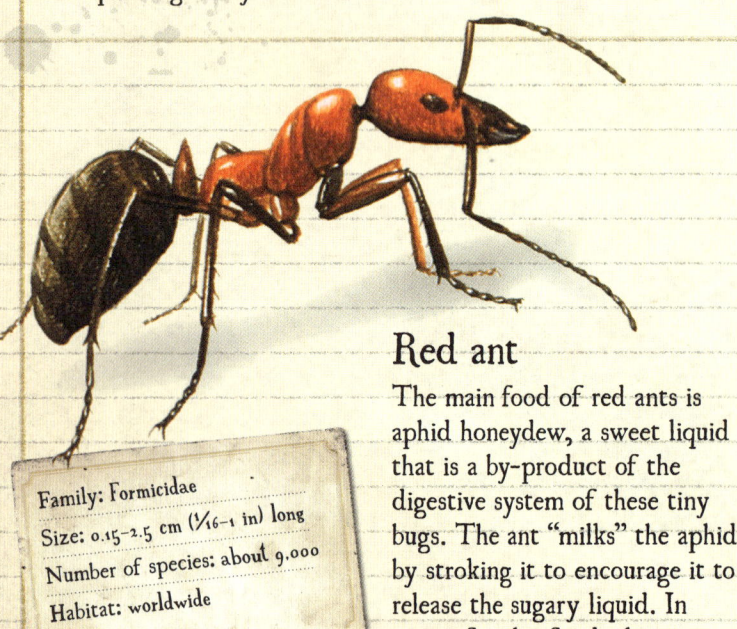

Family: Formicidae
Size: 0.15–2.5 cm (1/16–1 in) long
Number of species: about 9,000
Habitat: worldwide

Red ant
The main food of red ants is aphid honeydew, a sweet liquid that is a by-product of the digestive system of these tiny bugs. The ant "milks" the aphid by stroking it to encourage it to release the sugary liquid. In return for this food, the ants protect the aphids from predators – some even store the aphids in their nest over winter.

Family: Formicidae
Size: 0.15–2.5 cm (1/16–1 in) long
Number of species: about 9,000
Habitat: worldwide

Army ant
Unlike other ants, army ants do not build permament nests. They march in search of prey, and only periodically stop to produce eggs. The worker ants link their bodies together, making a temporary nest called a bivouac to protect the queen and young. When the young have developed, they move on.

Children's Animal Encyclopedia

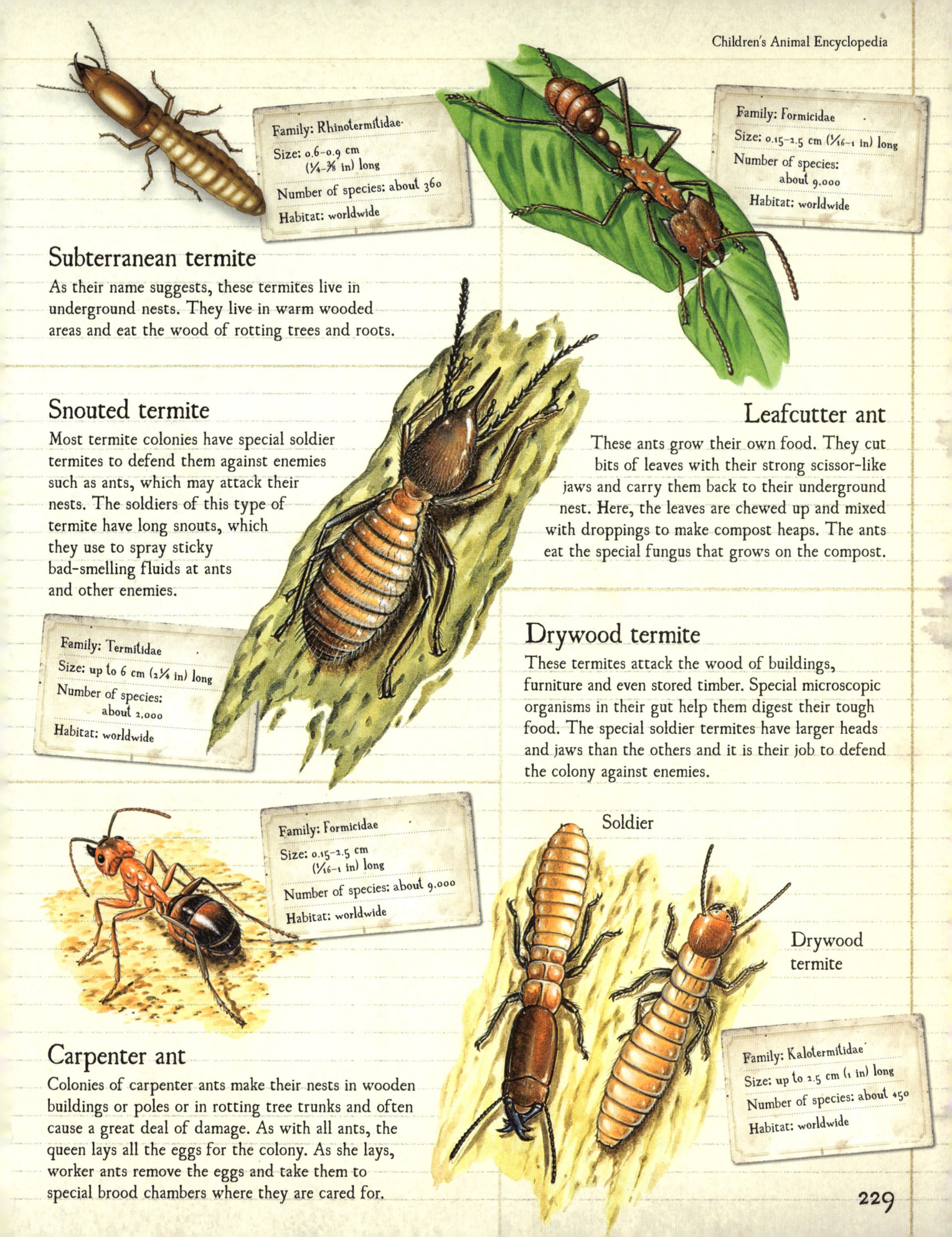

Family: Rhinotermitidae
Size: 0.6–0.9 cm (¼–⅜ in) long
Number of species: about 360
Habitat: worldwide

Family: Formicidae
Size: 0.15–2.5 cm (1/16–1 in) long
Number of species: about 9,000
Habitat: worldwide

Subterranean termite
As their name suggests, these termites live in underground nests. They live in warm wooded areas and eat the wood of rotting trees and roots.

Snouted termite
Most termite colonies have special soldier termites to defend them against enemies such as ants, which may attack their nests. The soldiers of this type of termite have long snouts, which they use to spray sticky bad-smelling fluids at ants and other enemies.

Family: Termitidae
Size: up to 6 cm (2¼ in) long
Number of species: about 2,000
Habitat: worldwide

Leafcutter ant
These ants grow their own food. They cut bits of leaves with their strong scissor-like jaws and carry them back to their underground nest. Here, the leaves are chewed up and mixed with droppings to make compost heaps. The ants eat the special fungus that grows on the compost.

Drywood termite
These termites attack the wood of buildings, furniture and even stored timber. Special microscopic organisms in their gut help them digest their tough food. The special soldier termites have larger heads and jaws than the others and it is their job to defend the colony against enemies.

Soldier

Family: Formicidae
Size: 0.15–2.5 cm (1/16–1 in) long
Number of species: about 9,000
Habitat: worldwide

Drywood termite

Family: Kalotermitidae
Size: up to 2.5 cm (1 in) long
Number of species: about 450
Habitat: worldwide

Carpenter ant
Colonies of carpenter ants make their nests in wooden buildings or poles or in rotting tree trunks and often cause a great deal of damage. As with all ants, the queen lays all the eggs for the colony. As she lays, worker ants remove the eggs and take them to special brood chambers where they are cared for.

SPIDERS AND SCORPIONS

Often confused with insects, the arachnids – which include spiders, scorpions, ticks and mites – are a separate group of invertebrates. They first lived on land at least 400 million years ago.

Today, arachnids include a wide range of body forms, but they have four pairs of legs and do not have wings or antennae. Most live on land and hunt other creatures to eat.

SPIDERS

Most spiders are harmless. Only a few have a venomous bite that is dangerous to people. In fact, spiders help us by keeping insect numbers under control. All are hunters and feed mostly on small insects. Some of the larger species catch birds and other small animals. All spiders can make silk with the special glands at the end of the body, but not all build webs. Spiders use silk to line their burrows and some make silken traps that they hold between their legs to snare prey. Young spiders use long strands of silk as parachutes to drift away and find new territories.

Family: Salticidae
Size: 0.3–1.5 cm (⅛–⅝ in) long
Number of species: about 5,700
Habitat: worldwide

Jumping spider
Unlike most spiders, the jumping spider has good eyesight, which helps it find prey. Once it has spotted something, the spider leaps on to its victim. Before jumping, it attaches a silk thread to the ground as a safety line along which it can return to its hideout.

Family: Theridiidae
Size: up to 1.2 cm (½ in) long
Number of species: about 2,400
Habitat: worldwide

Black widow spider
The female black widow has comb-like bristles on her back legs, which she uses to throw strands of silk over prey that gets caught in her web. She has a venomous bite. One drop is more deadly than the same amount of rattlesnake venom. Male black widows do not bite.

Family: Lycosidae
Size: 0.3–4 cm (⅛–1½ in) long
Number of species: about 2,400
Habitat: worldwide

Wolf spider
Fast-moving hunters, wolf spiders creep up on prey and seize it after a final speedy dash. Most do not make webs. Wolf spiders have excellent eyesight, which helps them find prey at night.

Children's Animal Encyclopedia

Family: Theraphosidae
Size: up to 28 cm (11 in) long
Number of species: about 1,000
Habitat: worldwide

Crab spider
This spider scuttles sideways like a crab. Some crab spiders are dark brown or black, but those that usually sit on certain flowers to wait for prey are brightly coloured to match the petals.

Family: Thomisidae
Size: 0.15-0.9 cm (1/16 - 3/8 in) long
Number of species: about 2,200
Habitat: worldwide

Red-kneed tarantula
Tarantulas are some of the largest of all spiders, with legs spanning more than 20 cm (8 in). Most hide by day and come out at night to hunt insects and other small creatures, which they kill with a venomous bite. Harmless to people, they are becoming popular pets. So many are collected for sale that they may soon become scarce in the wild.

Lichen spider
Mottled colours help keep this spider well hidden on lichen-covered tree bark. Tufts of tiny hairs on its legs break up any shadows which might otherwise reveal its presence. If the spider suspects an enemy is near, it flattens itself against the bark and is even more difficult to see.

Family: Sparassidae
Size: 0.9-3 cm (3/8 - 1 1/4 in) long
Number of species: about 1,150
Habitat: tropical

Family: Ctenizidae
Size: 0.9-5 cm (3/8-2 in) long
Number of species: about 130
Habitat: worldwide

Family: Scytodidae
Size: 0.9 cm (3/8 in) long
Number of species: about 230
Habitat: worldwide

Trapdoor spider
The burrow of the trapdoor spider has a hinged lid at the top. The spider waits in its burrow until it senses the movement of prey overhead. It then pops out of the door, grabs the prey and takes it back into its burrow.

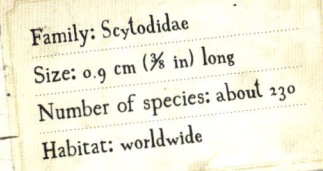

Spitting spider
This unusual hunter approaches its victim and spits out two lines of a sticky substance from glands near its mouth. These fall in zigzags over the prey, pinning it down. The spider then kills its prey with a bite.

231

Spiders

Family: Araneidae
Size: 0.15–5 cm
(1/16–2 in) long
Number of species: about 3,050
Habitat: worldwide

Golden-silk spider

The female golden-silk spider is eight or nine times the length of the male and may weigh a hundred times as much. Strangely enough the male's size is an advantage when he approaches the female to try and mate with her. Like any tiny insects that fly into her web, the male is too small to bother attacking so is left alone.

Purse-web spider

This spider builds a silken tube in a sloping burrow in the ground. The top of the tube extends above ground and is camouflaged with leaves. When an insect lands on the tube, the spider grabs it through the walls of the tube with her sharp fangs and drags it inside.

Family: Atypidae
Size: 0.9–3 cm
(3/8–1 1/4 in) long
Number of species: 49
Habitat: temperate

Family: Dipluridae
Size: about 3 cm (1 1/4 in) long
Number of species: about 180
Habitat: temperate

Funnel-web spider

This spider makes a funnel-shaped web that leads into an underground burrow. If a creature walks across the web, the spider senses the vibrations and rushes out for the kill. Funnel-webs prey on frogs and lizards as well as insects and have an extremely poisonous bite.

Common house spider

The house spider has long legs covered with strong bristles. It builds its large, flat web in any quiet corner of a house, garage or shed. It stays beneath the web, waiting for prey to get tangled up in its sticky strands, and then removes and eats the prey.

Family: Agelenidae
Size: 0.15–2 cm (1/16–3/4 in) long
Number of species: about 1,150
Habitat: worldwide

Family: Dysderidae
Size: 2 cm (¾ in) long
Number of species: about 530
Habitat: temperate

Woodlouse spider

These spiders have only six eyes – most spiders have eight. They spend the day hiding under stones and come out at night to hunt woodlice. Woodlice have strong external skeletons but this spider can pierce the body armour with its huge sharp fangs.

Green lynx spider

This fast-moving, active hunter does not build webs but chases its prey over plants, jumping from leaf to leaf. It has good eyesight, which helps it spot its prey, and its green colour helps to keep it hidden when it rests on leaves. The female spins a silken egg sac that she attaches to plants.

Family: Araneidae
Size: 0.15–3 cm (1/16–1¼ in) long
Number of species: about 3,050
Habitat: worldwide

Orchard spider

Although a member of the orb weaver family, the orchard spider does not make a web. She simply sits on the branch of a tree and grabs any moth that comes near with her strong front legs. She may release a scent that attracts the moths to her.

Family: Oxyopidae
Size: 0.3–1.5 cm (1/8–5/8 in) long
Number of species: about 500
Habitat: worldwide

Water spider

This is the only spider that lives its whole life in water. So that it can breathe underwater, it spins a bell-shaped home of silk, attached to water plants, and supplies it with bubbles of air collected at the surface. Then it sits inside its bell, waiting for prey to come near. It pounces on the prey and takes it back to the bell to eat.

Family: Pisauridae
Size: 0.6–2.5 cm (¼–1 in) long
Number of species: about 340
Habitat: worldwide

Family: Agelenidae
Size: 0.15–2 cm (1/16–¾ in) long
Number of species: about 1,150
Habitat: worldwide

Nursery-web spider

These spiders do not build a web to catch prey but to protect their young. The female carries her egg sac with her until the eggs are almost ready to hatch. Then she spins a web over the eggs to protect them while they hatch. She stands guard nearby.

ORB WEAVERS

Very few creatures build traps to catch their prey. Among the best-known are the orb weaver spiders that build the webs most often seen in our houses and gardens. There are about 3,050 species of these spiders living all over the world. Spiders build their webs with two types of silk that comes from glands at the end of the body. The silk is liquid when it comes out of the nozzle-like openings of small structures at the end of the abdomen, called spinnerets. One type of silk hardens into extremely tough, non-sticky thread; the other type is sticky and used for the centre of the web. Once the web is built, the spider waits near the centre or hides nearby, linked to the web by a signal thread. Through this, the spider can sense any movement or disturbance in the web. Once prey is caught in the sticky part of the web, the spider rushes over, bites it and wraps it in strands of silk to prevent it from escaping.

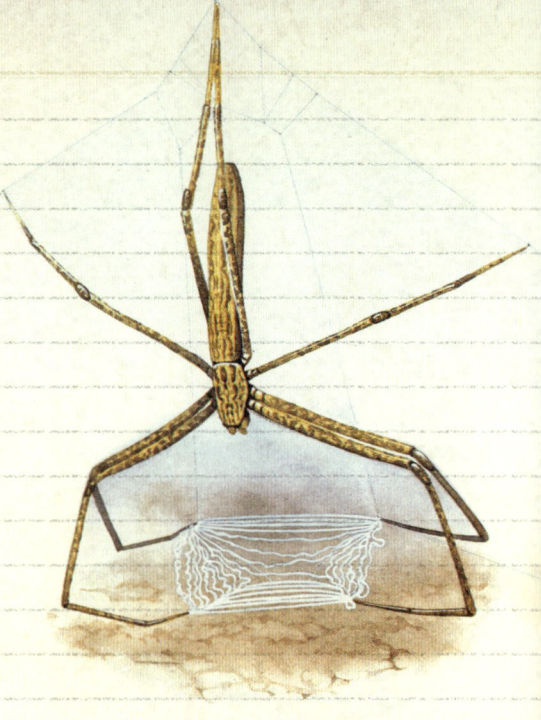

OGRE-FACED SPIDER

This spider takes its web to the prey. It makes a small but strong net of very sticky threads in a framework of dry silk. Once the trap is made, the spider hangs from a twig on silken lines, holding the net in its four front legs. When an insect comes near, the spider stretches the net wide so the prey flies into it and becomes entangled. The catch is then bundled up in the net and taken away to eat.

BUILDING A WEB

First, the orb weaver spider makes a framework of strong, non-sticky threads that are firmly attached to surrounding plants or other supports. Spokes are added and the spider spins a widely spaced temporary spiral. With everything locked in place, the spider then moves inwards, spinning the sticky spiral that will trap the prey and removing the temporary spiral. The whole process takes less than an hour and the spider may build a new web every night.

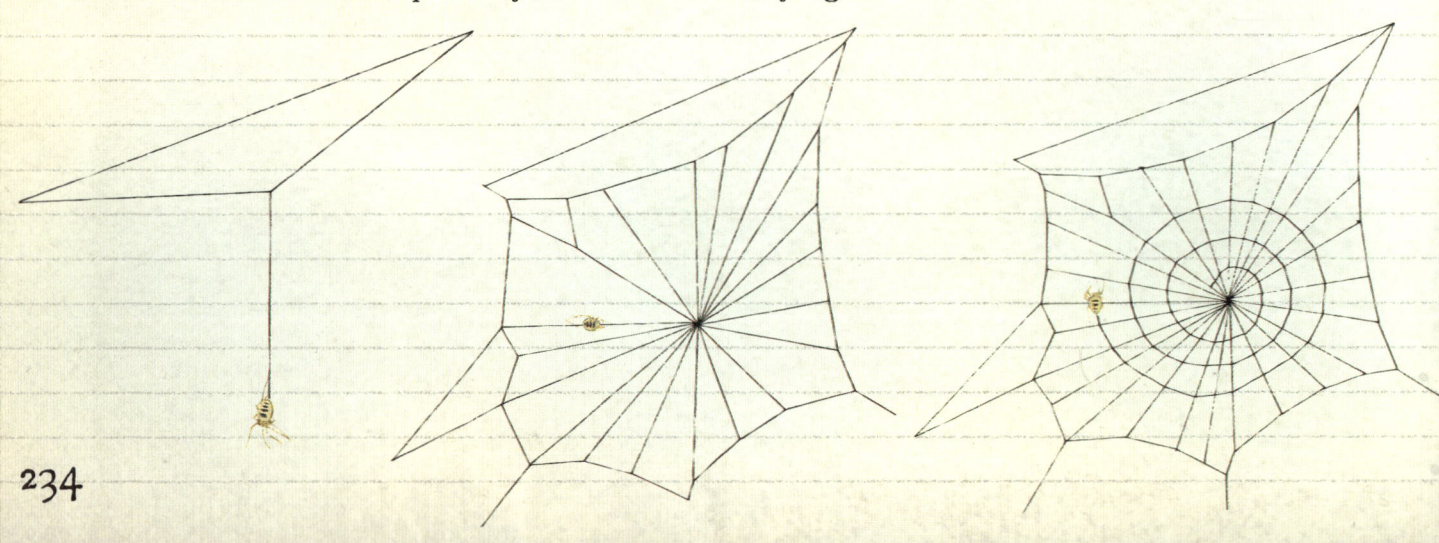

SHEET-WEB SPIDER

Yet another kind of trap is woven by this spider. It makes a flat, sheet-like web, which may measure as much as 30 cm (12 in) across, and lies in wait beneath it. Above the web there are many threads holding it in place. When a prey hits these threads it falls down on to the sheet web, where it is grabbed from below by the spider.

This orb web spider has caught a butterfly in her web and is wrapping the prey in threads of silk so that it cannot escape. She will then carry it off to eat in her hiding place near the web.

A WIDE WEB

The European garden spider, also known as the cross or diadem spider, builds a large orbital web that measures as much as 40 cm (15¾ in) across and catches butterflies, wasps, and flies. The spider has extra, claw-like structures on each foot that help it grip on to the dry lines of the web while avoiding the sticky threads. If the spider touches the sticky part, a special oily covering on its legs prevents it getting trapped.

Children's Animal Encyclopedia

235

SCORPIONS AND OTHER ARACHNIDS

There are about 1,500 kinds of scorpions living everywhere from deserts to rainforests in warm parts of the world. They use the venomous sting at the end of the body to kill prey and to defend themselves. A few kinds of scorpions have venom so strong that it can kill a human, but the sting of most is no worse than that of a bee or wasp. Also in the arachnid group are tiny mites and ticks. Mites eat aphid eggs and prey on other small insects. Some also live as parasites on other animals. Ticks feed on the blood of birds, mammals and reptiles.

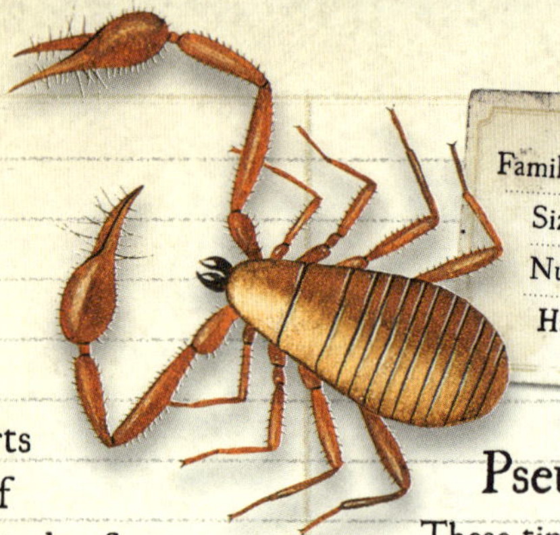

Family: Cheliferidae
Size: up to 0.6 cm (¼ in) long
Number of species: about 300
Habitat: worldwide

Pseudoscorpion

These tiny soil-dwelling relatives of the scorpion have venom glands in their pedipalps, which they use when attacking prey. They do not have a sting. Pseudoscorpions have silk glands and they spin cocoons in which to spend the winter.

Family: Solpugidae
Size: 0.6-6 cm (¼-2½ in) long
Number of species: about 190
Habitat: tropical

Wind scorpion

A group related to true scorpions, wind scorpions, also known as sunspiders, are fast-running hunters. Common in desert areas, they come out at night to hunt insects and even small lizards. They use their pedipalps and front legs as feelers.

Centruroides scorpion

This scorpion hides under stones on the ground during the day and comes out at night to seize insects and spiders in its powerful pincers. The female carries her newborn young around on her back for a few weeks until they are big enough to fend for themselves.

Family: Thelyphonidae
Size: 14.5 cm (5¾ in) long including tail
Number of species: about 110
Habitat: tropical North and South America

Family: Buthidae
Size: up to 12 cm (4¾ in) long
Number of species: about 650
Habitat: worldwide

Whip scorpion

Not a true scorpion, the whip scorpion has a long, thin, whip-like tail and no stinger. It has four pairs of legs but uses the first pair as feelers. The whip scorpion's other common name is vinegaroon because it can spray an acidic, vinegary liquid from glands near the base of its tail when threatened.

Children's Animal Encyclopedia

Velvet mite

Family: Trombidiidae
Size: up to 0.5 cm (3/16 in) long
Number of species: about 280
Habitat: worldwide

This mite gets its common name from the thick, soft hair that covers its rounded body. The adults are free-living, not parasites, and feed mostly on insect eggs. They lay their own eggs on the ground and when the larvae hatch they live as parasites on insects and spiders, feeding on their body fluids.

House dust mite

These mites are common in houses throughout the world. They feed on scales of skin found in house dust. Their droppings contain materials that can cause an allergic reaction or asthma (difficulty breathing) in some sensitive people.

Family: Pyroglyphidae
Size: 0.25–0.5 mm (1/100–3/100 in) long
Number of species: 20
Habitat: worldwide

Scorpion

Family: Scorpionidae
Size: up to 21 cm (8½ in) long
Number of species: about 200
Habitat: tropical

The scorpion finds prey mostly by its sense of touch, using fine hairs attached to nerves on the body, legs and claws to sense movements. It grabs the prey in its huge claws and then swings its sting forwards over its body to inject poison into its victim to paralyse or kill it before eating.

Harvestman

Also known as the daddy-long-legs, this relative of spiders has a rounded body without the narrow waist typical of spiders. All its legs are very long and thin but the second pair are the longest. Usually active at night, the harvestman hunts insects. The female lays her eggs in the ground where they stay through the winter and hatch out in the spring.

Family: Phalangiidae
Size: up to 4 cm (1⅜ in) long
Number of species: about 380
Habitat: worldwide

Tick

Family: Ixodidae
Size: ⅛–⅜ in (0.3–1 cm) long
Number of species: about 690
Habitat: worldwide

Ticks are parasites – they live by feeding on the blood of birds, mammals and reptiles. They stay on the host for several days while feeding, attached by their strong mouthparts. Some species may pass on diseases as they feed.

237

SNAILS, SLUGS AND OTHER LAND INVERTEBRATES

As well as insects and spiders, many other kinds of invertebrates spend their lives on land. Most molluscs live in the sea, but there are land species of slugs and snails. Woodlice are related to crustaceans, such as the sea-living crabs and shrimps. Earthworms are relatives of the segmented worms in the sea, but they spend their lives burrowing through the soil. All of these animals are common worldwide. Like insects and spiders, millipedes and centipedes are arthropods. They live everywhere from tropical rainforests to tundra. They may be mistaken for insects, but they have many more legs and do not have wings. Their bodies are sensitive to drying out in the sun and so they usually come out only at night.

Earthworm
Lumbricus terrestris

Earthworms are common in soil all over the world. They spend most of their lives underground and only come to the surface at night or in wet weather. Dead leaves and other plant material are their main food, but they also eat soil, digesting what they can and excreting the rest.

Size: up to 30 cm (11¾ in) long
Range: worldwide
Habitat: inhabited areas and farmland, deciduous forest, temperate grassland

Woodlouse
Armadillidium vulgare

A woodlouse is related to the crustaceans, like a crab or shrimp, but it has become adapted to live on land. Its body is made up of 13 segments and it has 7 pairs of legs. It hides in moist, dark places during the day and comes out at night to feed on decaying plants and tiny dead creatures.

Size: 1 cm (⅜ in) long
Range: worldwide
Habitat: inhabited areas and farmland, deciduous and tropical grassland and forest, northern forest

Great black slug
Arion ater

The slug is a mollusc, like a snail, but has no external shell. All land molluscs make mucus. This slime helps stop the slug's body drying out and allows the creature to move more easily. The slug leaves trails of slime wherever it goes and these help it find its way. It feeds mostly on rotting plant and animal material, which it finds by smell.

Size: 15 cm (6 in) long
Range: Europe and North America
Habitat: inhabited areas and farmland, deciduous forest, temperate grassland

Children's Animal Encyclopedia

Size: up to 13 cm (5 in) long
Range: worldwide
Habitat: deciduous forest, tropical evergreen forest

Size: 3 cm (1¼ in)
Range: Europe
Habitat: inhabited areas and farmland, deciduous forest

Armoured millipede
Polydesmus spp.

Armoured millipedes have a hard outer shell. They live in forests, where they feed on leaves and other rotting plants on the forest floor. They have poison glands and some can actually spray poison to defend themselves against enemies.

Centipede
Lithobius forficatus

The centipede moves fast on its 15 pairs of legs and preys on insects, spiders and other small creatures. It seizes prey in its sharp claws, which can inject a powerful poison to paralyse the victim.

Size: up to 9 cm (3½ in)
Range: Europe
Habitat: inhabited areas and farmland, deciduous forest

Millipede
Julus terrestris

Despite their name, long-bodied millipedes do not have a thousand legs – most have only a couple of hundred. They are slow-moving plant eaters that live under stones or tree bark or hidden inside rotting vegetation.

Garden snail
Helix aspersa

Different types of land snail live all over the world. All have a soft, slug-like body and a hard shell carried on the back. Most snails spend the day inside their shell and come out at night to find food such as leafy plants. They move by making rippling movements of the fleshy "foot" that makes up the underside of the body, sliding along on a layer of slime secreted by the foot.

Size: body: 9 cm (3½ in) long
Range: Europe
Habitat: inhabited areas and farmland, deciduous forest, temperate grassland

239

SEA CREATURES

As well as the thousands of kinds of fish that live in the oceans there is also a huge range of invertebrates. Marine invertebrates, including clams, crabs and jellyfish, live in every part of the ocean from the surface waters to the deepest sea. The most highly populated waters are those near the surface. Here, plenty of light penetrates to about 100 m (330 ft) and plant plankton thrive. These microscopic plants are eaten by animal plankton – tiny animals that drift in surface waters and are themselves eaten by larger sea creatures.

SPONGES, JELLYFISH AND RELATIVES

Sponges have such simple bodies that they look more like plants than animals. Their larvae are free-swimming, but adult sponges remain in one place on a rock or on the seabed. Sea anemones belong to a large group of creatures called cnidarians, as do coral and jellyfish. Most have a simple tube-like body and tentacles armed with stinging cells. Comb jellies are a separate group. They are small, translucent animals that float in surface waters. Lamp shells are shelled creatures that can anchor themselves to rocks or the seabed by a fleshy stalk.

Size: 15 cm (6 in) long
Range: Arctic, Atlantic and North Pacific oceans
Habitat: oceanic

Common comb jelly
Bolinopsis infundibulum

The comb jelly moves with the help of tiny hairs arranged in lines down its bag-like body. These hairs are called comb plates and they beat together to push the comb jelly through the water. It catches prey such as shrimp and other small creatures.

Size: up to 50 cm (19¾ in) long
Range: tropical waters worldwide
Habitat: coastal waters

Vase sponge
Callyspongia spp.

Sponges are among the simplest of animals. To feed, they draw water into the chambers of the body, where tiny particles of food are trapped and digested. The water also brings oxygen to the creatures and removes carbon dioxide.

Size: bell: 10 cm (4 in) wide; tentacles: 3 m (10 ft) long
Range: Atlantic, Indian and Pacific oceans
Habitat: oceanic

Mauve stinger
Pelagia noctiluca

Like most jellyfish, this creature has many stinging cells on its long tentacles. These cells protect it from enemies and help it to catch plankton to eat. Although known as the mauve stinger, it may be yellow, red or even brown in colour.

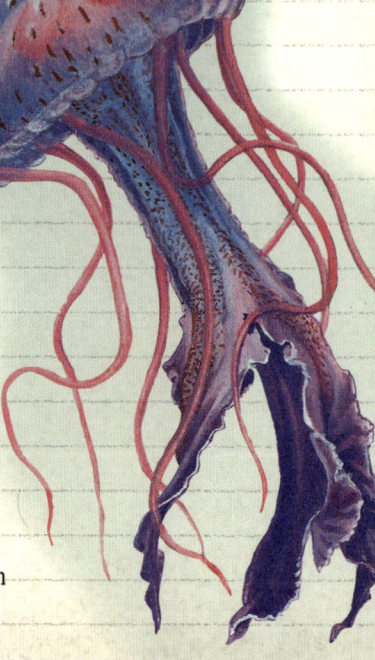

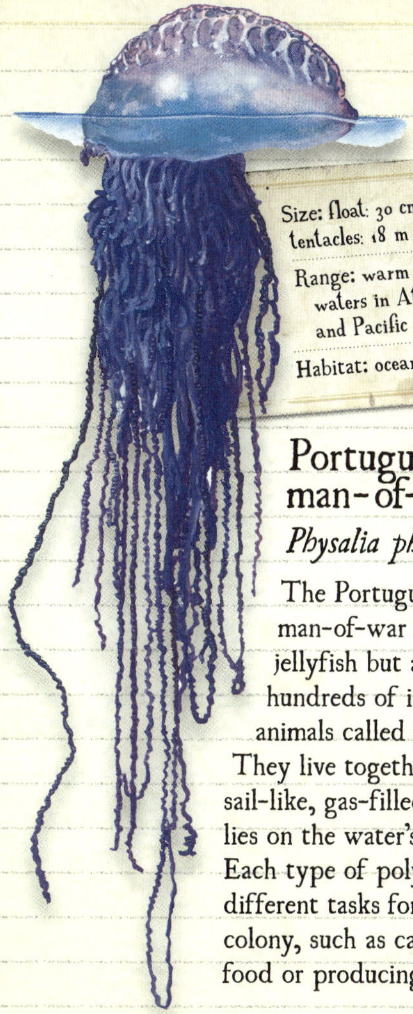

Children's Animal Encyclopedia

Size: float: 30 cm (11¾ in) long; tentacles: 18 m (60 ft) long
Range: warm and tropical waters in Atlantic, Indian and Pacific oceans
Habitat: oceanic

Portuguese-man-of-war
Physalia physalis

The Portuguese man-of-war is not a true jellyfish but a colony of hundreds of individual animals called polyps. They live together under the sail-like, gas-filled float that lies on the water's surface. Each type of polyp performs different tasks for the colony, such as capturing food or producing eggs.

Size: up to 38 cm (15 in) tall
Range: North Atlantic Ocean, Mediterranean Sea
Habitat: coastal waters

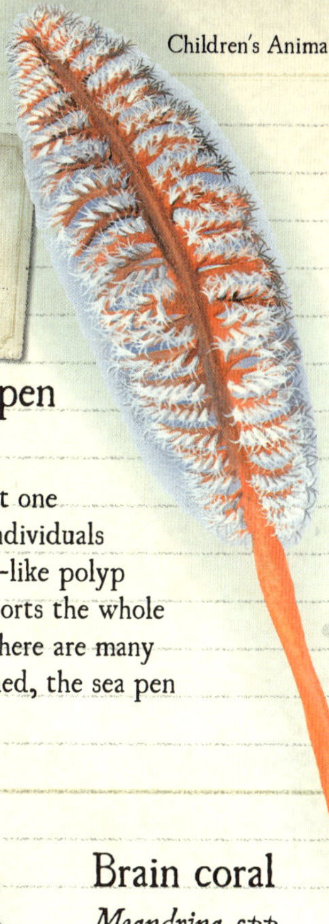

Phosphorescent sea pen
Pennatula phosphorea

The feather-like sea pen is not one animal but a group of many individuals called polyps. One large stem-like polyp stands in the seabed and supports the whole group. On the side branches there are many small feeding polyps. If touched, the sea pen glows with phosphorescence.

Brain coral
Meandrina spp.

Brain coral is most common in water 6–12 m (19½–39½ ft) deep. It lives in dome-shaped colonies of tiny anemone-like creatures called polyps. Each of the polyps has a hard skeleton. These make up the rocky base of the colony.

Size: Colony up to 1 m (3¼ ft) wide
Range: tropical Indian and Pacific oceans and Caribbean Sea
Habitat: coral reefs

Size: 3 cm (1¼ in) long
Range: Atlantic Ocean
Habitat: deep sea, coastal waters

Lamp shell
Terebratulina septentrionalis

The lamp shell belongs to a group of animals called brachiopods, members of which have lived on Earth for about 550 million years. It has two shells and a short stalk on which it can move around. When the shells open they expose folded tentacles lined with tiny hairs. These hairs drive water over the tentacles, which trap tiny particles of food.

Sea anemone
Urticina spp.

The sea anemone may look like a flower, but it is actually an animal that catches other creatures to eat. At one end of its body is a sucking disc that keeps it attached to a rock. At the other end is the mouth, surrounded by tentacles.

Size: up to 25 cm (9¾ in) tall
Range: Atlantic and Pacific coasts
Habitat: coast

CRUSTACEANS

There are about 70,000 species of crustaceans, including such creatures as barnacles, crabs, lobsters and shrimps. Woodlice live on land and there are some shrimps and other species in fresh water, but most crustaceans live in the sea. Typically, they have a tough outer skeleton, which protects the soft body within. The head is made up of six segments, on which there are two pairs of antennae and several different sets of mouthparts. The rest of the body may be divided into a thorax and abdomen, and carries the walking legs.

Size: up to 80 cm (31½ in), including stalk
Range: Atlantic and Pacific oceans
Habitat: oceanic

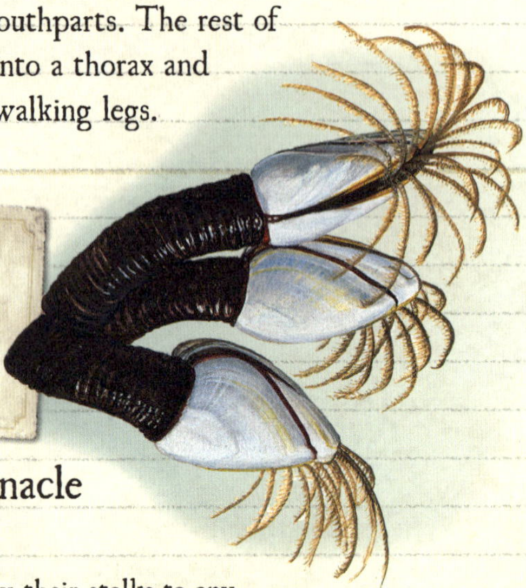

Common goose barnacle
Lepas anatifera

Goose barnacles live fixed by their stalks to any object floating in the open sea, including logs and buoys as well as boats. The barnacle's body is enclosed by a shell made of five plates. These open at the top so that the barnacle can extend its six pairs of feathery arms and collect tiny particles of food from the water.

Size: up to 1.1 m (3⅝ ft)
Range: North Atlantic coasts
Habitat: coast, coastal waters

American lobster
Homarus americanus

During the day this large crustacean hides in rock crevices, but at night it comes out to hunt. It uses its huge pincers to crack and tear apart prey such as molluscs and crabs. In the summer, the female lobster lays thousands of eggs, which she carries around with her on the underside of her body. The eggs hatch into shrimp-like larvae, which float in surface waters for a few weeks. They then settle on the seabed and start to develop into adults.

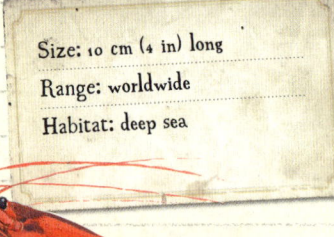

Size: 10 cm (4 in) long
Range: worldwide
Habitat: deep sea

Deep-sea shrimp
Pasiphaea spp.

The deep-sea shrimp's antennae are longer than its body. It spreads its antennae out in the water to help it find food in the darkness of the deep sea. It eats any dead and decaying matter that it comes across.

Size: up to 9 cm (3½ in) long
Range: Antarctic Ocean
Habitat: ocean seabed

Giant isopod
Glyptonotus antarcticus

A sea-living relative of the wood louse, the giant isopod lives in the Antarctic, where it catches any food it can find. It also scavenges on the seabed for dead and dying creatures. Antarctic isopods are much bigger than those elsewhere in the world.

Children's Animal Encyclopedia

Antarctic krill
Euphausia superba

Shrimp-like krill feed on plant plankton and tiny creatures that they sieve from the water. In turn, krill are the main food of many fish, penguins and even whales. A blue whale can eat as many as four million krill in a day. Krill are extremely common and sometimes occur in such large numbers that the sea looks red.

Size: up to 5 cm (2 in) long
Range: southern oceans
Habitat: oceanic

Size: up to 10 cm (4 in) long
Range: North Atlantic coasts
Habitat: coast, coastal waters

Size: up to 2.5 cm (1 in) long
Range: Atlantic coasts
Habitat: coast, coastal waters

Hermit crab
Pagurus bernhardus

Unlike other crabs, the hermit crab has no hard shell of its own. It protects its soft body by living in the discarded shell of another creature, such as a snail. The crab has large pincers on its first pair of legs, which it uses to grab its prey.

Amphipod
Gammarus locusta

This small crustacean lives on the lower shore under rocks or among seaweed, and feeds on tiny pieces of plant and animal matter. On its abdomen are three pairs of jumping legs. The female amphipod holds her developing young in a pouch on the underside of her body.

Pink shrimp
Pandalus montagui

Shrimps have much lighter shells than crabs or lobsters. The limbs on the abdomen are used for swimming, while some of those on the thorax are for walking and others are used as mouthparts.

Size: up to 12.5 cm (5 in)
Range: Arctic Ocean, north Atlantic coasts
Habitat: coast, coastal waters

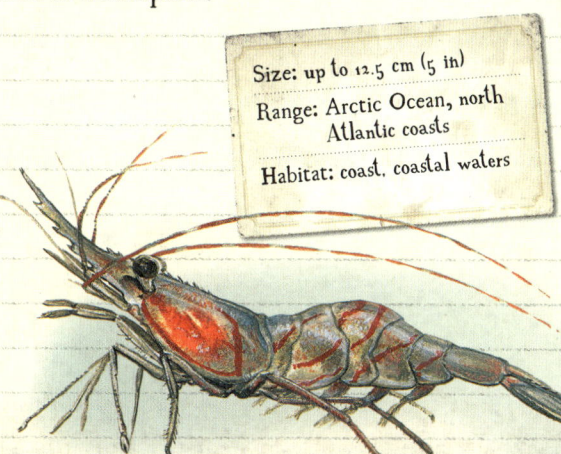

Size: up to 30 cm (12 in) wide
Range: North Atlantic coasts
Habitat: coast

Edible crab
Cancer spp.

Most crabs have a strong shell, which protects the body, and five pairs of legs. On the first pair are powerful pincers used to break open the shells of prey, such as molluscs. The other legs are smaller. Crabs live among rocks on the lower shore.

243

Molluscs

MOLLUSCS

There are at least 110,000 living species of molluscs. They are divided into three main groups: gastropods, such as limpets and snails; bivalves, which include clams, mussels and scallops; and cephalopods, such as squid, cuttlefish and octopus. Slugs and some kinds of snails live on land and there are freshwater snails and clams, but the greatest range of molluscs is found in the sea. In most molluscs, the body is divided into three parts: the head, which contains the mouth and sense organs; the body; and the foot, a fleshy part of the body on which the animal moves along. Most, but not all, molluscs have a tough shell that protects the soft body.

Size: up to 12.5 cm (5 in) long
Range: Atlantic Ocean and Caribbean Sea
Habitat: coral reefs

Atlantic deer cowrie
Macrocypraea cervus

This type of sea snail has a beautiful shiny shell. Unlike most snails, the cowrie's mantle can be extended to cover the outside of the shell and camouflage the animal. (The mantle is a thin fold of tissue, part of which makes the shell.) The opening of the shell is edged with 35 teeth.

Clam
Saxidomus nuttalli

The usual home of the clam is a burrow deep in a sandy or muddy seabed. It digs the burrow with its foot, a fleshy part of its body. Two long tubes extend from the shell. Water and food (tiny living particles) go in through one tube. The water then goes out the other tube.

Size: 15 cm (6 in) long
Range: North Pacific Ocean
Habitat: coastal waters

Size: 10 cm (4 in) long
Range: Atlantic coasts
Habitat: coastal waters

Iceland scallop
Chlamys islandica

The scallop has a soft body protected by two shells. A row of well-developed eyes can be seen when the shells are slightly parted. The scallop moves by flapping its shells together, forcing out jets of water that push it forwards.

Size: up to 10 cm (4 in) long
Range: Atlantic and Pacific coasts
Habitat: coast, coastal waters

Oyster
Crassostrea virginica

The oyster is a type of bivalve. It has a soft body protected by two hard shells, which are held together by strong muscles. It eats tiny pieces of plant and animal food, which it filters from the water. The water is drawn into the partly opened shell and any food is caught on tiny sticky hairs on the oyster's gills.

Common octopus
Octopus vulgaris

The octopus has eight long arms lined with suckers. It uses these to pull itself along, but it can also swim quickly by shooting jets of water out of its body. It spends much of its time hiding in crevices, then grabbing prey such as crabs, clams and shrimp.

Size: up to 100 cm (39½ in) long
Range: worldwide except polar waters
Habitat: coastal waters

Children's Animal Encyclopedia

Size: 40 cm (15¾ in) long
Range: Atlantic Ocean
Habitat: coastal waters

Lightning whelk
Busycon contrarium

This large whelk has a beautiful spiral shell with brown markings. It lives on sandy or muddy seabeds in shallow water and feeds mostly on other molluscs, such as clams, which it digs out of the mud.

Size: body: 15 cm (6 in) long
Range: Indian Ocean, Red and Mediterranean seas
Habitat: coral reefs

Chromodoris nudibranch
Chromodoris annulata

Nudibranches, or sea slugs, are related to snails, but they have no shells and are often brightly coloured. This species has a pair of horn-like projections and a clump of feathery gills on its back. Sponges are its main food.

Purple sea snail
Janthina janthina

This little snail cannot swim, but it drifts in the surface waters of the sea, clinging to a raft of bubbles. These are made from mucus the snail secretes, which hardens when it enters the water.

Size: 2.5 cm (1 in) long, including tentacles
Range: Atlantic, Indian and Pacific oceans
Habitat: oceanic

Longfin inshore squid
Doryteuthis pealeii

Size: up to 76 cm (30 in) long, including tentacles
Range: northwest Atlantic Ocean
Habitat: oceanic

The squid has a long, torpedo-shaped body, four pairs of arms, and one pair of much longer tentacles. Suckers on the arms and the tips of the tentacles help the squid grasp its prey – mostly fish and crustaceans. A fast swimmer, the squid moves by a type of jet propulsion, shooting water out of its body to force itself backwards through the water.

245

Rock clingers

ROCK CLINGERS

While most marine creatures swim or float freely in the water, some live firmly attached to rocks or other surfaces. This helps protect them from the waves that sweep over them twice a day as the tide comes in. Barnacles, one kind of rock clinger, are among the most common creatures on the shore. Huge colonies of them cover rocks and shore debris, and even attach themselves to other creatures such as mussels. Barnacles begin life as free-swimming larvae and spend a month or more floating in coastal waters, feeding on plankton. During its final larval stage, each barnacle finds somewhere to settle. It fixes itself to the surface with a cement-like substance that it makes in glands in its body. Once settled, it does not move again. Limpets, periwinkles and chitons can all cling to rocks by means of a sucker-like foot, which is so strong that they are almost impossible to move. But all these creatures can also move around on their own to graze on algae.

ROUGH PERIWINKLE

There are many types of periwinkle, each adapted for life in different parts of the shore. The rough periwinkle lives on stones and rocks higher up the shore than most other species.

CHITON

Unlike other molluscs, the chiton has a shell made up of eight sections held together by muscles. If in danger, the chiton can roll itself up like an armadillo.

COMMON LIMPET

As limpets move over rocks feeding on algae, they leave a sticky trail of mucus behind them. This helps each limpet make its way back to the exact same place on the rock after each feeding trip.

ACORN BARNACLE

When covered by water at high tide, the barnacle opens its shell at the top and puts out its feathery arms to gather plankton to eat. When the tide is out, the barnacle keeps its trapdoor top firmly closed.

Children's Animal Encyclopedia

COMMON MUSSEL

The threads that hold the mussel on to rocks are made as a sticky fluid inside a gland in the mussel's body. This fluid hardens to keep the mussel firmly in place. The shell is in two halves. These are normally held tight together, but they can be partly opened so that the mussel can filter tiny pieces of food from the water.

BLUE-RAYED LIMPET

Not all limpets cling to rocks. The blue-rayed limpet lives attached seaweed, which is anchored to rock or the seabed near the shore. The limpet grazes on the seaweed fronds, feeding on the seaweed itself and on small plants growing there, such as algae.

A colourful painted topshell clings to rocks on the seashore, surrounded by sea anemones and other creatures. The topshell, which is a cone-shaped kind of snail, feeds on tiny plants called algae growing on the rocks.

WORMS AND ECHINODERMS

There are about 21,000 species of segmented, or annelid, worms. They include earthworms on land, as well as some freshwater worms such as leeches, but most live in the sea. All have a body that is divided into a number of segments. All 7,000 species of echinoderms live in the sea. There are four main groups – brittle stars, starfish, sea cucumbers, and sea urchins and sand dollars. Many have a body that is divided into five radiating parts with a mouth at one end and an anus at the other. Most echinoderms move around using tiny stilts called tube feet, each tipped with a sucking disc.

Sea mouse
Aphrodita aculeata

Size: 18 cm (7 in) long
Range: Atlantic and Mediterranean coasts
Habitat: coast, coastal waters, deep sea

Despite its plump shape, the sea mouse is actually a kind of worm. Its upper side is covered with lots of greyish-brown bristles that give it a furry look and inspire its common name. The sea mouse spends much of its life under mud or sand in shallow water.

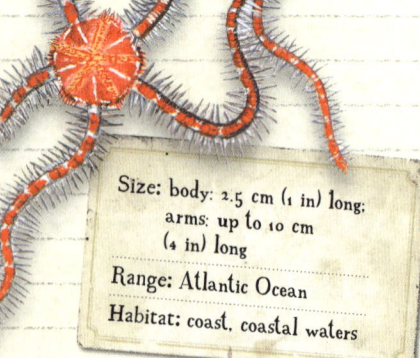

Sea lily
Crinoidea spp.

Size: up to 1.5 m (5 ft), including stalk
Range: worldwide
Habitat: deep sea

This relative of the starfish lives attached to a rock by a stalk. Its branching arms are lined with tiny sucker-like tube feet. When feeding, the sea lily spreads its arms wide and traps plankton and other tiny particles with its tube feet. The food is then passed down grooves lined with hairs to the mouth, at the centre of the body.

Long-spined urchin
Diadema antillarum

Sharp spines protect the urchin's rounded body from enemies. The urchin's mouth is on the underside of the body and has five teeth arranged in a circle for chewing food. By day these urchins stay hidden on the reef, but at night they come out to feed on algae.

Size: body 10 cm (4 in) wide; spines: 10-40 cm (4-15¾ in) long
Range: Atlantic Ocean and Caribbean Sea
Habitat: coral reefs

Common brittle star
Ophiothrix fragilis

Size: body: 2.5 cm (1 in) long; arms: up to 10 cm (4 in) long
Range: Atlantic Ocean
Habitat: coast, coastal waters

The brittle star has a central disc-like body and five long spiny arms, each separate from the other. The animal's mouth is on the underside of the disc. The brittle star uses its long arms to catch small crustaceans and other creatures.

Children's Animal Encyclopedia

Size: 12.5 cm (5 in)
Range: Atlantic Ocean and Caribbean Sea
Habitat: coral reefs

Size: up to 25 cm (9¾ in) long
Range: North Atlantic Ocean
Habitat: coastal waters

Magnificent feather duster
Sabellastarte magnifica

The body of this spectacular worm usually stays hidden in a flexible tube attached to a reef or the seabed. The tube is made of fine sand stuck together with a gluey substance made in the worm's body. The worm catches food with its crown of feathery gills.

Black sea cucumber
Holothuria forskali

Sea cucumbers are related to starfish, but they have long simple bodies. At one end is the anus and at the other is the mouth, surrounded by food-gathering tentacles. Rows of tiny tube feet run the length of the body. When disturbed, the sea cucumber ejects sticky white threads from its anus, which confuse the predator.

Common sand dollar
Echinarachnius parma

The sand dollar has a flattened disc-like body and a shell that is covered with short spines. On its underside are rows of tiny tube-like feet, which help the sand dollar gather tiny pieces of food from the water.

Size: 7.5 cm (3 in) wide
Range: North Atlantic and Pacific coasts, Arctic Ocean
Habitat: coast, coastal waters

Size: 12 cm (4¾ in) across
Range: western Atlantic Ocean and Caribbean Sea
Habitat: coral reefs

Green paddle worm
Eulalia viridis

This worm lives under rocks among seaweed, both on the shore and in deeper water. It has four pairs of tentacles on its head and lots of tiny leaf-like paddles down each side of its long body. It feeds mainly on other worms.

Size: up to 15 cm (6 in) long
Range: Northwest Atlantic coasts and Mediterranean
Habitat: coast

Thorny starfish
Echinaster sentus

Large spines cover the body and five arms of this starfish. Two rows of special feet, called tube feet, extend down each arm. The tube feet work together, extending and contracting, to move the starfish around as it searches for prey.

WHY DO ANIMALS BUILD NESTS?

While many animals manage without a nest or a home of any kind, others build structures that they use for shelter and for rearing their young in safety. This home may be specially built, like a bird's nest, or simply a natural hole or a sheltered spot. Homes may be made in trees, on the ground or in underground burrows. Birds generally use their nests only when breeding. They lay and incubate their eggs in nests and care for their young, but usually leave the nest once the young have gone. Some mammals, such as beavers and prairie dogs, spend much of their time in the homes they make. These may contain chambers for sleeping, caring for young and storing food. Insects such as bees, wasps, ants and termites also build elaborate homes.

The nest of the penduline tit hangs from the end of a slender twig, where it is hard for predators to reach it. The nest is woven from plant fibres and has an entrance near the top.

Children's Animal Encyclopedia

SHELTER

The female harvest mouse builds a nest as a shelter for her young. She finds some sturdy cereal stems and starts by winding the leaves of one stem around another to make a platform about 50 cm (19¾ in) above the ground. She then takes lengths of grass or leaves and uses these to weave a ball-like structure, which measures about 10 cm (4 in) across.

Stumps of trees used by beavers to build lodge

Dam

TERMITES

This large mound is made by a colony of small, soft-bodied insects called termites. The mound is made of soil mixed with the termites' faeces and inside is a complex nest. A maze of chambers and tunnels contains special areas for food storage and for eggs and young. Chimneys inside the mounds let air in and out and help keep the temperature in the nest comfortable.

BEAVERS

Beavers dam a stream with branches and mud to create a lake in which to store a winter food supply. A shelter, or lodge, is then made of branches by the dam.

INDEX

A

aardvarks 14
adalahs 188
adaptations 62–3
albatrosses 66, 80, 83
alewives 162
alligators 115, 116–17
amberjacks 172
amphibians 134–49
amphipods 243
anacondas 130
angelfish 154, 172, 174
angler fish 63, 155, 170, 171
annelid worms 197, 248
anoles 126
anteaters 14
antelopes 48, 50, 51
antennae 110
antlions 202, 203
ants 192, 222, 228–9, 250
apes 25
aphids 192, 207
arachnids 230–7
armadillos 14
arrow-poison frogs 134–5, 137, 148–9
arthropods 196, 238
avocets 74
axolotls 141
aye-ayes 20, 21

B

baboons 23
badgers 30, 31, 192
ballyhoos 181
bandicoots 11
barbels 170
barbets 94
barnacles 242, 246
barracudas 155, 172, 176
bats 16–19
beaks, birds' 67
beardfish 184
bears 26, 28, 29
beavers 55, 56, 250–1
bees 222–3, 226–7, 250
beetles 206, 209–13, 212, 213
bichirs 160
biddies 205
birds 64–109, 250
birds of paradise 108–9
birds of prey 86–91
bivalves 244
black drums 175
blennies 177
blind snakes 130
blood suckers 18
blue tangs 175
bluebirds 100
boa constrictors 130
boars 47
bongos 51
bony fish 155
boomslangs 131
bovids 48, 51
bowerbirds 71
bowfins 160
boxfish 190, 191
brachiopods 197, 240
bream 164, 165
breathing 36, 152, 155, 178
bristletails 198, 199
brittle stars 248
budgerigars 97
buffalo fish 164, 165
buffaloes 51, 193
bugs 206–8
bulbuls 102
bumblebees 222
bummalows 181
buntings 102
burbots 170
bushbabies 20, 21
butterflies 151, 214, 216, 218–19
butterflyfish 174
buzzards 86, 87, 88

C

caddis flies 217
caecilians 136, 141
caimans 117
camels 48, 63
camouflage 32, 62, 128, 158
capercaillies 70
capuchin monkeys 24
capybaras 60, 61
cardinals 101
caribou 49
carnivorous mammals 26–35
carp 164
cartilaginous fish 154, 156
cassowaries 71, 72
caterpillars 151, 216, 221
catfish 166–7
cats 26, 32–3
centipedes 196, 238, 239
cephalopods 244
cephalothorax 196
chameleons 112–13, 128–9
charr 169
cheetahs 33
chickadees 103
chimpanzees 25
chinchillas 60
chipmunks 55
chitons 246
chuckwallas 124
cicadas 206
cichlids 172
civets 26, 30
clams 240, 244
cleaner fish 192
clingfish 175
clownfish 193
cnidarians 197, 240
coatis 28
cobras 133
cockatoos 97
cockroaches 198–9
cocks of the rock 106
cocoons 221
cod 170–1

coelacanths 190
cold-blooded animals 115, 136
colobus monkeys 23
colonies 18, 85, 222, 226, 228, 246, 251
comb jellies 197, 240
communication 110–11
congo eels 138
corals 240, 241
cormorants 67, 80
cowries 244
coyotes 110
crabs 111, 196, 240, 242–3
crane flies 215
cranes 76, 77, 79
crickets 198, 200–1
crocodiles 115, 116–19
crows 67, 104
crustaceans 196, 238, 242–3
cuckoos 96
curassows 71
curlews 75
cusk-eels 170
cuttlefish 244

D

dams, beavers' 250
damselflies 204, 205
darters 194–5, 204
deer 48–50
dinosaurs 115
divers 78
dogfish 156
dogs 26, 110
dolphinfish 173
dolphins 36, 40, 41
dormice 60
dragonets 174
dragonflies 194–5, 202–5
dromedaries 48
ducks 67, 76, 78
dugongs 43

252

E

eagles 66, 67, 86, 87, 88, 90–1
earthworms 238
earwigs 198–9
echidnas 9, 10
echinoderms 197, 248–9
echolocation 16
eels 162–3
eggs *see* young
egrets 76, 78, 192
electric eels 168
elephant-snout fish 161
elephants 8, 44–5, 192
elk 49
emus 71, 73
eutherian mammals 9
exoskeleton 196

F

falcons 86, 89
false vampire bats 16, 19
feathers 66, 67
feeding
  arachnids 151, 234–5
  birds 67, 84, 90–1, 98–9
  fish 155
  insects 128, 151
  mammals 9, 18, 34
  reptiles 119, 128, 150
feet, birds' 67
filefish 191
finches 67, 105, 107
firebrats 199
fireflies 111, 211
fish 152–91
flamingos 76, 79
flatfish 188–9
fleas 206, 208
flies 214–15
flounders 188, 189
flycatchers 106
flyingfish 180
flying foxes 17
footballfish 171
four-eyed fish 183

foxes 27
frigatebirds 82
froghoppers 207
frogs 136–7, 142, 144–9
fruit flies 215

G

game birds 68–70
gannets 80, 82
garfish 180
gars 160
gastropods 244
gavials 116
geckos 124
geese 76
gerbils 58–9
gibbons 9, 25
gila monsters 126
gills 152, 155, 178
giraffes 48, 50
glow-worms 111
gobies 152, 172, 174
goldeyes 161
goldfish 164
gophers 55, 56
gorillas 9, 25
goshawks 87
grass snakes 131
grasshoppers 198, 200
graylings 169
great apes 25
great bustards 73
grebes 77
grenadiers 170
grosbeaks 103
ground birds 68, 171–3
grouse 70
grunions 182
guanacos 48
guinea pigs 60
gulls 81
guppies 182, 183
gurnards 186, 187

H

haddock 170, 171
hake 170

halfbeaks 180
hamsters 57
hares 54
harvestmen 237
hatchetfish 168
hawk moths 216, 220–1
hawks 66, 86, 87
hedgehogs 15
hellbenders 141
herrings 155, 162
hippopotamuses 46, 47
hoatzins 96
honey badgers 192
honeybees 226–7
honeycreepers 101
honeyeaters 105
honeyguides 192
hoofed mammals 46–53
hoopoes 94
hornbills 73, 96
hornets 224
horses 52–3
horseshoe bats 17
howler monkeys 24
hummingbirds 66, 67, 93, 98–9
hunting *see* feeding
hutias 60, 61
hyenas 26, 32

I

ibises 76, 79
Ichthyostega 137
iguanas 115, 125
insects 195, 196, 198–229
invertebrates 194–249
  land 238–9
  sea 240–9
isopods 242

J

jacamars 94
jacanas 75
jaguars 32
jawless fish 154, 156
jays 104

jellyfish 197, 240, 241
jerboas 60
John Dories 184, 185
jungle runners 126
junglefowl 69

K

kangaroo rats 56
kangaroos 13
katydids 201
kingbirds 103
kingfishers 95
kites 87
kiwis 71
koalas 12
Komodo dragons 127
kowaris 11
krill 243

L

lacewings 202, 203
ladybirds 211
Lambeosaurus 115
lampreys 156–7
lamp shells 197, 240
lanternfish 180, 181
lapwings 74
larks 100, 105
larvae 212, 216
leaf insects 62, 201
leeches 197, 248
lemmings 58
lemurs 20
leopards 33
Lepidoptera 216
lice 206–8
limpets 244, 246–7
limpkins 79
ling 170
lionfish 186
lions 33
lizardfish 180, 181
lizards 115, 124–9
lobsters 242
locusts 200
longclaws 105
lorikeets 97

Index

lorises 20
lungfish 190
lynx 32
lyrebirds 107
lyretails 182, 183

M

macaques 22
macaws 96
mackerel 154, 177
magpies 105
mambas 132
mammals 6–61
mammary glands 9
man-of-war fish 176
manakins 105
mandrills 22
manta rays 157
mantids 202
mantisflies 202, 203
marine mammals 36–43
marlins 177
marmosets 20
marsupials 8, 10, 11–13
martins 93
mayflies 205
meerkats 31
mice 57, 59, 251
midges 214
millipedes 196, 238, 239
mites 237
mockingbirds 101
mole-rats 57–8
moles 15
molluscs 197, 238, 244–5
mongooses 26, 30, 31
monk sakis 24
monkeys 22–4
monotremes 8, 9, 10
Moorish idols 175
moose 49
moths 110, 214, 216–17, 220–1
motmots 95
mouths, fish 155
mud daubers 225
mudpuppies 139
mullet 173
mummichogs 182, 183
mussels 244, 247
mustelids 26, 30–1
mutual benefits 192–3

N

narwhals 42
nautiluses 197
needlefish 180, 181
nests 118, 226, 228, 250–1
newts 136, 141
nightingales 100
nightjars 92
nudibranches 245

O

oarfish 184
octopuses 244, 245
okapis 50
olms 138
opahs 185
opossums 11
orang-utans 25
orb weaver spiders 234–5
orioles 106
ospreys 89
ostriches 66, 67, 71, 72
otters 30
owls 86
oxpeckers 193
oystercatchers 75
oysters 244

P

pacus 165
paddlefish 161
panchax 182, 183
pandas 28–9
parakeets 64–5
parasites 192, 193, 206, 237
parrots 64–5, 67, 92, 97
parulas 102
peafowl 68, 69
peccaries 46, 47
pelicans 81
penguins 80, 82–5
perch-like fish 172–7
periwinkles 246
pheasants 66, 69
pigeons 92, 95
pigs 46, 47
pikas 54
pike 168
pinecone fish 184
piranhas 164, 165
pirarucus 160, 161
pittas 107
placenta 8
plaice 189
plankton 240
platypuses 10
plovers 75
pocket gophers 55, 56
poisons and venoms 137, 143, 148–9, 150–1, 159, 230, 236
pollination 226, 227
pollock 171
pompanos 172
pond sliders 120
poorwills 93
porcupinefish 191
porcupines 60, 61
porpoises 40
Portuguese man-of-war 241
possums 12
potoos 92
pouches 8, 10, 11
prairie chickens 70
prairie dogs 55, 250
praying mantises 202
prehistoric animals 115, 137
primates 20–5
proboscis 220
pronghorns 48, 50
protection and safety 150, 192, 193
pseudoscorpions 236
ptarmigans 69
pufferfish 155, 190, 191
puffins 83
pupae 212, 216, 221
pythons 130

Q

quail 68
queens, insect 226, 227, 228
queleas 106
quetzals 94

R

rabbits 54
raccoons 26, 28
race runners 115
rainbowfish 182
rats 57, 59
rattlesnakes 133
rays 156–9
red pandas 28
redshanks 67, 74
reptiles 112–33
rheas 71, 73
rhinoceroses 52–3
roach 164, 165
roadrunners 72
robins 100, 101
rock clingers 246–7
rodents 54–61
roosting 19
roughies 184, 185
royal jelly 227

S

safety *see* protection and safety
sailfish 177
salamanders 136, 138–41
salmon 168, 169
sand dollars 248, 249
sand smelts 182
sardines 162
sauries 180
sawfish 156
sawflies 225
scallops 244
scorpionfish 186
scorpionflies 205
scorpions 230, 236–7
screamers 78
sculpins 186
sea anemones 193, 240, 241
sea basses 172, 173
seabream 173

254

sea creatures 240–9
sea cucumbers 248, 249
sea lilies 248
sea lions 36–7
sea mouse 248
sea pens 241
sea snails 245
sea snakes 132
sea urchins 197, 248
seabirds 74, 80–5
seahorses 154, 186–7
seals 36–9
searobins 186, 187
secretary birds 89
senses 8
seriemas 72
sharks 152–3, 154, 155, 156–9
sheathbills 80
sheepshead minnows 183
shrews 15
shrimps 242–3
Siamese fightingfish 172, 176
sidewinders 132
silverfish 198, 199
silversides 182
sirens 139
skates 158
skeletons 9, 115, 136, 155
skimmers 204
skinks 127
skuas 81
skunks 30, 31
slow worms 127
slugs 238, 244
smelts 168
snails 238–9, 244, 245, 247
snake lizards 127
snakeflies 202, 203
snakeheads 176
snakes 114, 124, 130–3, 150
snappers 173
sole 189
songbirds 100–9
sounds 150
spadefish 175
sparrows 107
sphinx moths 220–1
spider monkeys 24
spiders 151, 195, 196, 230–5

spiny-eels 163
sponges 197, 240
spring peepers 145
springhares 55, 56
squid 244, 245
squirrelfish 184, 185
squirrels 55
stag beetles 212–13
starfish 248–9
stargazers 176
starlings 100
stick insects 201
sticklebacks 186, 187
sting rays 159
stingers 240
stinkbugs 206
stoats 30
stonefish 186
stoneflies 203
storks 76
sturgeon 160–1
suckers 164
suckling 9
sun bears 29
sunbirds 104
sunbitterns 77
sunfish 191
swallows 66, 93
swans 76, 77
sweetlip emperors 174
swifts 66, 92, 93
swordfish 172, 177

T
tadpoles 137, 149
tamarins 20, 21
tanagers 102
tapirs 52
tarantulas 231
tarpons 162
tarsiers 20
Tasmanian devils 12
tench 164
tenrecs 15
termites 222, 228–9, 251
terns 80
terrapins 120
thorax 196

ticks 237
tigers 7, 34–5
tinamous 71
tits 250
toads 136, 142–3, 145, 150
tonguefish 189
topshells 247
tortoises 114, 116, 121
toucans 67, 97
tragopans 68
tree frogs 145
tree snakes 132
treehoppers 206
Trichoptera 216
triggerfish 190
tropicbirds 82
trout 169
trunks 44
tuataras 115, 125
tuna 178–9
turacos 96
turbot 188
turkeys 70
turtles 114, 116, 120–3
tusks 44, 45
Tyrannosaurus rex 115
tyrannulets 103

V
vampire bats 18–19
venoms *see* poisons and venoms
vertebrates *see* amphibians; birds; fish; mammals; reptiles
vicuñas 48
vipers 133
vlei rats 58
voles 58–9
vultures 66, 87, 89

W
wading birds 74–5
wallabies 8, 13
walruses 36
warblers 67, 111
warm-blooded animals 8

warthogs 46
wasps 222, 224–5, 250
water snakes 131
waterbirds 74, 76–9
webs 230, 234–5
weedy seadragons 187
weevils 210
whale sharks 152, 157
whalefish 185
whales 9, 36, 40–3
whelks 245
whipsnakes 114
wild boars 9, 47
wild cats 32
wildebeest 51
wings 66, 196
wolverines 30
wolves 26–7
wombats 12
woodchucks 55
woodcocks 75
woodcreepers 103
woodlice 238
woodpeckers 95
workers, insects 226, 227, 228
working together 192–3
worms 197, 238, 248–9
wrasses 172
wrens 101

Y
yaks 51
young
  amphibians 137, 149
  birds 66, 84–5
  fish 154
  insects 212, 221
  mammals 8, 9, 18, 34, 38
  monotremes and marsupials 8, 9, 10, 11
  nests 250, 251
  reptiles 114–15, 118–19

Z
zander 155
zebras 52, 53, 62–3

ACKNOWLEDGEMENTS

PICTURE CREDITS
(t=top, b=bottom, l=left, r=right, c=centre, fc=front cover)

FLPA
6-7 Paul Sawer/FLPA, 64-65 Tim Fitzharris/Minden Pictures/FLPA, 110bl Paul Sawer/FLPA, 112-113 Frans Lanting/FLPA, 134-135 Chris Mattison/FLPA, 151tr Photo Researchers/FLPA, 152-153 Fronline/Fronline/FLPA, 194-195 Dave Pressland/FLPA

OXFORD SCIENTIFIC FILMS
35tr Frank Schneidermeyer/Oxford Scientific Films, 38bl Rick Price/Oxford Scientific Films, 44tr Martyn Colbeck/Oxford Scientific Films, 62t Alastair Shay/Oxford Scientific Films, 63t Eyal Bartov/Oxford Scientific Films, 62-63 Stan Osolinski/Oxford Scientific Films, 85t Colin Monteath/Oxford Scientific Films, 99br Michael Fogden/Oxford Scientific Films, 108bc Hans Reinhard/Oxford Scientific Films, 110cr Alastair Shay/Oxford Scientific Films, 111tl Jorge Sierra/Oxford Scientific Films, 118tr David Cayless/Oxford Scientific Films, 129bl David Haring/Oxford Scientific Films, 148cl John Netherton/Oxford Scientific Films, 150bl Alastair Shay/Oxford Scientific Films, 151b Michael Fogden/Oxford Scientific Films, 158tr Gary Bell/Planet Earth Pictures, 179bl Richard Herrmann/Oxford Scientific Films, 192cr Anthony Bannister/Oxford Scientific Films, 192bl Andrew Plumptre/Oxford Scientific Films, 193b David B Fleetham/Oxford Scientific Films, 193tr Steve Turner/Oxford Scientific Films, 212tr Stephen Dalton/NHPA, 220tr Bob Fredrick/Oxford Scientific Films, 226br David Thompson/Oxford Scientific Films, 235cr Oxford Scientific Films, 247bl Paul Kay/Oxford Scientific Films, 250tr Roland Mayr/Oxford Scientific Films, 251cr Stan Osolinski/Oxford Scientific Films

NHPA
18tr Haroldo Palo Jr./NHPA, 251tl Roger Hosking/NHPA

ARTWORK CREDITS
MAMMALS: Graham Allen, John Francis, Elizabeth Gray, Bernard Robinson, Eric Robson, Simon Turvey, Dick Twinney, Michael Woods
BIRDS: Keith Brewer, Hilary Burn, Malcolm Ellis, Steve Kirk, Colin Newman, Denys Ovenden, Peter D. Scott, Ken Wood, Michael Woods
REPTILES AND AMPHIBIANS: John Francis, Elizabeth Gray, Steve Kirk, Alan Male, Colin Newman, Eric Robson, Peter D. Scott
FISH: Robin Boutell, John Francis, Elizabeth Gray, Elizabeth Kay, Colin Newman, Guy Smith, Michael Woods
INSECTS, SPIDERS AND OTHER INVERTEBRATES: Robin Boutell, Joanne Cowne, Sandra Doyle, Bridget James, Steve Kirk, Adrian Lascom, Alan Male, Colin Newman, Steve Roberts, Bernard Robinson, Roger Stewart, Colin Woolf